Criminal Justice
Policy & Planning

Wayne N. Welsh
Temple University

Philip W. Harris
Temple University

anderson publishing co.
2035 Reading Road
Cincinnati, OH 45202
800-582-7295

Criminal Justice Policy and Planning

Copyright © 1999
     Anderson Publishing Co.
     2035 Reading Rd.
     Cincinnati, OH 45202

    Phone 800.582.7295 or 513.421.4142
  Web Site www.andersonpublishing.com

Library of Congress Cataloging-in-Publication Data

Welsh, Wayne N., 1957-
    Criminal justice policy and planning / Wayne N. Welsh, Philip W. Harris.
      p.   cm.
    Includes bibliographical references and index.
    ISBN 0-87084-341-9 (pbk.)
    1. Criminal justice, Administration of. 2. Criminal justice, Administration of--United States.
  3. Criminal justice, Administration of--Planning. I. Harris, Philip W. II. Title.
HV7419.W45 1999
364.973--dc21   98-10895
                                                     CIP

Cover digital composition and design by Tin Box Studio, Inc.

EDITOR Ellen S. Boyne
ASSISTANT EDITOR Sharon L. Boyles
ACQUISITIONS EDITOR Michael C. Braswell

Acknowledgments

The authors are grateful to their families for all their love and patience, especially during those times when we sequestered ourselves to do the writing and research for this book. Thank you, Dea and Ilana, and Ellen and Elisabeth.

We appreciate the thoughtful guidance provided by Michael Braswell, Acquisitions Editor for Anderson, and the helpful comments of Victor Kappeler at Eastern Kentucky University. Comments by Professor Frank Cullen at the University of Cincinnati on an earlier version of this manuscript were most valuable in shaping this manuscript and bringing it to fruition.

The first author gratefully acknowledges the support of a Research Fellowship awarded by the Crime and Justice Research Institute in the fall of 1998, which greatly helped to complete this work.

Last, but not least, we thank the many fine men and women in criminal justice agencies, community programs, the private sector, and local, state and federal government with whom we have had the good fortune to work and learn from in our criminal justice research.

Contents

Chapter 3
Setting Goals and Objectives   77

Chapter 4
Designing the Program or Policy   111

Chapter 5
Developing an Action Plan   135

Chapter 6
Developing a Plan for Monitoring Implementation   157

Chapter 7
Developing a Plan for Evaluating Outcomes

Chapter 8
Initiating the Program or Policy Plan

Preface

The purpose of this book, broadly speaking, is to acquaint students, practitioners and policymakers with scientific techniques for analyzing criminal justice problems and developing solutions. By necessity, we analyze existing criminal justice interventions, asking to what degree such efforts have been guided by logic and planning, rather than partisan politics or untested hunches.

Change, some of which is planned, touches every aspect of our lives. In criminal justice, new interventions aimed at reducing crime seem to spring up constantly. Some notable interventions of recent years include "three strikes and you're out" laws (aimed at incapacitating repeat felony offenders), "Megan's Laws" (aimed at registering convicted sex offenders upon their release from prison), a myriad of "community corrections" programs, the "war on drugs" and other strategies, but to what degree are such interventions guided by a rational planning approach? What problems do they attempt to address, and what causal theory about crime do they assume? What difficulties could have been anticipated (e.g., a shortage of prison space; criticisms that programs or policies are inconsistent, unfair or even unconstitutional)?

Our point is this: what we call "planned change" encompasses a multitude of criminal justice policies, programs and projects that are developed, implemented, revised, torn down and recreated every year. We are interested in how such policies, programs and projects are currently developed, and how they *should be* developed. Poor planning and faulty problem analysis, we argue, are the primary reasons that so many criminal justice interventions fail to live up to their promises.

Consider the example of "three strikes" laws. Evidence suggests that the laws are unfair, expensive and ineffective. As Walter Dickey[1] argues, "When the law's hidden costs and unintended consequences are assessed, its simple goal is obscured by effects that are alarming in their scope" (p. 62). We illustrate some of the pitfalls of poor planning below, using the seven-stage framework that guides our work.

The Pitfalls of Poor Planning: "Three Strikes" Legislation

1. Problem Analysis: The proper starting point for program or policy planning is to ask what problem needs to be addressed. How does a specific issue become targeted for change, and why? How big is the problem, where is it, who is affected by it, and so on? What evidence has been used to demonstrate a need for change?

There is a widespread misconception that crime rates have been steadily rising in recent years, and that an increasingly larger portion of serious crimes are committed by recidivating felons. Nowhere in state or federal "three strikes" legislation can any evidence for such conclusions be found. In fact, crime rates have remained stable or gone down since the early 1990s, while recidivism rates have remained remarkably stable. It is doubtful that any coherent problem analysis guided policy development.

Assumptions speak faster and louder than facts, and politicians may too eagerly cater to the perceived public will, rather than documented problems. "Three strikes" laws are a rapid and visible response to public outcries following heinous or well-publicized crimes.[2] "We have a serious crime problem in this country," according to Walter Dickey, a University of Wisconsin law professor. "We are sold this as a solution. It gets all kinds of energy and attention, and yet it is relatively ineffectual."[3]

2. Goals and Values: Before designing programs or policies, we must be clear about the specific outcomes they are expected to achieve, and what specific values guide choices to select one course of action over another.

The intent of "three strikes" laws is to incapacitate violent offenders for long prison terms—25 years to life. If the law successfully increases the imprisonment rate, according to this logic, fewer offenders will be free to victimize the population. The laws have no *specific* deterrent effect if those confined will never be released, but their *general* deterrent effect could, at least in theory, be substantial. Legislators convey the message that certain crimes are deemed especially grave and that people who commit them deserve harsh sanctions.

Values such as *equity* (fairness) may be compromised by such laws. A California study[4] found that blacks were sent to prison under the "three-strikes" law 13 times as often as whites. Forty-three percent of the "three strikes" inmates in California were African-American, although African-Americans made up only 7 percent of the state's population and 20 percent of its felony arrests. In analyses of the federal sentencing guidelines, researchers found that African-Americans received longer sentences than whites, not because of differential treatment by judges but because they constituted the large majority of those convicted of trafficking in crack cocaine—a crime Congress had singled out for especially harsh mandatory penalties.[5] Controversy still ensues over exactly what "three strikes" laws are expected to achieve, and whether numerous unintended consequences, including racial disparity, could have been avoided.

3. *Program or Policy Design:* For any program or policy to have a chance at being effective, it is essential that the target population and all provisions, procedures and services be clearly spelled out ahead of time. In other words, there should be absolutely no doubt about who does what to whom in what order, how much or how often. This has clearly not been the case for "three strikes" laws.

One might expect some consistency among "three strikes" laws in different states and between state and federal "three strikes" laws. In reality, sentencing and parole eligibility vary dramatically from state to state, with some calling for third-time offenders to receive life without parole. In others, prisoners are eligible for parole after 30 or 40 years. Even within a single state such as California, there is considerable variability in how state laws are interpreted and used in different counties.[6]

Target populations for "three strikes" laws seem particularly poorly defined. In California, about 1,300 offenders have been imprisoned on third-strike felonies and more than 14,000 criminals for second-strike felonies. California's law calls for a doubling of the prison sentence for a second felony and for a sentence of 25 years to life for a third conviction. The California law was written to cover 500 felonies, including many nonviolent offenses. Some of the felonies include petty theft, attempted assault and burglary. Thus, about 85 percent of all those sentenced under the "three strikes" laws were involved in nonviolent crimes. For instance, 192 marijuana possessors have been sentenced for second and third strikes, compared with 40 murderers, 25 rapists and 24 kidnappers.[7]

4. *Action Planning:* Prior to implementing a new policy such as "three strikes" legislation, a systematic plan is needed that assigns responsibilities for communication, coordination and completion of specific tasks required to enact the new law. Everyone involved must clearly understand their roles and responsibilities. Possible obstacles and sources of resistance should be anticipated and sought out. By the time the new "three strikes" laws are implemented, everyone should understand and accept their roles. Evidence suggests the opposite.

State prosecutors have avoided the "three strikes" laws because they see little need for them with existing sentencing laws.[8] Another reason is that some laws were narrowly written, making them difficult to apply. Plea bargaining and charge bargaining have become common methods for circumventing "three strikes" laws.

The criminal courts rely on a high rate of guilty pleas to speed case processing and avoid logjams. Officials offer inducements to defendants to obtain guilty pleas. "Three strikes" laws disrupt established plea-bargaining patterns by preventing a prosecutor from offering a short prison term (less than the minimum) in exchange for a guilty plea. However, prosecutors usually can shift strategies and bargain on charges rather than on sentences. The findings of research on the impact of mandatory sentencing laws are instructive.[9] Officials make earlier and more selective arrest, charging and diversion decisions; they also tend to bargain less and to bring more cases to trial.[10] Indeed, 25 percent of "three strikes" cases go to trial compared with 4 percent overall for felonies.[11]

5. Monitoring: Following implementation of a policy such as "three strikes" legislation, it is essential to monitor; that is, collect data to determine to what degree the actual provisions, procedures or services are actually being implemented as designed. Adjustments may be needed, but no valid evaluation can be conducted if the laws are not being properly implemented. That would be tantamount to arguing that "x caused y" when we have no idea what "x" (the policy) was. "Three strikes" legislation fares badly on this criterion also.

At the federal level, where "three strikes" legislation was included in the 1994 crime bill, the law had been used on only nine occasions two years later. Twenty-four other federal cases were pending.[12] At the federal level, the long-term impact is minimal because less than 2 percent of violent felonies are resolved in federal courts.

"Three strikes" statutes simply are not being used in many of the 22 states—including Pennsylvania and New Jersey—that passed similar laws[13]. Tennessee, New Mexico, Colorado and North Carolina have not used them at all. Wisconsin has applied its law only once. Georgia has handed out five life sentences, and Indiana has had 10 convictions. Washington, the first state to pass such a law in 1993, has had more than 60 convictions, but the state's corrections director says those criminals would have faced stiff sentences anyway under existing laws.[14]

6. Evaluation: We need measurable evidence that any policy, particularly an expensive one such as "three strikes" legislation effectively and efficiently achieves what it was intended to do (i.e., reduce crime, protect public safety). The existing evidence is not encouraging.

Steve Telliano, press secretary for California Attorney General Dan Lungren, defended the state's "three strikes" law, saying California's crime rate dropped dramatically since the law's passage in March 1994.[15] Such claims are much in dispute. Although 25,000 repeat felons have been incarcerated in California, and annual drops of about 7 percent in the state Crime Index were observed in the two years following passage of the law, crime rates had already been decreasing for two years prior to the passage of the laws, consistent with national trends. Indeed, many other social and economic factors beside "three strikes" laws affect crime rates, including trends in the labor force and changes in the population of young males (the most high-risk group).[16]

The California law has created a need to build 15 new prisons over the following five years at a cost of $4.5 billion. California's prison population was expected to grow by 70 percent by the end of 1999, resulting in a 256 percent capacity rate, meaning that without new prisons, three inmates would be housed in space for one.[17]

Although "three strikes" laws have not yet been formally evaluated, the costs and benefits of California's law have been simulated.[18] Assuming that the law would produce incapacitation effects but not deterrent effects, researchers projected it would:

- triple California's prison population over the next 25 years, creating a prison population about equal in size to that of the entire United States prison population in 1980

- cost an average of $5.5 billion more each year for the next 25 years than the previous law, for a cumulative additional cost of $137.5 billion

- reduce serious crime by 28 percent, at a total correctional cost of about $16,300 for each crime averted

The effects on future California budgets of funding the "three strikes" law were estimated. In their calculations, the researchers assumed that health and welfare costs would not increase (an assumption they labeled as unlikely) and that educational spending for grades K through 12 would increase only as a direct result of foreseeable demographic changes. They found that corrections would consume 18 percent of state spending by the year 2002—double the 1994 percentage. Together, corrections, health and welfare, and K-12 education would consume 99 percent of the state's budget by 2002, leaving just 1 percent to fund everything else.

7. Reassessment and Review. Evidence suggests that felons are neither widely aware of the provisions of new "three strikes" laws nor deterred by them.[19] Even worse, violent behavior could be unintentionally increased, inciting some felons to murder witnesses or resist arrest by police officers to avoid getting caught.

Better planning in each of the areas discussed above could have reduced such disappointing consequences. Other policy options and/or revisions should now be considered, including presumptive sentencing, periodic administrative review (e.g., sunset provisions), limitations on the duration and scope of the laws, and provisions requiring legislators to fund the costs of passing "three strikes" laws.[20]

In spite of the pitfalls of poor planning, it is possible to address and reduce even the most pressing problems in criminal justice. One should be skeptical, even critical, but not cynical. We invite students, practitioners, politicians, academics and planners to subject their own assumptions, decisions and plans to scrutiny. We discuss several successful (and unsuccessful) case studies in this book, and we plan to analyze others in a separate volume. Where the costs of unsuccessful intervention are high, in terms of human suffering as well as finances, we can and must do better in devising solutions to criminal justice problems.

As authors, the challenge we face is to present and communicate the methods of analyzing problems and interventions in a clear, concise manner. We have found no existing book adequate for the task. Some are simply far too jargonistic or technical; others are idiosyncratic, abstract or unfocused. To make life even more difficult for us, no existing book presents these methods using criminal justice problems and interventions. This book attempts to meet these challenges. No doubt, it is less than perfect, and we welcome all comments and suggestions for improvements. Could advocates of planned change do any less?

Endnotes

1   Dickey, Walter J. (1997). "The Impact of 'Three Strikes and You're Out' Laws: What Have We Learned?" *Corrections Management Quarterly,* 1(4): 55-64.

2   Parent, Dale, Terence Dunworth, Douglas McDonald, and William Rhodes (1997). *Key Legislative Issues in Criminal Justice: Mandatory Sentencing* (NCJ 161839). Washington, DC: U.S. Department of Justice, Office of Justice Programs, National Institute of Justice.

3   Cannon, Angie (1996). "Survey: 'Three-strikes' Laws Aren't Affecting Crime. The Federal Government and States Aren't Hastening to Use Them. California is the Notable Exception." *The Philadelphia Inquirer,* 10 September 1996.

4   Greenwood, Peter W., et al. (1994). *Three Strikes and You're Out: Estimated Benefits and Costs of California's New Mandatory-Sentencing Law.* Santa Monica, CA: RAND, 1994.

5   McDonald, D.C., and K.E. Carlson (1993). *Sentencing in the Courts: Does Race Matter? The Transition to Sentencing Guidelines, 1986-90.* Washington, DC: U.S. Department of Justice, Bureau of Justice Statistics.

6   Ibid., note 1.

7   Ibid., note 4.

8   Ibid., note 4.

9   Tonry, Michael (1987). *Sentencing Reform Impacts.* Washington, DC: U.S. Department of Justice, National Institute of Justice.

10 Ibid., note 2.

11 Ibid., note 1.

12 Ibid., note 3.

13 Ibid., note 4.

14 Ibid., note 3.

15 Ibid., note 3.

16   Ibid., note 1.

17   Ibid., note 4.

18   Ibid., note 4.

19   Ibid., note 1.

20   Ibid., note 2.

CHAPTER 1

INTRODUCTION

CHAPTER OUTLINE

▶ *Examples of criminal justice interventions* include intermediate sanctions, mandatory arrest for domestic assault, Drug Awareness Resistance Education (DARE), "three strikes and you're out" legislation, juvenile waiver laws, comprehensive drug courts and domestic violence courts.

▶ *Planned change* is any project, program or policy, new or revised, intended to produce a change in some specific problem. It is limited in scope, it is aimed at improving quality of life for its clients, it includes a role for consumers, and it is guided by a "change agent."

▶ *The three approaches to planned change are: policy, program and project.*

▶ *The need for planned change has been sharpened by three trends: (1) declining resources, (2) accountability, and (3) expansion of knowledge and technology.*

▶ *The perils of planned change:* Any change to existing procedures and conditions is likely to be resisted. Two broad approaches to change should be carefully considered: collaborative strategies and conflict strategies.

▶ *A seven-stage model for planned change* specifies the sequence of steps required for analyzing a problem, determining its causes, and planning and carrying out some intervention. The seven stages consist of (1) analyzing the problem, (2) setting goals and objectives, (3) designing the program or policy, (4) developing an action plan, (5) developing a plan for monitoring program/policy implementation, (6) developing a plan for evaluating outcomes, and (7) initiating the program or policy design.

There are many different types of "programs," "policies" and "projects" in criminal justice: different interventions within government (federal, state and local), community and private agencies. In fact, one could argue that these many interventions comprise a majority of what criminal justice really is all about: a series of constant innovations and experiments attempting to discover what works to meet the goals of criminal justice (e.g., to reduce criminal behavior, to protect public safety). These numerous innovations attempt to change individuals, groups, organizations, communities and even societal and cultural norms in some cases, in order to improve the achievement of criminal justice goals. Criminal justice, then, is much more than just the daily business of police, courts and corrections, which forms the grist for many university courses and professional training in criminal justice. Figure 1.1 includes just a few examples of recent criminal justice interventions.

Figure 1.1

Examples of Criminal Justice Interventions

- Intermediate sanctions to reduce jail crowding (e.g., intensive supervision probation, boot camps, electronic monitoring)

- After-school delinquency prevention programs

- Drug treatment programs for convicted offenders

- Drug Awareness Resistance Education (DARE)

- Operation Weed and Seed (dual policy of first stamping out drug sales in specific communities, then "seeding" community with protective economic and social resources)

- Shelters, counseling and victim assistance for abused women

- "Three strikes and you're out" legislation, which aims to put away repeat offenders for long periods of time

- Mandatory arrest policies for suspected spouse abusers

- "Megan's Laws" (laws specifying the public's "right to know" where released child molesters are going to live)

- Juvenile waiver laws (serious juvenile offenses may be transferred to adult courts or automatically tried as adult offenses)

- Comprehensive domestic violence and drug courts, which provide assessment and treatment services in conjunction with criminal sanctions

The problem is that many criminal justice interventions often fall short of their goals because of poor planning, implementation and evaluation. It is fair to say that we have not yet discovered what works. What we truly need, though, is not *more* programs, or *new* programs, per se: we need *better* programs. We need a better understanding of planned change to improve the effectiveness of such interventions. Such change is ubiquitous in governmental, community, private and nonprofit agencies. This book provides a systematic framework for analyzing and improving existing interventions, but also for planning new ones so as to maximize chances of success.

Planned Change versus Unplanned Change

> ### Definition
>
> *Planned Change:* Any project, program or policy, new or revised, intended to produce a change in some specific problem. The intended change may occur within individuals, groups, organizations, systems of organizations, communities, cities, regions, states or, much more rarely, within entire cultures or societies.

Planned change involves planning. Planning means that some person or group of persons has explicitly thought about a problem and developed a specific solution. However, solutions (interventions) vary considerably in the degree to which thorough, explicit or deliberate planning has been undertaken.

As the examples and case studies in this book will illustrate, interventions are often poorly planned or even unplanned. *Unplanned change* means that little explicit or proactive planning has been undertaken at all. Instead, unplanned change often comes about as a reaction to a crisis, a dramatic incident publicized by the media, a political opportunity, a lawsuit against criminal justice officials or an untested set of assumptions about a specific problem. Unplanned change, even if it is motivated by sincere intentions, is likely to be ineffective and expensive.

Planned change improves the likelihood of successful intervention, but it cannot guarantee it. Even when planned change is successful, it may not be permanent. Planned change is dynamic, like the problems it seeks to address. People who play critical leadership roles come and go over time, initial shock about a problem and enthusiasm about an intervention abates, the political environment changes, other problems demand greater attention, and the impact of the intervention may be

Figure 1.2

The Birth of a Program or Policy: Examples

1. A county boot camp program for juvenile offenders is created after the Federal Crime Bill allocates millions of dollars in start-up funding for boot camp programs.

2. A nonprofit organization working with juveniles in poor neighborhoods applies for state funding after reading a solicitation for proposals to develop after-school delinquency prevention programs.

3. Following several tragic school shootings during the 1997-98 school term, hundreds of school districts across the United States announce that they are revising their disciplinary policies and installing tougher security measures.

4. A parolee shoots and kills a police officer after a routine traffic stop. Intensive scrutiny and revision of state parole policies immediately follows.

5. After the ACLU files a lawsuit alleging unconstitutional conditions of confinement in state prisons, a state corrections commissioner signs a court-approved agreement (a consent decree) to implement expensive policy changes such as building new prisons, improving health care, increasing inmate educational and treatment programs and increasing the number of prison staff. Some elected officials accuse the commissioner of using the lawsuit to "shake down" the state government for more money for prisons.

How much planning do you think guided the development of these interventions?

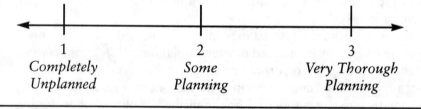

1	2	3
Completely Unplanned	*Some Planning*	*Very Thorough Planning*

unknown. Good planning, however, increases the odds of success by explicitly considering such factors.

In general, planned change differs from unplanned change in at least three ways:[1]

1. *Planned change is limited in scope, and specific.* It is confined to specific goals and achievable objectives; it seeks to develop clear, precise definitions of problems before developing solutions.

2. *Planned change includes a role for consumers.* Programs and policies must consider the unique perspectives and needs of the people affected by the intervention. In addition to the targets of the inter-

vention (inmates in a halfway house, for example), "consumers" include those within a specific area likely to be affected by an intervention. Neighbors, local schools and crime victims are examples of consumers who may be affected by a halfway house program. Cooperative planning of the intervention is an important part of program planning, monitoring and evaluation.

3. *Planned change is guided by a "change agent."* Someone must be responsible for coordinating the planning and development of a new program, or the revision of an old one. Such an individual will guide the analysis of the problem to be solved, search for causes of the problem and review similar interventions in use elsewhere, and facilitate the collaboration of clients, staff and consumers involved in the planning process. This individual may come from various backgrounds: he or she may be a program director appointed by a specific agency such as county probation, a university professor with a research grant, a director of a nonprofit agency such as an ex-offender program, a consultant hired by a criminal justice agency to formulate a plan, or perhaps even a state representative who introduces new legislation authorizing the use of boot camps for certain offenders as an alternative to incarceration.

Three Approaches to Planned Change: Policy, Program and Project

There are three general approaches to planned change, which differ in terms of their specificity and complexity. The most specific type of intervention is a *project,* the next most specific is a *program* and the most complex and comprehensive is a *policy.*

Definitions

1. *Policy: A rule or set of rules or guidelines for how to make a decision.* Policies vary on the complexity of the rule or guidelines *(simple-complex)*, and the amount of discretion afforded to those who apply policies *(constrained-flexible)*. How an instructor calculates grades in a course is a matter of policy, and students are typically informed of this policy at the start of a course. The existence of a grading policy helps to ensure that all students are treated fairly. Similarly, police officers are required to read *Miranda* warnings to people they have arrested, before beginning to ask questions that might be used in court against the defendant. Both of these examples pertain to relatively simple rules designed to protect the interests of individuals. Discretion is relatively constrained, although specific exceptions have been formulated by instructors and by the Supreme Court. Sometimes policies are much

Definitions, *continued*

more complex: the federal government may construct a social policy, such as President Lyndon Johnson's War on Poverty in the 1960s, designed to address large-scale social and economic problems. Organizations, too, create policies specifying how they are going to expend their resources: the U.S. Health Department's emphasis on juvenile violence prevention was tied to its budget in such a way that specific resources were set aside to deal with this important social problem. Another example includes the 1989 changes in the federal Juvenile Delinquency Act, which required states to assess and address the problem of minority overrepresentation in juvenile detention facilities. States were required to comply with this requirement in order to qualify for the large federal block grants on which state justice agencies depend. In each of these three cases, the policy was relatively complex (different rules and guidelines applied to different situations, and guidelines were quite broad) and flexible (the policy allowed decisionmakers to use discretion to develop or fund specific programs). Complexity and flexibility do not always correspond: for example, state sentencing guidelines are generally complex (different rules apply to different offenders and offenses), but vary considerably in the amount of discretion afforded to the sentencing judge. We address these issues in more depth in Chapter 4.

2. *Program: A set of services aimed at achieving specific goals and objectives within specified individuals, groups, organizations or communities.* For example, a local Boys' and Girls' Club decides to address the problem of minority overrepresentation in juvenile justice by creating an after-school program for minority juveniles residing in a high-risk community. Another example is a boot camp correctional program that is created to reduce the amount of time that offenders spend in custody. Offenders are sentenced to an intensive, short program of rigorous physical and academic services that is followed by probation rather than time in prison. Theoretically, such programs reduce the cost of corrections, increase the rehabilitative impact of corrections and satisfy the aim of retributive punishment. Programs, then, consist of services that are linked together by a single set of goals and an organization.

3. *Project: A time-limited set of services provided to particular individuals, groups, organizations or communities, usually focused on a single need, problem or issue.* Projects are usually intensive efforts by groups within an organization, system of organizations or a community to achieve a short-term objective. Evaluating a community corrections program, instituting a crackdown on drunk driving or conducting an assessment of needs for a computerized information system are examples of projects.

While the distinction between programs and projects is sometimes ambiguous, depending on whether the intervention is intended to be permanent or short-term, the distinction between programs and policies deserves more careful attention. Two examples illustrate the differences between a program and a policy, the two most common types of change. In each of the two cases in Figure 1.3, a program is but one small component of a much larger policy formulated at the local, state or federal level. In each case, a policy (legislation) authorized or mandated the use of specific programs for certain populations.

Figure 1.3

Problem	Program	Policy
• Jail overcrowding	Boot camps	Federal Crime Bill
• Drug abuse	Operation Weed and Seed	The federal "war on drugs"

Boot camps, rigid military-style drill camps intended as an alternative to incarceration for certain offenders, were mandated and funded by the Violent Crime Control and Law Enforcement Act of 1994. The federal government allocated $24.5 million in competitive funds available for boot camps in 1995 and authorized $7.9 billion in the time period between 1996 and 2000.

Operation Weed and Seed, a U.S. Department of Justice initiative launched in 1992 as part of President Bush's continuing "war on drugs" campaign, is a two-pronged community intervention. First, law enforcement agencies and prosecutors cooperate in "weeding out" criminals who participate in violent crime and drug abuse, and attempt to prevent their return to the targeted area. Second, "seeding" involves the development of community services including prevention, intervention, treatment and neighborhood revitalization. In each case, sweeping federal policy led to the formulation and funding of specific programs.

Policies, therefore, often contain the authorization or impetus for many specific programs, but policies often provide only very general prescriptions for what kind of approach should be used to solve specific problems. We can begin to see that the development of many programs and policies arises out of a political process that determines not only which problems will receive attention and priority in the first place, but what kind of intervention approach (e.g., changing individuals versus changing specified conditions in a community) will be used to address those problems.

The Need for Planned Change

The quest to find "what works" to achieve the goals of criminal justice has not yet been fulfilled and is not likely to be anytime soon. In fact, many people (policymakers, academics, politicians and citizens) disagree profoundly about the desirability of certain intervention approaches (e.g., drug treatment for convicted offenders versus tougher criminal sanctions to reduce drug abuse). Even if there were not such strong disagreement in values, it would still be difficult to find widespread agreement about how effective specific interventions have been (e.g., school-based drug prevention campaigns such as DARE).

Several factors fuel the debates about program effectiveness. For one thing, it is usually difficult to evaluate the long-term effects of social interventions. There are many different social variables to measure and control for, and this complexity often defies measurement. In addition to difficulties involved in measuring the objectives of specific interventions, the objectives themselves may be poorly defined. Alternatively, the problem may be poorly defined. Another possibility is that both the problem and the goals are well-defined, but the intervention was not implemented correctly, and thus we cannot have faith in any outcome results obtained by evaluation, whether they point to program success or failure. Indeed, evaluation results that do not address implementation problems should be treated suspiciously.

We will address all of these issues in more detail in subsequent chapters, but our point is that there is currently very little consensus about "what works" in criminal justice. A major reason for this lack of consensus, we argue, is a lack of sufficient attention to principles of planned change. At least three trends have sharpened our needs for planned change over the past 20 years:[2] (1) declining resources, (2) increased accountability, and (3) the expansion of knowledge and technology.

Declining Resources

Since 1980, there have been huge cuts in social services, especially programs affecting the poor and minorities (e.g., subsidized health care, welfare reform, daycare for working parents). Part of the explanation for these changes lies in the increased public concern over high taxes. However, it is obvious that taxes are the basis for the provision of public services, and cuts in taxes mean cuts in services (somewhere). Cuts in social services, according to some, may have magnified social problems that already existed. For example, the problem of homelessness in the 1980s was likely exacerbated by huge cuts in funds available for mental health care, inadequate funding for substance abuse treatment programs, and rising health-care costs.[3]

Partly as a consequence of declining resources, many groups have organized to promote change, both legally (through lawsuits) and politically (by advocating for changes in laws and government programs). Advocacy efforts have often succeeded in raising awareness about a particular problem and stimulating change. A good example is provided by the problem of domestic violence. Women's groups have organized and protested for numerous changes throughout history, including the right to vote and the right to work. Advocacy by women's groups in the 1970s and 1980s led to changes in police and court policies for dealing with sexual harassment, rape and domestic violence. Such advocacy contributed greatly to the perception that existing programs and policies were not working, and that some kind of change was needed.[4] One can find numerous examples of other groups that have campaigned for change and contributed to changes in existing policies and programs (e.g., groups protesting welfare reforms that restrict eligibility and benefits; groups advocating for programs and policies to address problems of homelessness, AIDS, etc.).

Accountability

As public resources have dwindled, agencies have increasingly been called upon to demonstrate their effectiveness and efficiency in meeting goals. There has been suspicion by many that public money has not always been spent wisely.

A case in point is provided by the former Law Enforcement Assistance Administration (LEAA), created in 1968 when Congress passed the Omnibus Crime Control and Safe Streets Act.[5] Intended to strengthen the efficiency and effectiveness of comprehensive planning to address criminal justice problems, the LEAA made large block grants available to local and state criminal justice agencies to develop systematic planning processes and to establish criminal justice planning as a profession. A major goal was to improve comprehensive planning by cooperating criminal justice agencies, rather than the piecemeal, "every agency for itself" mode that prevailed.

However, vagueness in LEAA application guidelines as well as ambiguity about what a "comprehensive plan" should contain, led to the submission of "wish lists" by police, courts and corrections agencies for everything from typewriters to handcuffs. LEAA funds were used less to develop and improve comprehensive planning than to supplement state and local justice budgets. Lack of monitoring and accountability by the LEAA contributed to questionable uses of these grants. For example, police departments used funds to purchase equipment such as squad cars or helicopters, rather than submitting plans to strengthen their organizational planning capacity. Such permissiveness in funding is rare today. Granting agencies, whether government, private or nonprofit, usually have strict reporting, monitoring and evaluation requirements for any agency receiving funding.

Expansion of Knowledge and Technology

We have greater technological abilities than ever before. These changes have created both new opportunities for change and new problems. Improvements in computing technology over the past 20 years have dramatically increased our information collection, storage and retrieval capabilities. As a result, we have ready access to many types of criminal justice data, including information about reported crimes, police arrests, convictions, sentencing, prison time served, parole and recidivism. Naturally, improved data collection and access mean that our ability to identify specific needs and problems has improved. For example, improved justice information systems have contributed to the increased visibility of problems such as racial disparities in sentencing[6]. Our ability to collect and compare data on the processing of thousands of defendants in different regions over time has never been greater. High-powered computers and statistical packages make it possible to control statistically for various legal (e.g., previous criminal record) and nonlegal factors (e.g., race, socioeconomic status) that influence sentencing. There are no longer disputes about whether sentencing disparities exist but about where, why and how much they exist.[7]

Other technological changes have improved our ability to detect crime and monitor offenders. Computerized fingerprint identification systems have greatly reduced the amount of time required to scan and match individual prints, and both regional and national data banks of criminal information and fingerprints are now available to criminal justice agencies for investigation purposes. Electronic monitoring equipment has made it possible for probation and parole agencies to cost-effectively supervise certain offenders in a community, rather than a prison setting, at least as part of their sentence. Sophisticated drug testing equipment available today has made it possible to detect minute amounts of drugs in an individual's body, leading to huge increases in the number of parolees who fail to complete their parole terms successfully and return to jail.

Computers have also increased the ability of researchers to discover what works. Data on the effectiveness of a program or policy can be tracked rapidly and with greater precision than ever before, thus enabling criminal justice systems to learn from their experiences and continuously improve their interventions. For example, the effects of juvenile correctional programs on individual youths are increasingly the subject of outcome-based monitoring systems.

As computerized information systems have grown, a whole new field of crime, dubbed "computer crime," has evolved, in which perpetrators attempt to break into secure computer systems of individuals and corporations, usually for the purpose of illegally obtaining classified information or money. Methods of detecting, investigating and prosecuting this whole new category of crime are evolving rapidly, but seemingly slower than the rate of growth in the crime itself.

The Perils of Planned Change

Any change to existing procedures and conditions carries a certain amount of risk. The proposed change is likely to be resisted by someone, perhaps even its intended beneficiaries (e.g., a city successfully lobbies for state funds to build a new prison but then faces vigorous protests from different communities being considered for the location of the new prison). Regardless of the specific change proposed, universal consensus is rare; resistance is the norm.

In many cases, people fear and resist change because it may threaten their job security or bring about unwanted scrutiny (e.g., citizen review boards of complaints against police). There is often a fear that the change might only make things worse. For example, in July of 1996, following the crash of TWA Flight 800, suspicions that a terrorist bomb was responsible led to tough new federal anti-terrorism legislation introduced in Congress. The bill met resistance by both Democrats and Republicans because of certain provisions that would have greatly enlarged the circumstances under which police could use wiretaps on private telephone numbers. Regardless of the many varied reasons for which resistance emerges in any specific case, those who propose change must be prepared for disagreement and resistance. Again, *planned* change, rather than *unplanned* or *poorly planned* change, can go a long way toward minimizing resistance, especially if the "change agent" (the person or agency that has introduced the proposed intervention) has involved different constituents in the planning process from the beginning.

Even prior to beginning work on planning a specific intervention, the change agent should have identified potential sources of resistance and considered the potential costs and benefits of two very different approaches to handling resistance: (1) collaborative strategies, or (2) conflict strategies.[8]

Definitions

Collaborative strategies emphasize participation from those affected by change. Individuals, groups or organizations who are known to oppose the intervention in part or *in toto* are included in the design and planning of the intervention. For example, a police commissioner might ask police officers about their views on community policing before it is adopted as a department policy and imposed on them. State sentencing commissions might ask judges about their perceived difficulties in sentencing before drafting, adopting or imposing sentencing guidelines on them.

Conflict strategies, on the other hand, approach resistance in an adversarial manner. Those who resist the proposed change are seen as opponents who must either be persuaded or coerced to change their views. Such strategies are more likely to come into play where opposing parties have a strong history of disagreement; leaders favor a dictatorial, authoritarian style of management; resources are scarce and there is much disagreement over allocation; the stakes of the proposed change are high (i.e., large benefits to certain parties and perhaps large costs to others); time pressures are great; or the likelihood of successfully suppressing the opposition is perceived (correctly or incorrectly) as high. A good example is provided by brutality lawsuits launched against local police departments. Because citizens perceived the existing system of reviewing complaints as ineffective and heavily biased in favor of police, legal reform in complaint review procedures has evolved. Another example is provided by lawsuits against local, state and federal prisons for overcrowding and other conditions of confinement. Such lawsuits, some lasting as long as 13 years, usually followed a period of unsuccessful and rancorous discussion and negotiation.[9] Changes eventually resulted, but at considerable cost to human and fiscal resources.

While the actual outcomes of either strategy are impossible to predict without knowing detailed circumstances of the case in question, there are several serious costs associated with conflict strategies that generally make them unattractive options:

- They create greater resistance.
- They require greater resources.
- They create more unexpected effects.
- Change tends to be temporary (capitulation) rather than long-term.

A Seven-Stage Model for Planned Change

A model specifies the sequence of steps required for: (1) analyzing a problem, (2) determining its causes, and (3) planning and carrying out some intervention. For our purposes, a model may be used to plan new interventions, analyze existing interventions, or both (e.g., revising a current program). In the first case, certain critical activities can be enacted (or avoided) to increase the likelihood that a proposed intervention will effectively produce a desired change in a specific problem. In the second case, critical activities and decisions that inform the planning process can be identified and analyzed to help us to understand why a particular intervention did or did not produce effective results.

Our model of planned change is based on a "problem-solving model" (i.e., developing solutions to specific problems through a rational process of planning). The 1968 President's Commission report,[10] *The Challenge of Crime in Free Society*, was extremely influential in shaping current conceptions of criminal justice as a *system*[11] and it stimulated attempts to improve criminal justice programs and policies through comprehensive, coordinated planning. As Mark Moore[12] suggests, "The Crime Commission had two big things in mind: (1) how to produce an effective, decent criminal justice system, and (2) how to deal with crime . . . They also had a managerial or implementation vision, which was a theory about how the processes and institutions of the criminal justice system needed to be developed . . ." (167-168). This vision was to be guided by data and knowledge rather than ideology and passion.

The Commission's report was the major impetus for passage of the Omnibus Crime Control and Safe Streets Act of 1968 and the creation of the federal Law Enforcement Assistance Administration (LEAA) discussed earlier in this chapter. While rational criminal justice planning and the "social justice" it was intended to foster remain elusive, those lofty goals remain as relevant as ever. Reflecting on the positive contributions of the President's Commission report, Moore notes that, "The authorization to experiment has been spread widely, and that turns out to be a very good thing for society" (pp. 176-177). At the same time, the goals of rationality and social justice have proven far more difficult to achieve than originally expected.[13]

We present our model here with a program approach in mind, but we have generalized it to include the development of policies. That is, the stages are described with the assumption that a program or policy is being developed or analyzed. Because projects differ from programs and policies mainly in terms of their shorter duration and more focused intervention approach, this seven-stage model can also be applied to the project approach to problem solving. The seven stages of the program model are briefly described here; each is dealt with in more detail in separate chapters. A summary of the seven stages is provided in Figure 1.4.

Table 1.1 A Systematic Approach to Program and Policy Development and Analysis

Stage 1. Analyzing the Problem	Stage 2. Setting Goals and Objectives	Stage 3. Designing the Program or Policy	Stage 4. Developing an Action Plan	Stage 5. Developing a Plan for Monitoring Program/Policy Implementation	Stage 6. Developing a Plan for Evaluating Outcomes	Stage 7. Initiating the Program or Policy Design
Document the need for change	Write goal statements	Choose from different intervention options	Identify resources needed	Design instruments to collect monitoring data	Develop outcome measures based on objectives	Planning for failure: avoid exaggerated claims.
Describe the history of the problem	Write specific outcome objectives for each goal	Program design: • Define the target population	Plan to acquire or reallocate resources	Designate responsibility to collect, store and analyze data	Specify the research design to be used	Planning for success: ongoing reassessment, learning and revision are crucial.
Examine potential causes	Seek participation in goal setting	• Define target selection procedures • Define program components and activities	Specify dates to complete implementation tasks	Develop information system capacities	Identify potential confounding factors	Learning and adapting; successful interventions must adapt to change.
Examine previous interventions	Specify an impact model	• Write job descriptions of staff and specify skills required	Develop mechanisms of self-regulation	Develop mechanisms to provide feedback to stakeholders	Identify users and uses of evaluation results	Initiate the program or policy design from Stage 3.
Identify relevant stakeholders	Identify compatible and incompatible goals in the larger system	Policy design: • Define the target population of the policy	Specify a plan to build support		Reassess the entire program/policy plan	Initiate the Action Plan from Stage 4.
Conduct a systems analysis	Identify needs for interagency collaboration	• Identify the responsible authority				Initiate Monitoring of Program/Policy (Stage 5 plan).
Identify barriers and supports		• Define the provisions and procedures of the policy				Collect and analyze evaluation data; provide feedback to stakeholders (Stage 6 plan).
						Reassess the entire program/policy plan and make necessary modifications to increase fit with environment.

Stage 1: Analyzing the Problem

The first step is to analyze the problem. We should carefully collect information about dimensions of the problem, the history of the problem, who is affected by the problem and potential causes of the problem. For example, we ask the following questions: What and where is the problem? How big is it? How long has the problem existed? Do different groups of people have different definitions of the problem? Who is affected by the problem? What causes the problem? What theories do we have? What kinds of interventions have been tried elsewhere? Who is likely to support a certain course of action, and who is likely to resist it?

The pitfalls of faulty problem analysis are enormous and can completely subvert effective intervention. Many interventions fail not necessarily because the intervention itself is flawed, but because it addresses the wrong problem (or an inadequately defined problem). Major activities at this stage include the following:

- Document the need for change: collect and analyze data about the problem.

- Describe the history of the problem.

- Examine potential causes of the problem.

- Examine previous interventions that have tried to change this problem.

- Identify relevant stakeholders (those who have a legitimate interest in the problem and/or the intervention).

- Identify barriers to change and supports for change.

- Conduct a system analysis.

This last step, the system analysis, involves conducting research on the system within which the problem exists. Most problems are produced by more than one source and most solutions affect more than one part of a system. It is important, then, to learn as much as possible about how different decisions interact to produce the problem. For example, prison overcrowding is not simply the result of judges sending more people to prison: changes in laws pertaining to drug crimes, increases in drug-related violence, and the development of sentencing guidelines for judges all contributed to increasing prison populations. Unless we understand *how* these and other changes affected the prison population, we stand little chance of constructing an effective solution.

Example 1.1

Prostitution as a Problem

After a series of well-publicized police sweeps and arrests, a community identifies prostitution as a serious *problem* in need of change. The presumed *cause*, determined by intuition rather than careful analysis, is that police have simply not taken the problem seriously enough. The proposed *intervention*, then, is a police crackdown, with intensive law enforcement targeted in areas frequented by prostitutes and their customers. However, what if these causal assumptions were wrong, or left out something important? What if it turns out that the problem is mainly limited to the summer months, and the majority of prostitutes are teenage runaways trying to make money to survive? Such information might lead to a very different type of intervention: perhaps shelters, crisis counseling, or job training and assistance.

Stage 2: Setting Goals and Objectives

Every intervention attempts to achieve some kind of outcome (i.e., some change in the problem), but sometimes it is difficult to figure out what it is. *Goals* are broad aims of the intervention (e.g., reduce drug abuse); *objectives* specify explicit and measurable outcomes. It is amazing how many expensive and otherwise well-designed interventions fail to define adequately the desired outcomes of the intervention. Without specific, agreed-upon criteria for success, it would be impossible to determine whether any intervention worked. If you don't know where you are going, as the saying goes, don't be surprised when you don't get there. Major activities at this stage include the following:

- Seek participation from different individuals and agencies in goal setting.

- Write goal statements specifying the general outcome to be obtained.

- Write specific outcome objectives for each goal: these should include a time frame for measuring impact, as well as a specific measure of impact.

- Specify an impact model: this is a description of how the intervention will act upon a specific cause so as to bring about a change in the problem.

- Identify compatible and incompatible goals in the larger system: where do values of different stakeholders overlap or conflict?

- Identify needs and opportunities for interagency collaboration. For example, police and prosecutors may need to collaborate to make the drunk driving law work. Prosecutors might hold training sessions with police to educate them on the nature of evidence required to obtain convictions under the new law. Police officers, in turn, can educate prosecutors about the likelihood of obtaining different kinds of evidence.

Example 1.2

The Goals of Drunk Driving Laws

A new state law is passed that provides tougher sentences for drunk drivers. A mandatory 48-hour jail sentence is imposed on second-time offenders; a mandatory three-month jail term is imposed on three-time offenders. The goal is obvious: to reduce drunk driving. Six months after the law is passed, there is widespread disagreement about whether the law is working. Advocates of the law point to a 10 percent reduction in drunk driving arrests. Critics point to insurance statistics that indicate an increase in traffic accidents involving alcohol. Who is right? Does the law work or not? After much discussion, both sides realize that they lack an agreed-upon criterion for judging the outcome of the intervention. Eventually, they agree that a desirable outcome (change in the problem) is that one year after the law was passed, there should be a 30 percent reduction in auto fatalities caused by drunk driving. The difficulty, it turns out, is that no specific objective was defined before the law was passed, and without such an objective, multiple and conflicting criteria for deciding "outcome" could be debated endlessly.

Stage 3: Designing the Program or Policy

Designing the program or policy is one of the most crucial and time-consuming stages in the planning process. It is much more detailed than often realized, and it often requires considerable review of information collected during the first two stages of planning. It involves specifying, in as much detail as possible, who does what to whom, in what order, and how much? It is the "guts" of the program or policy, including its staff, its services and its clients. While the planning steps for programs and policies are generally similar, at the design stage we find it best to distinguish activities for programs and policies separately. Major activities for program design include:

- Define the target population. Who is to be served or changed? This often involves specifying some level of need (e.g., level of drug involvement) and characteristics of intended clients (e.g., age, gender, geographic residence).

- Define client selection and intake procedures. How are clients selected and recruited for the intervention? For example, boot camp programs are often intended for first-time, nonviolent offenders. A list of eligible clients might be obtained from court records; an application from the client may be required; an interview and screening process may be required to determine the client's suitability for the program.

- Define program components. The precise nature, amount and sequence of services provided must be specified. Who does what to whom, in what order, and how much? Boot camp programs, for example, might contain several components: military-style drills and physical training; academic or vocational education; life skills or problem-solving training; drug awareness education; social-skills training.

- Write job descriptions of staff, and define the skills and training required. How many and what kind of staff are required to operate the program? What specific duties will they carry out? What kind of qualifications do they need, and what further training will be necessary? How much money is needed for staff salaries and training?

Major activities for policy design include:

- Define the target population of the policy. Which persons or groups are included and which are not? For example, legislators in various states had to write specific requirements for inclusion and exclusion under new "three strikes" laws. Which offenders (e.g., felony vs. misdemeanor) and offenses (e.g., violent vs. property) should be included?

- Identify the responsible authority. Who is required to carry out the policy, and what will their responsibilities be? For example, what role will judges, prosecutors, defense attorneys and others play in any case, and how can we ensure that each understands "three strikes" policy correctly? Will each party understand their individual responsibilities and options? Will they need special training or orientation? Are additional court or prison resources required?

- Define the provisions of the policy. A policy should identify the sanctions, services, opportunities or interventions that will be delivered, as well as the conditions that must be met in order for the policy to be carried out. Under a new "three strikes" policy, for example, state legislators had to write specific rules for how case processing and sentencing decisions were to be made: when and how would the District Attorney's office make charging decisions under the new law? How would pretrial motions be handled? Would trials be conducted in private or in public? What are the appropriate terms of incarceration?

- Delineate the procedures that must be followed. Individuals responsible for implementing a specific set of rules must clearly understand the specific actions to be taken to ensure that the policy is carried out consistently. For example, "three strikes" laws specify decisions regarding the charging, processing and sentencing of repeat offenders. These might include the court's procedures for notifying a suspect and his or her attorney that the suspect is about to be charged under "three strikes" laws, including delivery of written notice, and clearly specifying the suspect's legal rights and options under the new law. Procedures may also specify who signs such forms, other individuals or agencies that need to be notified, and records that must be maintained.

Example 1.3

The Design of a Boot Camp Program

There are many different kinds of boot camp programs in use today. Knowing that "reforming offenders" is the program's mission, however, tells us very little about what the treatment is or how it is delivered. One specific boot camp offers a mix of rigid military discipline with treatment approaches. Ransom and Mastrorilli[14] provide the following description of the Massachusetts Boot Camp Program.

"The Massachusetts Boot Camp is an intensive 16-week modified therapeutic community focusing offenders on a course of behavioral change. The camp provides a balance of military-style discipline, community service, and programming (substance abuse, adult basic education, wellness and life skills), focusing on accountability in a public safety, behavioral leveraged-treatment model.[15] In the Massachusetts Boot Camp, inmates receive approximately 30 hours of programming per week. All sessions begin and end with positive, upbeat music played at a high volume to stimulate motivation. During classes, classical music is used to produce an altered state of consciousness. Instructors frequently focus interactions on positive recovery-based themes: Give 110%, be all you can be, participate . . . take the first step, see the situation clearly. The classrooms and barracks are filled with mind maps (visual symbols) representing decision-making techniques; the 12 steps of recovery; tools of recovery; being honest, open, and willing; and following good, orderly direction" (p. 309).

There are many more questions we could ask about program services, as well as staff and clients, but even this brief description illustrates that any specific boot camp program is likely to have its own unique design. Knowing simply that it is a "boot camp" does not tell us very much at all.

Stage 4: Developing an Action Plan

Once the design is complete, the next stage is to develop an "action plan" that specifies the sequence of tasks that need to be completed in order to launch or "implement" the program or policy successfully. These include technical and interpersonal tasks (e.g., identifying and acquiring the necessary resources for the program, locating office space and/or meeting space, hiring and training staff, designing client intake and reporting forms, purchasing equipment and supplies, setting dates and assigning responsibility for the completion of specific tasks). Major activities at this stage include the following:

- Identify resources needed and make cost projections: How much funding is needed?

- Plan to acquire or reallocate resources: How will funding be acquired?

- Specify dates by which implementation tasks will be accomplished, and assign responsibilities to staff members for carrying out tasks.

- Develop mechanisms of self-regulation (create mechanisms to monitor staff performance and enhance communication).

- Specify a plan to maintain and build support base; anticipate sources of resistance and develop responses.

Example 1.4

Action Planning for a Delinquency Prevention Program

The excerpt below is from a funding proposal submitted by a community-based delinquency prevention program applying for state funds. Major program components include: a seven-day challenge course in which juveniles are encouraged to examine their lives and set goals, one-to-one mentoring of youths by adult "committed partners"; and weekly "follow-through" meetings of all mentors and clients. The proposal spells out, in considerable (but necessary) detail, exactly who is responsible for completing a myriad of tasks required to launch the program. The entire action plan covers training, travel, site costs, seven-day course costs, and follow-through costs. The following excerpt covers some of the major training tasks only, but it gives one the flavor of the detailed sequence of tasks to be specified in an action plan.

> **Project Coordinator Training and Development.** Through structured workshops and meetings, the *Consultant* will train and support the development of the applicant's staff person designated to be responsible for the successful management of the year-long project. The Consultant will train this *Program Coordinator* to enroll and manage community volunteers to function on-site as: *Facilitators*,

Example 1.4, *continued*

Committed Partners, Course Production Team, Coaches, Situation Intervention Team, and Security. The program coordinator will also be trained to target and enroll *Youth Participants* through presentations to appropriate youth serving agencies and to ensure maximum benefit from their participation in the program. The consultant will also train and support the project coordinator in successfully managing the year-long follow-through program (Training hours by quarter: First = 260 hours, Second = 195 hours, Third = 195 hours, Fourth = 130 hours. Total training hours = 780; average cost per training hour = $10.26).

Facilitator Workshop. This three-day session empowers prospective Facilitators, by their discovery of what is available to them in their participation in the Program, to ensure the success of the Youth participating in the program (one Workshop Leader for three days @ $350 per day = $1,050).

Youth Enrollment Workshops. These workshops are designed to train the requisite teams of volunteers to successfully enroll 30 youth in the Program and enable them to support these youth in keeping their word through Departure (two Youth Enrollment Coaches for five days apiece @ $350 per day = $3,544).

Committed Partner Training. Committed Partners are trained to support the Youth in participating fully in the seven-day course and the Follow-through Program (one Workshop Leader for three days @ $350 per day = $1050).

Volunteer Enrollment Training (Course Production Team, Coaches, Situation Intervention Team and Security). Over the course of three days this segment will prepare the Course Production Team to execute the seven-day Course. The Team is presented with what they can expect to encounter in the process of producing a seven-day Course and what will be expected of them in order to accomplish this remarkable result. This training also empowers the Coaches and Situation Intervention Team to support the Facilitators and Youth in participating fully in all seven-day Course activities, keeping their agreements and responding to breakdowns (three Trainers for three days apiece @ 350 per day = $3,150).

Stage 5: Developing a Plan for Monitoring Program/Policy Implementation

At this stage, we attempt to find out if the program or policy was implemented properly. Sometimes referred to as "process evaluation," *monitoring* refers to the collection of information to determine to what degree the program/policy design or blueprint (Stage 3) is being carried out as planned. Data is collected to find out what is actually being delivered to clients (e.g., observations, surveys, interviews). The purpose is to identify gaps between the program on paper (design) and the program in action. Adjustments then need to be made to revise either the design of the program or policy (e.g., program components) or to make what is being done conform to the intended design. We ask the following types of questions at this stage: Are program/policy activities actually being carried out as planned? Is the intended target population being reached? Are staff carrying out their assigned responsibilities? Major activities at this stage include the following:

- Design monitoring instruments to collect data.

- Designate responsibility for data collection, storage and analysis.

- Develop information system capacities.

- Develop mechanisms to provide feedback to staff, clients and stakeholders.

Example 1.5

Monitoring Implementation of Delinquency Prevention Programs

In response to changes in the federal Juvenile Delinquency Act of 1989, The Juvenile Advisory Committee of the Pennsylvania Commission on Crime and Delinquency (PCCD) commissioned research in 1990 to analyze minority overrepresentation in that state. The subcommittee concluded that actions should be taken to slow the entry or reentry of minorities into the juvenile justice system and it recommended the development and support of community-based prevention activities. After identifying jurisdictions with the highest rates of minority overrepresentation in juvenile arrests, PCCD funded five programs in Harrisburg for 1991-92 and later added four programs in Philadelphia beginning in the fall of 1992. As evaluators of these programs, we undertook the following monitoring study[16].

First, using program documents such as funding proposals and published program brochures, we developed a "Documents/Rhetorical Model" (full description) of each program's activities and objectives. These served as a basis for subsequent interviews with program staff and administrators to obtain their perceptions of specific activities, intended objectives, and linkages between the two. Next, we reinterviewed program personnel two or three times to gain information about program components, objectives, staff responsibilities and expected performance for clients. This information was used to revise the original program models (indeed, program activities and objectives changed substantially during the first two years of operations), eventually resulting in an up-to-date "evaluable model" of each program containing only clearly specified program activities, and only feasible, measurable objectives.

After identifying program services, we asked two general questions: (1) How are program services actually being delivered? and (2) Are there any gaps between the program on paper and the program in action? Informa-

Example 1.5, *continued*

tion sources included program documents, interviews with program staff and clients, and our observations of each program in action.

Program Records. Program directors were asked to provide examples of all recordkeeping measures, including agency referral forms, program intake forms, weekly activity schedules, client attendance reports, and any information in client files pertaining to services delivered and client responses. We examined such documents to determine how clearly each program identified services delivered to clients in terms of time, costs, procedures and products (e.g., three life skills classes of one hour duration each were offered each week by one staff person). We determined whether the information collected by each program was adequate to document the number and type of referrals received from different agencies, the program's procedures for selecting and admitting clients, and the nature and frequency of services delivered to each client. This information was necessary to fulfill reporting needs to PCCD, referring agencies and evaluators.

Direct Observation. Researchers visited each program site at least three times annually to observe delivery of services. Program staff were contacted in advance and the reasons for the visits were explained (e.g., to demonstrate accountability; to build collaborative relationships with program personnel; to facilitate program planning and development). The confidentiality of client and staff responses was ensured. Observers obtained information about the frequency, duration and nature of services delivered, using a "data guide"[17]: we gave observers a protocol consisting of several questions that they were required to answer from their observations.

Participant Interviews. A valuable perspective on services provided can be obtained from clients, for clients should have detailed, firsthand knowledge of the program. Of course, information provided by clients may be limited by clients' subjectivity and their possible suspicion of researchers. For example, clients may want to make the program "look good" by exaggerating its positive benefits, or they may wish to make it "look bad" by exaggerating its negative features. Even so, their views provide a valuable source of information to cross-check against information obtained by other methods (observations, inspection of program documents, and staff interviews). Individual clients were interviewed for approximately 30 minutes.

As a result of this monitoring study, we identified 10 high-priority issues for program planning and development. We detected gaps in target selection procedures (e.g., clients were often selected on the basis of availability rather than need); client attendance and attrition were problematic (many clients attended irregularly, and many dropped out early); and program records were not being kept consistently (e.g., one program stopped keeping regular attendance data after a few months, others periodically failed to complete required intake forms for new clients). Philadelphia programs were required by PCCD to respond to our recommendations by developing corrective action plans. Although PCCD funding had already elapsed in Harrisburg, program directors were receptive and responsive to our feedback.

Stage 6: Developing a Plan for Evaluating Outcomes

The goal of this stage is to develop a research design for measuring program or policy outcome (a specific, intended change in the problem, as defined by objectives). Did the program or policy achieve its intended objectives? Why or why not? Note that all planning, including the formulation of an evaluation plan, should precede the actual start-up of the program or policy (Stage 7). Major activities at this stage include the following:

- Develop outcome measures based on objectives.

- Specify the research design to be used.

- Identify potential confounding factors (factors other than the program that may have influenced measured outcomes).

- Identify users and uses of evaluation results.

- Reassess the entire program or policy plan.

Example 1.6

Evaluating Intensive Supervision Probation

Intensive Supervision Probation (ISP) in New Jersey[18] required that eligible participants first serve a few months in prison. ISP then provided a level of punishment between probation and ordinary terms of imprisonment. Major program components included intensive supervision contacts (e.g., face-to-face contacts with probation officers, curfew checks, drug tests, checks with employers, monitoring performance of community service, monitoring restitution payments, monitoring participation in drug treatment and other court-ordered services) and immediate revocation for failure to abide by program rules. The program design included the required payment of fines, required employment, required community service work (at least 16 hours per month), special counseling (those with an identified problem such as drug or alcohol dependence must participate in specialized counseling and treatment) and community sponsor and network team support (each client had a community sponsor and other support persons who helped monitor client progress and provide help and assistance).

The ISP program had four major objectives, and researchers devised measures for each objective. The first objective was that ISP should *improve the use of scarce prison resources* (save prison space). The measure for this objective was the number of "bed-days saved," calculated by multiplying the number of offenders by the average sentence they would have served had they remained in prison. The second objective was that the program should be *cost-effective*, compared to ordinary incarceration. This measure was calculated by comparing the average cost per offender in ISP with the

Example 1.6, *continued*

average cost of incarceration for the same time period. Researchers also used employment figures to calculate income generated by ISP offenders working in the community. The third objective was to *prevent criminal behavior* of selected offenders. The measure, a common outcome in criminal justice studies, was recidivism rates. The fourth objective was to *deliver appropriate intermediate punishment in the community.* This objective was measured by an attitude survey about ISP administered to criminal justice officials, and the rate of withdrawal of applications by offenders due to strict program criteria.

Program goals and objectives were well-defined and, for the most part, basic program components (service delivery) were adequately implemented. The research design was a posttest-only design, whereby ISP participants ($N = 375$) were compared on outcomes, such as recidivism, to a matched comparison group (matched for criminal records and background factors) of similar inmates ($N = 130$) who completed their prison terms through normal procedures, rather than participating in ISP.

Compared to ordinary imprisonment and parole, ISP achieved slight reductions in recidivism (after two years, ISP participants had recidivism rates about 10 percent lower than did offenders in the matched control group), saved prison space (62,000 bed-days saved) and was substantially more cost-effective than prison (average cost of ISP was $13,000; the average cost for incarceration for the same period was $20,000-21,000). Due to ambiguous measures, it was not clear whether the fourth objective regarding delivery of appropriate intermediate punishment in the community was achieved. Results of a survey of criminal justice officials suggested that ISP was less severe than it should be, but the officials surveyed were not well informed about the program. Researchers concluded that well-implemented and well-maintained ISP programs such as New Jersey's can provide an effective, appropriate mode of punishment for felons who are neither dangerous nor habitual criminals.

Stage 7: Initiating the Program or Policy Plan

Only after planning has addressed the previous six stages is the program or policy actually ready to be launched. None of the prior six stages, including monitoring and evaluation, should come as an afterthought. To increase the likelihood of success, all six stages of planning should ideally be completed prior to the initial start date. If a review of the planning process uncovers any discrepancies at any of the six prior stages, these gaps should be carefully addressed before proceeding. Stage 7, then, involves putting into motion the program or policy design and action plan (Stages 3 and 4), monitoring program or policy implementation (Stage 5), and, if appropriate, evaluating outcomes (Stage 6).

Once evaluation data is analyzed, feedback is provided to all stakeholders, and the program/policy design should be thoroughly reassessed to determine where revisions are necessary. At the end of the process, the change agent asks whether further adjustments are necessary to meet objectives. What are the strengths and weaknesses of the program or policy? Decisions may have to be made about whether a program should be launched (or continued), and whether it should receive funding. Major activities at this stage include the following:

- Initiate the program/policy design and action plan.

- Begin monitoring program/policy implementation.

- Make adjustments to the program/policy plan as gaps are found.

- Decide whether the program/policy is ready to be evaluated.

- Collect and analyze evaluation data.

- Provide feedback to users and stakeholders.

- Reassess the entire program/policy plan and make modifications or revisions.

This last point is extremely important. Several writers have commented on the importance of "mutual adaptation" as necessary in order for a program or policy to be implemented successfully. [19] Lots of changes are made in the criminal justice system, but few of them stick. One important reason for this is that the innovation and the organizational environment did not fit well enough. In every case of planned change, both the innovation and the environment must change if the new program or policy is going to work.

Imagine a family adopting a 12-year-old child. The family system has to make room for this new member and shift some of its time, attention and emotional resources to meet the child's needs. At the same time, the child needs to make changes. She must learn the family's rules, routines and norms, and learn the idiosyncrasies of each family member. Both the child and the family adapt interactively in response to each other's actions and reactions.

In much the same way, successful implementation of a new program requires mutual adaptation. In New York City, for example, staff at the Center for Alternative Sentencing and Employment Services (CASES) wanted to make sure that their clients fit the target population: jail-bound, not probation-bound, offenders. The program was designed to provide intensive community services that would enable offenders to stay in the community. The system analysis showed, however, that judges in the different boroughs of New York used different criteria for placing offenders in jail. In Queens, for example, judges required fewer jail sentences for offenders than did judges in Manhattan. In order to prevent the CASES program from being used for probation-bound cases, staff adjusted the criteria for accepting clients to the sentencing patterns in each borough. Adaptation of the program increased its chances of achieving its objective (keeping offenders in the community).

Conclusion

A systematic plan is necessary for any change effort. Good intentions are rarely sufficient to bring about successful change. We must beware of the "activist bias,"[20] by which well-intentioned advocates of change assume that they already know what the problem is and what is needed. Such advocates may insist that we desist all this prolonged planning and simply "get on with it." The perils of unplanned or poorly planned change should by now be obvious: expensive, poorly articulated, poorly implemented, ineffective programs and policies that are unable to compete successfully for scarce funds. There are four key points to remember about this seven-stage, systematic model of planned change that you are about to explore:

1. *Program and policy planning is an interactive and ongoing process.* It is crucial to review and modify planning (as needed) at each stage of the analysis. This takes time, but it is time well spent.

2. *A rational planning approach provides a framework for developing logical and effective programs and policies.* The default (too often) is to use unarticulated and untested assumptions to guide planning.

3. *Participation and communication with all stakeholders (e.g., program staff, clients, individuals or agencies whose cooperation is needed, funding sources, citizens affected by the intervention, elected representatives) throughout the change process are keys to success.*

4. *Rarely does planning go smoothly.* While we strongly believe that the advantages of systematically attending to the elements of planning discussed in this book can greatly improve the chances of developing effective policies and programs, we recognize that the environments in which this planning occurs are messy and unpredictable. It takes willpower, a clear vision of what you want to accomplish and lots of communication to remain rooted in the planning process. Planned change increases the likelihood of successful intervention; it cannot guarantee it.

In the next seven chapters, we provide detailed discussions of the seven stages of planning and introduce you to many of the major concepts and terms that you will need to master. We have placed a great deal of emphasis on providing you with case studies that illustrate these concepts and will help you to discover how these concepts can be applied in a variety of criminal justice contexts. Of course, it is practice in the real world of policymaking and program development that will enable you to exploit fully the lessons of planning.

What's to Come

Chapter 2: This chapter discusses one of the most critical and overlooked stages of planning—defining and understanding the problem or issue that is driving the planning process.

Chapter 3: Once we have an understanding of the problem or issue, then we can identify what we want to achieve. Chapter 3 discusses the ways in which goals and objectives are framed so that we can communicate about the direction in which we want our change effort to move and can know when we are heading in the right direction.

Chapter 4: In this chapter, you will learn how to design effective policies and programs. Design involves a number of critical decisions, such as who specifically will benefit from the intervention—something that will affect greatly our ability to achieve our goals.

Chapter 5: Next we will learn about some of the more pragmatic aspects of planning that are essential to the real world of planning, including budgeting and cost projections, orienting staff and assigning responsibility for completion of specific implementation tasks.

Chapter 6: This chapter gets us into the area of accountability. We decided what we wanted to do and who would do what. Now we need to make sure that we do it. We need to monitor our activities and learn about when and why we drift away from what we set out to do.

Chapter 7: How can we learn about what's working and what's not? How can we improve upon our past performance? These are questions that we discuss in the context of evaluation. The methods of evaluation are important to understand in order to avoid drawing invalid conclusions.

Chapter 8: Finally, Chapter 8 brings us into the arena of experience. As we begin to carry out our plans, new information is created that requires a response. Our program or policy may have looked good on paper, but it will have to adapt to the real world of people and organizations and competing goals, and to the results of evaluation data.

DISCUSSION QUESTIONS

1. Describe three trends that have increased the need for planned change.

2. Define *planned change* and give an example.

3. Define *unplanned change* and give an example.

4. Define and describe an example of each of the following: (1) policy, (2) program, and (3) project.

5. Why are collaborative strategies of change preferable to conflict strategies? Explain.

6. Briefly describe the first six stages of planned change (analyzing the problem, setting goals and objectives, designing the program, developing an action plan, monitoring program implementation, and evaluating outcomes). What are the major questions we need to ask at each stage?

7. How did the 1968 President's Commission Report influence thinking about criminal justice planning?

8. Give an example of *mutual adaptation*.

EXERCISE 1.1

Describe briefly, in three paragraphs: (a) a problem in criminal justice (why is it a problem?) (b) what is one possible cause of this problem? (c) what is one possible intervention (a program or policy, as defined earlier in this chapter) that might change this problem?

EXERCISE 1.2

Review the example described in the preface ("The Pitfalls of Poor Planning: 'Three Strikes' Legislation"). Briefly illustrate how the seven-stage model of planned change can be used to analyze an existing policy. Give one example for each of the seven stages.

Endnotes

1   Kettner, Peter M., John M. Daley, and Ann Weaver Nichols (1985). *Initiating Change in Organizations and Communities*. Monterey, CA: Brooks/Cole.

2   Ibid., note 19.

3   Rossi, Peter (1989). *Down and Out in America: The Origins of Homelessness*. Chicago: University of Chicago Press.

4   Buzawa, Eve S., and Carl G. Buzawa (1990). *Domestic Violence: The Criminal Justice Response*. Newbury Park, CA: Sage.

5   Hudzik, John K., and Gary W. Cordner (1983). *Planning in Criminal Justice Organizations and Systems*. New York: Macmillan.

6   Tonry, Michael (1995). *Malign Neglect: Race, Crime, and Punishment in America*. New York: Oxford University Press.

7   Lynch, Michael J., and E. Britt Patterson (1990). "Racial Discrimination in the Criminal Justice System: Evidence from Four Jurisdictions." In Brian E. MacLean and Dragan Milovanovic (eds.) *Racism, Empiricism, and Criminal Justice*. Collective Press.

8   Ibid., note 19.

9   Welsh, Wayne N. (1995). *Counties in Court: Jail Overcrowding and Court-Ordered Reform*. Philadelphia, PA: Temple University Press.

10   President's Commission on Law Enforcement and Administration of Justice (1967). *The Challenge of Crime in a Free Society*. New York: Avon Books.

11   Walker, Samuel (1992). "Origins of the Contemporary Criminal Justice Paradigm: The American Bar Foundation Survey, 1953-1969." *Justice Quarterly*, 9: 47-76; see also Chapter 2 of this book.

12   Moore, Mark (1998). "Synthesis of Symposium." In U.S. Department of Justice, *The Challenge of Crime in a Free Society: Looking Back, Looking Forward*, pp. 167-178. Symposium on the 30th Anniversary of the President's Commission on Law Enforcement and Administration of Justice. (NCJ 170029) Washington, DC: U.S. Department of Justice, Office of Justice Programs.

13   U.S. Department of Justice (1998). *The Challenge of Crime in a Free Society: Looking Back, Looking Forward*. Symposium on the 30th Anniversary of the President's Commission on Law Enforcement and Administration of Justice. (NCJ 170029) Washington, DC: U.S. Department of Justice, Office of Justice Programs.

14   Ransom, George, and Mary Ellen Mastrorilli (1993). "The Massachusetts Boot Camp: Inmate Anecdotes." *The Prison Journal*, 73:307-318.

15   Valle, S. (1989). "Accountability for Addicted Inmates." *The Counselor*, March/April:7-8.

16   Welsh, Wayne N., Philip Harris, and Patricia Jenkins (1996). "Reducing Overrepresentation of Minorities in Juvenile Justice: Development of Community-Based Programs in Pennsylvania." *Crime & Delinquency*, 42 (1):76-98.

[17]   Rossi, Peter H., and Howard E. Freeman (eds.) (1993). *Evaluation: A Systematic Approach* (5th ed.) Thousand Oaks, CA: Sage.

[18]   Pearson, Frank S. (1990). "Evaluation of New Jersey's Intensive Supervision Program." *Crime & Delinquency,* 34:437-448.

[19]   Berman, P. (1981). "Thinking About Programmed and Adaptive Implementation: Matching Strategies to Situations." In Ingram, H., and D. Mann (eds.) *Why Policies Succeed or Fail.* Beverly Hills, CA: Sage; Harris, P., and S. Smith (1996). "Developing Community Corrections: An Implementation Perspective." In A.T. Harland (ed.) *Choosing Correctional Options That Work: Defining the Demand and Evaluating the Supply.* Thousand Oaks, CA: Sage; McLaughlin, M. (1976). "Implementation as Mutual Adaptation: Change in Classroom Organization." In Williams, W., and R.F. Elmore (eds.) *Social Program Evaluation.* San Diego: Academic Press.

[20]   Sieber, Sam D. (1981). *Fatal Remedies.* New York: Plenum.

CHAPTER 2

ANALYZING THE PROBLEM

CHAPTER OUTLINE

▶ *Document the need for change:* Collect and analyze data to define what the problem is, where it is, how big it is and who is affected by it. What evidence of the problem exists?

▶ *Describe the history of the problem:* How long has the problem existed? How has it changed over time?

▶ *Examine potential causes of the problem:* What causes the problem? What theories do we have? The intervention to be chosen must target one or more specific causes supported by research.

▶ *Examine previous interventions* that have tried to change this problem, identify the most promising interventions and choose a preferred intervention approach. We need to analyze available information to direct decisions about a possible course of action.

▶ *Identify relevant stakeholders:* Do different groups of people have different definitions of the problem? Who is affected by the problem?

▶ *Conduct a systems analysis:* Conduct research on the system within which the problem exists, and determine how the system may create, contribute to or maintain the problem.

▶ *Identify barriers to change and supports for change:* Who is likely to support a certain course of action, and who is likely to resist it?

Some preliminary analysis is needed to identify the issues involved in trying to change a particular problem. This important analysis sets the stage for all subsequent planning activities. Beware of the *activist bias,* the notion that we already know what to do, so let's get on with it. In almost all cases, the person who expresses such a view has a vague definition of the problem and its causes, and little knowledge of successful interventions. Without intending to, he or she is advocating a process of unplanned change that maximizes the likelihood of a poorly planned, poorly implemented, ineffective intervention. The many hours of hard work and the motivation that must surely guide any successful change effort should not be wasted on unplanned change. How we analyze the problem guides what kind of interventions we initiate. If problem analysis is flawed, subsequent program or policy planning is also likely to be faulty.

Document the Need for Change

We begin analysis of a problem by examining information about the problem. We are interested in questions such as: How do we define the problem? How big is it, and where is it? Is there a potential for change? We especially want to provide evidence for the existence of a need or problem. We need to be very careful here. Many problems are socially constructed by the media, politicians or even criminal justice officials. By "socially constructed," we mean that certain problems are perceived, and decisions are made to focus attention and resources on a particular problem.[1] However, perceptions of a problem and reactions to it may be quite different than the actual size or distribution of a problem. We need methods to document, describe and analyze problems. At minimum, we need to be sure that a problem actually exists before taking any specific action, but we also need to know about the size and distribution of the problem in order to plan effective solutions.

Although the distinction is somewhat arbitrary, it is often worthwhile to differentiate a need from a problem. Students often point out that many "conditions" could be stated either way: for example, if victims of domestic violence lack access to shelters, then is there not only a need but also a problem, such as repeat incidents of abuse of this population? However arbitrary the distinction may appear at first glance, it might make a large difference in the problem analysis (what kind of information we collect), analysis of causes (explanations of why certain conditions are lacking, versus why other conditions are present) and identification of relevant interventions (do we attempt to provide services that fill an important gap, or do we attempt to apply some intervention to change a problem?). Needs and problems are clearly related, but not identical.

Example 2.1

School Violence: A Problem Out of Control?

In Arkansas in 1998, two boys, ages 12 and 14, were convicted of killing a teacher and four schoolmates after carefully planning their attack with guns taken from the collection of the older child's grandfather. Following several other widely publicized shootings on school properties during the 1997-98 school term, hundreds of school districts across the United States announced tougher disciplinary policies and security measures. While dramatic incidents fuel perceptions that school violence is out of control, available data suggest a more modest interpretation. Information on student victimization, for example, is collected through the School Crime Supplement (SCS), added to the National Crime Victimization Survey in 1989 and repeated in 1995.[2] Only 4.2 percent of students reported any violent victimization in 1995, up slightly from 3.4 percent in 1989. Fewer than 20 children under the age of 14 commit murders in any given year,[3] and homicides committed by juveniles account for only about 14 percent of all homicides for which an offender is identified.[4] Fortunately, tragedies such as the Arkansas incident are quite unusual. Thorough and localized problem analysis should precede the revision or development of school policies in any district. It is not clear from the Arkansas example that school violence is out of control or that revision of school policies is the proper solution.

Definition

Need: A *lack* of something that contributes to the discomfort or suffering of a particular group of people. For example, we might argue that there is a need for drug treatment programs for convicted offenders, or that there is a need for shelters for abused women. In each case, an existing lack of services perpetuates the difficulties experienced by the target population.

Definition

Problem: The *presence* of something that contributes to the discomfort or suffering of a specific group. For example, we might argue that a specific community experiences a high rate of robberies committed by addicts to buy drugs, or that there is a high rate of repeat incidents of abuse of women applying to courts for protection orders. In each case, there is a clearly defined condition present that perpetuates the suffering of a particular group of people.

Next, we attempt to apply some boundaries to the problem. For example, we might begin by stating a concern with juvenile violence. However, we are quickly overwhelmed with information not only about the problem, but also by different causal explanations and different interventions. Are we really concerned with all types of juvenile violence, or with more specific settings? Are we really interested in specific types of violence, such as gang violence, school violence, gun-related violence, drug-related violence, interpersonal conflicts versus violence committed against strangers, or instrumental (goal-oriented) versus affective (emotional) violence? This is an important point. We need to do some research first to narrow our definition of the problem. It is entirely possible that we might decide to focus not only on a specific type of violence, but also upon a specific age group (say, middle-school children), a specific jurisdiction (e.g., a community with a high rate of violence, or a specific city, county or state) or a particular demographic group (e.g., poor children living in inner-city slums). Whatever our reasons for choosing to set boundaries in particular ways (perhaps for personal reasons or because of political or theoretical interests), identifying boundaries involves making judgments about how widely or narrowly to define a problem. How specific or comprehensive should the change be? Where are potential causes and potential interventions located (e.g., at the individual level? group? community? organizational? social structural)?

We first attempt to document the need for change through an analysis of existing conditions. Is there a problem? How big is it? What is the level of "need"? What is the evidence for a problem? One way of documenting a problem is to look at its incidence versus its prevalence.

Definitions

Incidence versus Prevalence

Incidence: The number of *new* cases of a problem within a specific time period (e.g., the number of new cases of AIDS diagnosed in the calendar year 1998).

Prevalence: The *existing* number of cases of a particular problem as of a specific date (e.g., the total number of people in the United States with AIDS as of December 31, 1998).

Where do we find this kind of statistical information, as well as more descriptive information about the problem? We usually need to look at some kind of data to estimate the degree and seriousness of a problem. There are several techniques available; we'll briefly review four of them. Wherever time and resources allow, it is always desirable to use as many techniques as possible to converge upon a specific problem.

Figure 2.1

Data Collection Techniques: Documenting the Need for Change

- **Key informant approach:** We could conduct interviews with local "experts" to assess the level of need or seriousness of a problem (e.g., community leaders, police officers, social service agents, clergy, etc.). One problem with this technique is that people to be interviewed need to be selected carefully for their expertise. We need to be aware that their views may be biased or inaccurate.

- **Community forum:** We could bring together a wide variety of people interested in a particular problem. Through discussion and exchange of ideas, we attempt to identify major problems or needs to be addressed. One common difficulty is that the most vocal groups may not necessarily be representative of a given community (e.g., special interest groups).

- **Community survey:** We may decide to conduct a survey by sampling part of a community or specific areas in a city. We might ask people, for example, "how serious would you rate the following problems in your community . . .?" A common problem with this technique is that it requires skilled researchers, and it can be very expensive and time-consuming.

- **Social indicators:** These are statistics reflecting some set of social conditions in a particular area over time. For example, the U.S. Bureau of Census collects and reports extensive data on unemployment, housing, education and crime. Common problems include difficulty in collecting data on certain questions (e.g., underreporting of illiteracy due to embarrassment), samples that are unrepresentative of the population (e.g., the last census missed a large segment of transient urban dwellers) and questions about the accuracy (reliability and validity) of some data.

Social indicators are perhaps the most accessible and widely used type of data for analyzing criminal justice problems. For example, the Uniform Crime Reports (UCR), collected by the FBI, consist of all crimes reported to the police, and all police arrests for specific crimes. These figures are available for each state, and for the nation as a whole. These figures are widely used to calculate changes in the homicide rate, for example, from year to year. Another widely used indicator is the National Crime Victimization Survey (NCVS), which is a survey administered to a national probability sample, asking respondents to report whether they have been a victim of specific crimes within a specific time period (e.g., the previous six months), as well as other information about any victimization, such as degree of injury suffered, and characteristics of the offender (if known).

Examination of social indicators often leads to the definition of a problem and attempts at change. For example, as part of a Community Corrections Program Development Project, the National Institute of Corrections entered into a contract with researchers at Temple University in 1993 to provide consultation for agencies developing specific community corrections programs. Orange County and Los Angeles Probation Departments filed a joint application that was selected for assistance under this project. Their analyses identified a small group of juveniles (about 8 percent of the juveniles in their study) who accounted for the great majority of repeat referrals to juvenile court. Program planning efforts for this targeted "high-risk" population came to be known as the "8% Program." Various county agencies (probation, health care, mental health, social services and the schools) participated in a multi-agency task force to address program planning.

Figure 2.2

Examples of Social Indicators for Criminal Justice Problems

One extremely valuable source of criminal justice data is the *Sourcebook of Criminal Justice Statistics*, an annual publication by the U.S. Department of Justice. It is available on the internet at *http://www.albany.edu/sourcebook/* or in the Government Documents section of most libraries. Here are a few examples.

- *Drug use by high school seniors.* In 1996, in response to the question "On how many occasions, if any, have you used marijuana/hashish during the past 12 months?" 35.8% of high school seniors reported using these drugs at least once. This figure was up from 21.9% in 1992, but down from 40.6% reporting such use in 1985.[5]

- *Jail overcrowding.* In 1994, 45,618 state prisoners were being held in local jails across the United States because of overcrowding in state facilities. With few exceptions, state prison populations typically exceeded their rated capacities by a considerable amount.[6]

- *Domestic violence.* Of all assaults committed in 1994, according to results from the National Crime Victimization Survey, fully 48.5% were committed by a "nonstranger" (acquaintance, a spouse, ex-spouse, parent, child, brother/sister, other relative, boyfriend/girlfriend).[7]

Social indicators are extremely useful in identifying the seriousness of a problem, how it varies across groups (e.g., income), and how it is changing over time (is it getting better or worse?). Such data are not without biases, however, and the potential user needs to be aware of these.[8] For example, crime victimization measures such as the NCVS may be biased by numerous factors (e.g., respondent misunderstanding of questions or crime definitions; faulty recall of incidents and time periods; deliberate underreporting due to fear, embarrassment or the respondent's participation in illegal activities). Police-reported crime rates such as the UCR also carry potential biases, including police errors in recording and coding crime incidents. Many crimes are never even reported to the police for various reasons (e.g., victim or witness fear, embarrassment or mistrust of the legal system). Social indicators, like the problems they measure, can be viewed as social constructions rather than objective indicators of reality. As Reiss and Roth suggest: "Any set of crime statistics, therefore, is not based on some objectively observable universe of behavior. Rather, violent crime statistics are based on the events that are defined, captured, and processed as such by some institutional means of collecting and counting crimes . . ."[9]

Example 2.2

The New York Crime Story: Fact or Fiction?

Should we hesitate before praising public officials for observed decreases in crime rates (or blaming them for increases)? New York Mayor Rudolph Giuliani and former Police Commissioner William Bratton claimed that reductions in police-recorded crime rates from 1991 to 1996 (including a 55 percent decrease in homicide rates) were due to improved crime-fighting strategies and a "zero tolerance" for crime. There are some reasons to be skeptical.[10]

- The decline in the murder rate began in 1991, three years before either Giuliani or Bratton took office.

- Murder and violent crime rates dropped nationwide for the same time period; New York was not unique.

- Public officials assumed that police policies and resources are the major influences on crime statistics. Much criminological research over the past 30 years suggests otherwise.

- Don't many different factors other than the police influence crime statistics? How about an improved economy, lower unemployment rates, increased incarceration rates over the past 10 years, and so on?

- Battles between drug dealers over turf have dissipated, especially in large urban areas. Many experts feel that drug wars temporarily drove up homicide rates in the late 1980s and early 1990s.

Examples: Documenting the Need for Change

The following examples are recent newspaper stories. Examine how each one covers the points discussed above.

Example 2.3

Inmate total is over twice the '85 level. The inmate population reached 1.6 million in 1995. One in every 167 Americans was in prison.[11]

WASHINGTON—The flood of men and women into America's jails and prisons continued last year, bringing their total—1.6 million—to more than double the inmate count in 1985, the Justice Department said yesterday.

At the end of 1995, there were 600 inmates per 100,000 U.S. residents, up from 313 in 1985. At the end of 1995, one in every 167 Americans was incarcerated.

And an estimated 7,888 children under 18 were being held in local jails last year, a 17 percent increase over the year before, the agency said.

More than three-quarters of those juveniles had been tried or were awaiting trial as adults—a statistic reflecting the increasingly tough public attitude toward youth crime.

Rapid prison population growth in recent years—reflecting a national wave of tough antidrug laws—has strained state and federal budgets as corrections officials have raced to find bed space for 841,200 additional people since 1985, or more than 1,600 new beds every week.

The Federal Bureau of Prisons operated 26 percent over capacity in 1995, while state prison systems reported operating between 14 percent and 25 percent above capacity, the new Justice Department study showed.

The combined federal, state and local prison population grew 6.8 percent last year, slightly lower than the 8.4 percent average annual growth recorded since 1985.

The fast pace of growth reflects a number of trends, including tough mandatory sentencing for some drug crimes and new state and federal provisions designed to hammer repeat offenders.

Judges have less opportunity to be lenient because of new laws that provide for specific prison terms rather than maximum-to-minimum ranges formerly specified.

Prisoners are generally a youthful group, because the vast majority of serious crimes are committed by young men. But because of longer sentences in recent years, the prison population is aging—with more middle-aged prisoners than before.

Politicians and experts on crime are divided over whether the large increase in the number of Americans behind bars has contributed to recent drops in violent-crime rates across the nation.

Example 2.3, *continued*

A number of cities, including New York, have reported significant drops in homicide rates in recent years.

Some experts have described the continuing fast pace of prison growth as a time bomb with potentially devastating economic and social consequences.

More than 60 percent of men in state prisons have children, most of whom are under 18. Nearly 80 percent of women prisoners are mothers. About 6 percent of them come to prison pregnant.

A third of the nation's state prisoners were in three states—California, Texas and New York.

The prison boom has been biggest in the states with the toughest sentences. Texas also had the highest per-capita incarceration rate in the nation, 653 prisoners with sentences of more than a year per 100,000 residents.

Other states with high rates of incarceration included Louisiana, Oklahoma and South Carolina. The states with the lowest incarceration rates were North Dakota, Minnesota and Maine.

Forty-three percent of 1995's prison-population increase was accounted for by Texas (9,571), Florida (6,711), North Carolina (5,726), the federal system (5,216) and Pennsylvania (4,108).

Pennsylvania's 1995 prison-population growth—14.5 percent—ranked sixth in the nation, behind North Carolina, Mississippi, Idaho, Wyoming and Nebraska.

Women accounted for just 6.1 percent of all state and federal inmates and 10.2 percent of those in local jails. There were 63,998 women held in state or federal prisons at the end of 1995 and 52,452 in local jails at midyear.

About two-thirds of the nation's 1.6 million prisoners are in state and federal prisons, where felons serving sentences of more than a year are normally held. The other third are in local jails, which usually hold people awaiting trial or serving sentences of less than a year.

The state prison population increased by 66,843 last year, while federal prisons held 5,216 more than in 1994, the Justice report showed.

Example 2.4

Sharp Rise Reported in Teenagers' Drug Use. In all, 10.9% of Youths in a Survey Admitted Using Drugs. That's a 105% Jump Since '92.[12]

WASHINGTON—Teen drug use rose an alarming 105 percent between 1992 and 1995, the government reported yesterday.

The National Household Survey on Drug Abuse, released by the Department of Health and Human Services, found that the percentage of adolescents between the ages of 12 and 17 who admitted to using illicit drugs in the month preceding the survey increased from 5.3 percent in 1992 to 10.9 percent in 1995, or 105 percent. It also found that:

Youth drug use rose 24 percent between 1994 and 1995.

Monthly marijuana use among youths is up 105 percent since 1992, and 37 percent between 1994 and 1995.

Monthly use of LSD and other hallucinogens is up 183 percent since 1992, and rose 54 percent between 1994 and 1995.

Monthly cocaine use rose 166 percent between 1994 and 1995.

Experts blamed everyone from parents to the media for decreased vigilance in the drug war since the late 1980s, when aggressive drug-fighting efforts appeared to be pushing usage lower in every segment of American society.

Republican presidential candidate Bob Dole saw the problem through a political filter.

"This is nothing short of a national tragedy," he told the Veterans of Foreign Wars convention in Louisville, Ky. "Starting next January, I'm going to make the drug war Priority No. 1 once again."

Dole promised to hold a White House Summit on Drug Abuse in January if elected. In recent months, other Republicans have alleged a lax attitude toward drugs in the Clinton White House.

The Clinton administration expressed concern about the new report's findings but said they were too important to be merely fodder for political attacks.

"The one thing we can't do is to turn drug use among young people into a political football, because that is the wrong message for kids," presidential spokesman Michael McCurry said. "They'll just think it's an issue for the politicians and not something that they have to accept responsibility for."

Health and Human Services Secretary Donna E. Shalala, joined by drug czar Barry McCaffrey, also rejected the Republican criticism yesterday, calling teen drug abuse an urgent, bipartisan issue that every adult must help solve.

"Kids don't know yet whether they're Republican or Democratic," Shalala said at a news briefing. "We must let them know that using drugs is like skydiving without a parachute—that there is no soft landing at the end."

Example 2.4, *continued*

Today, more teens are smoking marijuana and sampling cocaine and heroin at "astounding" rates, McCaffrey said. "What's worse," he said, "too many believe these drugs are not addictive, and fewer have a negative view of drug use than youths did in the '70s and '80s."

Shalala and McCaffrey also released data from the Drug Abuse Warning Network (DAWN), an HHS division, that underscored the sharp rise in drug use by teens. The network monitors the number and pattern of drug-related emergencies and fatal overdoses in 21 major metropolitan areas.

The most current DAWN figures for 1995 found that for youths ages 12 to 17:

- Marijuana-related emergency-room problems rose 96 percent since 1992.

- Emergency-room admissions for heroin use rose 58 percent from 1992 to 1995.

- Cocaine-related admissions rose 19 percent from 1992.

Although overall rates of drug use for the general population are stable, McCaffrey said youths who start with "gateway" drugs such as marijuana and alcohol are particularly vulnerable.

"Drug exposure in America now starts in the sixth grade," McCaffrey said. "It's not enough to have [an antidrug] program, or a yearly antidrug lecture. We need consistent effort, from kindergarten through the 12th grade."

One expert thinks partisan sniping only delays solutions.

"We don't get very far as a nation when we lay blame instead of focusing our energies on youths," said Lloyd Johnston, chief researcher on a 1995 University of Michigan study on teen drug use.

In Johnston's survey of 50,000 students, one-fifth of eighth graders, one-third of high school sophomores, and nearly 40 percent of seniors said they had used an illicit drug during the last year.

Johnston thinks that in the '90s, parents, communities and legislators "dropped the ball" in teaching young people about drugs' dangers.

"The drug issue fell off the national screen at around the time of the Gulf War, and it never really got back on," Johnston said. Now, there are fewer public-service announcements, campaigns, and school-based programs than during the '70s and '80s, Johnston said.

Also, some baby-boom parents are ambivalent about warning their children about drugs, having sampled them themselves. But Johnston said that should not stop them. "They shouldn't have a problem in telling kids that they made the wrong choice back then."

Ultimately, McCaffrey thinks drug education and prevention strategies are the best responses.

"A 12-year-old who smokes marijuana is 79 percent more likely to develop a deadly addiction later in life," he said. "Our best hope is to reduce the impact and the exposure to drugs for American children."

Describe the History of the Problem

As part of a problem analysis, we need to know something about the history of the problem: how long has a given problem existed, and how has it changed over time? Some of this information will have been gathered through research methods such as "key person" interviews, community forums, surveys, or through examination of social indicators. Most likely, however, we will need to look further in published literature for specific, important historical events that shaped the definition of something as a social problem in need of attention, and how responses to the problem changed over time. What significant event or events helped shape the perception of certain conditions as a social problem in need of change? Such historical events often include lawsuits, legislation, dramatic public events or specific social indicators such as crime statistics.

Lawsuits often fuel the perception of a problem, as they did with domestic violence. Liability issues led police to consider seriously the calls for reform. The first of several major cases was *Thurman et al. v. City of Torrington, Conn.*[13] After the defense successfully demonstrated that police showed deliberate indifference to continued pleas for help from Thurman, the court awarded her $2.3 million in damages. This case not only raised awareness of the problem of domestic violence but also led many police departments to favor a presumption of arrest.

Legislation may also create an important push for change. For example, changes in the federal Juvenile Delinquency Act of 1989 led to state initiatives to reduce minority overrepresentation in juvenile justice (see Example 2.5 below).

Dramatic, violent, well-publicized events often demand the recognition of a problem, as did prison riots at New York's Attica prison in September of 1971, which resulted in enormous damages and the deaths of 32 inmates and 11 guards. Attica riots led to the most intensive investigation of prison violence in United States history to date.

One useful technique for summarizing the history of responses to a problem is to construct a "critical incidents" list: a chronology of specific events explaining how a problem was recognized as such and how a specific type of intervention has developed. Once again, we caution readers that reactions to a problem are social constructions, not objective indicators of the problem.

Example 2.5

A Critical Incidents List: Reducing Minority Overrepresentation in Pennsylvania Juvenile Justice.[14]

In response to changes in the federal Juvenile Delinquency Act of 1989, the Juvenile Advisory Committee of the Pennsylvania Commission on Crime and Delinquency (PCCD) concluded that action should be taken to slow the entry or reentry of minorities into the juvenile justice system. It recommended the development and support of community-based prevention activities. The following is a brief "critical incidents" list specifying the major historical events in this effort.

- **1985 - 1988:** There was intensive lobbying by various groups at the federal level to address the problem of minority overrepresentation in juvenile justice. Advocates documented the problem by pointing to various reports indicating that minority youth made up a majority of the juveniles housed in secure detention facilities, even though they constituted only a small proportion of the overall juvenile population in each state.

- **1989:** The federal Juvenile Delinquency Act (JDA) was amended. States were required to address problems in their jurisdictions in order to qualify for federal block grants: a large, indispensable source of state funds for juvenile justice programs and operations.

- **1990:** The state of Pennsylvania formed the Minority Confinement Subcommittee, a division of the state Juvenile Advisory Committee, to address provisions of the JDA. They commissioned a research study to assess the problem. Preliminary results clearly showed a problem: minority youth made up about 75 percent of all youths confined, a proportion more than six times their representation of 12 percent in the state juvenile population.

- **Spring of 1991:** PCCD held an informational session for various groups active in community-based programming for minority youth in Harrisburg, and solicited proposals from various agencies interested in obtaining state funding to address the problem. Five programs were funded.

- **Fall of 1991:** The state commissioned an evaluation of the Harrisburg programs by a team of researchers at Shippensburg University.

- **April of 1992:** The state extended its initiative to Philadelphia, once again inviting various groups active in community-based programming to an informational session and solicited proposals from agencies interested in obtaining state funding to address the problem. Four programs were funded.

Example 2.5, *continued*

- **September of 1992:** The state commissioned an evaluation study of the Philadelphia programs by researchers at Temple University. The same team of researchers took over the evaluation of the Harrisburg programs. The four Philadelphia programs formed a coalition consisting not only of their own staff and directors but also solicited the involvement of other agencies who were interested in the problem and whose cooperation was needed (e.g., probation, police, courts and schools). Monthly coalition meetings began.

- **January of 1993:** While two of the Philadelphia programs had begun selecting and accepting clients late in 1992, full-scale intake of clients began in January of 1993. The evaluation study began at the same time.

Examine Potential Causes of the Problem

Examining the potential causes of the problem is a critical stage of problem analysis. Different causes imply different solutions. If you choose a solution before you examine causes, it is likely that your intervention will be ineffective. Any intervention should be aimed at a specific cause or causes. By attempting to change one or more causes, the goal is to bring about a specific change in the problem. Causes mediate the effect of an intervention on a problem.

When we talk about examining causes, we are analyzing the etiology of a problem, the factors that cause or contribute significantly to a specific problem or need. A *theory* attempts to describe and explain relationships between cause and effect (e.g., a specific problem). A theory will describe causes of a specific problem, and it will outline proposed relationships between different causes. A theory may also suggest solutions to a problem: it provides a logical rationale for using one intervention over another.

Causes may be identified at different levels of analysis ranging from individual to social structural:

- *Individual:* Presumed causes lie within individuals (e.g., personality traits such as "aggressiveness").

- *Group:* Presumed causes lie within the dynamics of particular groups to which a person belongs (e.g., patterns of roles and relationships within a family).

- *Organizational:* Presumed causes lie within the particular culture and procedures of a specific organization such as the police, courts or prisons (e.g., how police are recruited, selected or trained).

- *Community:* Presumed causes lie within the behavioral patterns and dynamics existing within a specific community (e.g., community "cohesiveness," the degree of involvement in community organizations such as churches and community associations; attitudes toward deviance; supervision of juveniles).[15]

- *Social structural:* Presumed causes lie within the underlying social structure of society (e.g., the unequal distribution of wealth and power engendered by the economic system of capitalism) or its cultural attitudes regarding behaviors such as drug use, sexuality, education, crime, and so on. Factors commonly examined at this level of analysis include poverty, unemployment and discrimination.

We argue that any individual or agency who proposes any intervention always has some theory about what causes what and at least a "hunch" about what kind of strategy would solve a specific problem and why (even if they haven't clearly thought about it or articulated it). In planned change, we very carefully think about such theories and articulate them before we begin an intervention. In other words, we must explicitly tell the rest of the world what our causal assumptions about a specific problem are, and we must support these assumptions before proposing a specific type of change.

Where do you find causes and theories? Causes and theories are discovered by reading published material, and doing library research on the problem. One should look at journal articles, books and government and agency reports (e.g., from numerous branches of the U.S. Department of Justice, including the National Institute of Justice). There are many varying theories of different kinds of social behavior, including criminal behavior. While some theories are very general, and most theories are constantly refined and applied to specific problems, we highly recommend that anyone proposing a criminal justice intervention acquire at least a basic knowledge of criminological and criminal justice theories, either through taking a course on criminological theory or by reading one of several excellent books on criminological theory.[16] As we investigate causes, we should be guided by two major questions:

- What is the *evidence* for competing theories? No intervention should be aimed at causes that are not supported by empirical evidence of some sort.

- What kind of *intervention* is suggested by a particular causal theory? How can a specific cause be affected by an intervention?

Example 2.6

Causes and Correlates of Domestic Violence

There are at least four general categories of causes (theories) or correlates of domestic violence.[17]

- individual
- family structural
- organizational
- social structural

Individual Theories: Researchers often examine characteristics of offenders and victims that increase the likelihood of domestic violence. Causes or contributing factors that lie within offenders, according to researchers, have included poor self-control, low self-esteem, immaturity, depression, stress, poor communication skills and substance abuse. Characteristics of victims contributing to domestic violence have included low self-esteem, psychological dependence and passivity.

Family Structure Theories: Certain kinds of family structures or roles may create high potential for violence. For example, social isolation of families neutralizes potential support and increases risk of abuse. The best family-centered predictors of spouse abuse are family conflict over male substance abuse as well as conflicts over control in the relationship. Such conflicts tend to escalate over time. Also, children who have been victimized themselves or who have witnessed domestic violence in the home may be at higher risk for domestic violence (the "violence begets violence" theory).

Organizational Theories: Processes within criminal justice agencies may unintentionally contribute to domestic violence. In particular, reluctance by police to arrest suspected abusers received much criticism in the 1970s. Research pointed to at least five reasons for the "hands-off" police response to domestic violence:

- *Police culture and training*: Police are socialized into a "crime-fighting" culture; they dislike tasks that imply a "social worker" role.

- *Disincentives*: Police performance is often evaluated on the basis of numbers such as arrest rate and clearance rate, not mediation skills.

- *Perception of danger in domestic assault cases*: Although widely perceived as such among police officers, it is a myth that domestic violence calls are the most likely to result in officer deaths.

Example 2.6, *continued*

- *Perceived futility*: Police perceive, often accurately, that few arrests for domestic violence actually result in successful prosecution (e.g., victims drop charges; prosecutors decline to proceed).

- *Fatalistic attitudes*: Police have lamented legal restraints (e.g., search and seizure) on their own use of power. They are sensitive to the potential liability involved in domestic violence cases.

Social Structural Perspectives: Broad-based patterns of gender inequality in our Western society are seen by many researchers as significant contributors to high rates of domestic violence. For example, patriarchal (male-dominated) religions have been said to affirm a family structure dominated by the authority and power of males. Economic patterns have also discriminated against women: women's traditional role as housewife was not as highly valued as men's breadwinner role, and women have historically been more economically dependent on men as a result. Other researchers point to the influence of a class-based social system: men have traditionally exerted domination over women in all areas of private and public life. According to this view, culturally sanctioned sexism is the problem to be addressed, rather than deviant individuals or dysfunctional families. We live in a stratified society, it is suggested, in which men retain more power and social advantage than women.

Examine Previous Interventions

As we did in documenting the need for change, and in our analysis of causes, some thorough research is needed to discover what types of interventions have been attempted to change a specific problem. Often, a single study will report both causal factors and the intervention that was designed to address those factors, but this is not always the case. The planner or analyst must attempt to find out what major interventions have addressed the problem of interest, and they should identify which specific causes the intervention was attempting to modify.

Again, excellent sources of information about interventions are "key persons" working in justice-related positions, as well as criminal justice journals and books, and (especially) government reports. Numerous databases can be searched by key words and terms. Excellent criminal justice literature searches can be conducted on-line, via computer software (disk or CD-ROM) and in printed index format. These include the National Criminal Justice Reference Service (NCJRS) sponsored by the U.S. Department of Justice, and the *Criminal Justice Abstracts*. It is necessary to familiarize oneself with the various search instruments and techniques available, preferably at a well-equipped university library. A good reference librarian is a valuable source of assistance.

Identify Relevant Stakeholders

Next, we identify the "stakeholders" in the change process. A *stakeholder* is any person, group or agency who has a legitimate interest in the problem and/or the proposed intervention. We need to decide whose views should be considered in the planning process. Some stakeholders will provide essential cooperation; others provide potentially fatal opposition. If the intervention is to be successful, it is important that the right individuals, groups and organizations be involved in the planning process. Otherwise, the project may run into insurmountable difficulties stemming from a lack of adequate information, resources or cooperation. Who, then, should be included in the planning phase?

- experts?

- agency heads?

- agency staff?

- clients?

- community groups?

- business people in the neighborhood?

- other community organizations (e.g., church, school)?

Before we can answer these questions, we need to review the information we have already collected, and answer some key questions. For example, what expectations do various individuals and groups have for change? What results are expected? Are there differences of opinion?

We can think of potential stakeholders in terms of several roles that participants may play in the change process.[18] Major roles include the following:

- **Change Agent System:** Who begins the planning process to design an intervention? Who actually gets the ball rolling to address the problem? The change agent system usually includes the change agent and his or her sanctioning institution (e.g., the State Department of Corrections announces plans for developing boot camps). Change agents, as noted previously, come from many different backgrounds: legislators, criminal justice policymakers, professional planners, administrators and service professionals.

- **Initiator System:** This includes those who bring the problem to the attention of the change agent. They raise awareness of a problem (e.g., professional lobbyists, national groups such as the ACLU, National Organization of Women, the Urban League, etc.).

- **Client System:** This includes the specific individuals, groups, organizations or communities that are expected to benefit from the change (e.g., juveniles, families and their communities might be expected to benefit from a delinquency prevention program that requires performance of community service).

- **Target System:** This includes the persons, group or organization that need to be changed in order to reach objectives. For example, to reduce domestic violence, do we need to change abused women? their spouses? the police response? the court response?

- **Action System:** This includes all those who, in some way, assist in carrying out the change plan, including program planning, implementation, monitoring and evaluation. Particularly important, however, is the actual agency responsible for programming or service delivery (e.g., a nonprofit agency called Impact Services, Inc. runs an after-school delinquency prevention program called the Checkmate Program in north Philadelphia). Primarily, then, the action system includes the actual service providers who implement the change.

Sometimes, overlapping roles are possible. For example, the change agent may be part of both the target system and the action system. For example, a police commissioner orders sweeping changes in police policy for dealing with domestic assault complaints. In such a case, the change agent, by virtue of overlapping roles, enjoys a degree of credibility or authority with both patrol officers (the target system) and their supervisors who are responsible for implementing the new policies (action system). Overlapping roles may also enhance continuity: for example, in cases in which the same person who initiates change (initiator system) also carries it out (action system) with the cooperation of other participants. On the other hand, there are clearly instances in which overlapping roles are not desirable. For example, the person or agency actually carrying out the intervention should never be held responsible for the monitoring and evaluation of performance, because of their potential subjectivity or bias.

Conduct a Systems Analysis

Current thinking about criminal justice as a system was largely influenced by the 1967 President's Commission report (see also Chapter 1). There is now little doubt that criminal justice problems and policies are shaped by the interactive actions and decisions of various individuals and agencies in any jurisdiction (e.g., a particular city, township, county or state). At the same time, criminal justice projects, programs and policies are shaped in a volatile political environment. Diverse interest groups and agencies compete for attention, and fragmented decisionmaking is common.[19] Because criminal justice officials and agencies often act without consideration of how their decisions might affect those elsewhere in the system, the criminal justice system has often been called a "nonsystem."[20] While the past 20 years have been characterized by increased coordination, harmony and cooperation among criminal justice units, there is still a long road to travel.[21]

A *system* can be defined as "all aspects of criminal justice case processing that relate to punishment or sanctions from the time of arrest—including decisions about pretrial custody—through the execution and completion of a sentence—whether that sentence is served in the community and/or in a correctional institution."[22] All individuals, groups and organizations that play a role in such decisions in a specific jurisdiction are part of the relevant system.

The change agent, whether a consultant, a criminal justice or government official or an academic, must identify relevant individuals and agencies in the policy environment: those whose decisions may have shaped the problem and those whose decisions may potentially shape the development and implementation of change (i.e., new or modified policies, programs or projects). Once identified, the change agent must consider how various officials and agencies have impacted the problem and solutions in the past and how they might do so in the future. Many of the problems we seek to address in criminal justice are "systems" problems. Consider the following examples:

Example 2.7

Examples of "Systems" Problems

Jail Overcrowding. Jails interact extensively with law enforcement agencies, courts, probation and local government. Local police decide whether to arrest and book accused offenders and thus control the major intake into the jails. Local courts influence jail populations through pretrial release decisions and sanctions for convicted offenders. Charging decisions by district attorneys influence the efficiency with which pretrial suspects are processed. Probation may administer both pretrial release programs, such as "ROR" (release on own recognizance), and intermediate sanctions for sentenced offenders, such as electronic surveillance, intensive supervision probation and work release. County government is responsible for financial and personnel allocations to each of these agencies. In turn, county government decisions are affected by financial allocations and criminal justice legislation determined at the state level.[23]

Sentencing Disparities. Concerns about disparities in sentencing (individuals committing similar offenses often receive very different penalties), the use of judicial discretion (wide variations in sentences across different

Example 2.7, *continued*

judges and jurisdictions) and perceptions of either excessive leniency or harshness have led to the development and revision of state and federal sentencing guidelines. However, actual "sentencing" policy in any jurisdiction is an outcome resulting from the input of numerous individuals and agencies. Judges obviously impose criminal sanctions, but they must do so within the limits of state criminal statutes, set by the state legislature. Prosecutors make decisions about charging, which depend upon the strength and quality of evidence supplied by police, the ability and willingness of witnesses to testify, and so on. Prosecutors' charging decisions determine which criminal statutes apply to a case, and thus influence legal procedures and outcomes in any case. Pretrial service providers make decisions about which defendants are eligible for release pending trial, which in turn critically affect a defendant's ability to assist in the preparation of his or her defense. Defense attorneys participate in negotiations with prosecutors regarding admissible evidence, appropriate charges, potential plea bargains, and so on. Probation usually prepares a presentence report on convicted offenders, and their recommendations influence judicial options for sanctioning. At the time of sentencing, elected judges also consider the values of their constituents, their colleagues and local justice officials. Judges must be at least to some degree aware of and responsive to their local political environment.[24]

Guidelines for Systems Analysis

While the methods for analyzing systems tend to be complex, we offer several basic guidelines for conducting a systems analysis. A model developed by the Center for Effective Public Policy assumes that in order to understand the criminal justice system in any jurisdiction, it is essential to examine the full range of sanctions that are imposed upon offenders. A *criminal justice system assessment* involves gathering and analyzing information that may exist in the experiences of individual decisionmakers, in agency information systems and databases, and in agency reports and communications. In general, "a system assessment is a collaborative effort to synthesize individuals' experiences with the criminal justice system into a shared understanding of how things work now. This provides a common base upon which to evaluate the present, to shape a common vision for the future and to make that vision a reality."[25]

This model assumes the presence of two key elements: (1) a set of policymakers committed to understanding and shaping their system of sanctions to operate in a more collaborative manner (i.e., a "policy team"), and (2) a team of outside consultants committed to working with the jurisdiction to complete the assessment. It prescribes a set of assessment activities that constitute information collection, analysis and vision-building. Refer to Case Study 2.3 at the end of this chapter for a specific example. Sources of data for systems analysis are summarized in Table 2.1.

Table 2.1 Data Sources for Criminal Justice Systems Analysis

Stakeholders (Interviews/Forums)	Documents/Social Indicators
Local and state policymakers involved in justice activities: judges, prosecutors, public defenders, corrections officials, police, sheriff, jail administrator, community corrections personnel, probation officers, bail bond agents.	• Annual reports of local and state justice agencies • City and state budgets; agency budgets • Criteria for various sanctions as expressed in agency policies, mission statements, etc. • Any agency and committee reports on the problem • Community corrections plans • Newspaper accounts • Minutes of criminal justice policy committees
Key legislators (state and local) and committee staff involved in criminal justice legislation; county commissioners.	• Reviews of past and pending litigation • Legislative study commission reports
Sentencing commission staff.	• State sentencing guidelines
Staff of agencies involved in the sanctioning process, especially those who have responsibility for data collection, reports, research (e.g., court clerk, booking staff of the jail, research staff in justice agencies, information system managers, criminal justice coordinators).	• Jail booking records • Court data systems • Presentence investigation reports • Information system documentation and codebooks • Court and probation files
Citizens, service organizations, business organizations, churches, neighborhood organizations and community groups.	• Records of any public opinion polls or community forums on criminal justice issues • Newspaper accounts
Private business groups; board members of large private and nonprofit organizations that fund or supervise justice-related activities.	• Minutes of meetings • Newspaper accounts
Association or union representatives for police, corrections or court staff.	• Union contracts
Private-sector service providers that work with police, courts and corrections (e.g., drug, alcohol, sex offender, educational, job training and mental health treatment providers who accept criminal justice referrals).	• Internal agency documents and listings of referral sources and treatment providers • Service directories • Standards and audits for private care providers
Faculty in local law schools and universities who have conducted policy analyses and research on the problem.	• Research reports

1. Describe the Problem. What is the problem, issue, crisis or impending disaster that has suggested that a systems analysis might be helpful? What has brought certain officials to the table to discuss some problem, such as jail crowding, sentencing legislation, a high-profile crime such as child sexual abuse, or community concerns about drugs? Special attention should be devoted to assessing the problem as it exists in an entire system (e.g., all case-processing decisions that influence jail populations), not in just one separate part (e.g., jail admissions, daily populations and discharges).

2. Describe the Roles and Responsibilities of Different Levels, Branches and Agencies of Government. There is enormous variety across jurisdictions in how typical justice functions are distributed. At the state level, for example, typical actors and agencies include a Commissioner and Department of Corrections, the Attorney General, the Probation and Parole Department, officials in the State Planning Agency and/or the Governor's Office of Criminal Justice, a Senate Judiciary Committee, and so on. There is usually some kind of sentencing commission, community corrections board or other state body that sets policy and/or makes decisions about the distribution of justice funds (e.g., the Pennsylvania Commission on Crime and Delinquency oversees such functions). The actual structure and operation of policing, courts and corrections varies substantially by state and locality. Various public and private agencies at the county level may provide pretrial assessment and services, prevention and treatment programs, halfway houses, and so on. We want to find out what agencies have responsibility for which elements of the sanctioning system, and how they relate to each other.

3. Describe the Funding Environment. Who pays for what in a specific jurisdiction? To what degree are agencies and programs funded by local, state or federal funds? Private-sector funds? Nonprofit agency support? There is often tension between state and local governments over budget responsibility for public services such as criminal justice, education and health. For example, state law requires cities and counties to enforce the criminal code of the state but usually provides only about one-third of the funding needed for local courts. Community corrections programs are likely to be funded by a variety of sources—public, private and nonprofit. We need to understand, then, how funding is provided for various elements of sanctioning, the level of funding provided for each, whether the funding is likely to decrease or increase, and what conflicts or changes are likely in the near future.

4. Describe the Role of the Private Sector (if any). Private-sector agencies have been involved in criminal justice for many years, through treatment programs, halfway houses, and so on. Their role has increased tremendously in recent years to include pretrial services, urine screening, electronic monitoring, offender assessments, residential programming and even secure detention. We want to answer questions such as the following: What proportion of and what types of sanctions are provided by private and public sector agencies? What are the criteria for contracting with private providers? How does this distribution of resources influence availability, targeting, funding, use and offender performance? Are unique incentives (e.g., profitability) associated with the use of some particular sanctions over others? What effects do these incentives have on criminal justice processing and outcomes?

5. Describe How Discretion is Distributed Throughout the System. Responsibility for sanctions varies greatly among different agencies in different jurisdictions. As such, we need to find out who has discretion regarding particular decisions in the sanctioning process. Note that this task is distinct from the "roles" question above; we want to determine not only *which* decisions different agencies and individuals exert discretion over, but also *how* they use that discretion. For example, what are the typical options available to prosecutors in charging and dismissal decisions? How much discretion do parole, probation and the Department of Corrections have regarding the timing of release, and the use of prerelease programs such as furlough and halfway house placements? How often are the recommendations in a presentence investigation followed by the judge? In general, we seek to determine answers to the following questions: Where does discretion exist in case processing and dispositions? How much discretion does each individual and agency possess in relation to a specific sentence or sanction? Who else influences that decision?

6. Describe the Existing Continuum of Sanctions. Here, we seek to formally identify all possible sanctions available in a particular jurisdiction, through both the public and private sectors. Sanctions may be punitive, incapacitative or rehabilitative in nature. In addition to jail or prison beds, we want to record treatment slots, educational programming slots and community-service slots. We want to know the number of slots available, average length of stay, per-day costs, and methods of referral or access.

7. Describe the Offender Population. We need to know about the volume and characteristics of offenders who move through each stage of criminal justice processing and sanctioning. We seek to understand what types of offenders are receiving which types of sanctions. Ideally, sanctions should be appropriate to individual offenders (e.g., seriousness of offense, past record, specific needs and level of risk). For example, are scarce jail and prison beds being used for the most high-risk offenders? Are community sanctions being used for appropriate offenders?

8. Describe the Policy Environment. Sentencing and sanctioning policy in any jurisdiction is usually the result of formal or informal interactions between various policymakers. At the local level, formal efforts often take the form of collections of public and private officials as well as citizens appointed to criminal justice coordinating councils, intermediate sanctions policy groups, community corrections advisory boards and similar groups. In many cases, individual actors and agencies communicate haphazardly and informally. The key question here is whether a jurisdiction exhibits the readiness to begin and engage in a more formal "systems" policy process. The Center for Effective Public Policy places considerable emphasis upon building effective "policy teams" to examine systems issues such as intermediate sanctions. Policy teams consist of key decisionmakers in the local criminal justice system: those who have the authority to make major decisions, and those who are willing to make a commitment to system-level policy analysis and development. It is assumed that no single individual is capable of developing system policy, and that problems and responses will occur randomly and unpredictably if no system-level policy is put into place. Questions to ask include the following: What pressures are there for policymakers to meet to discuss a specific problem? Does the necessary leadership and commitment exist to engage in a group policy-making process? What is happening in the jurisdiction that might distract policymakers from this effort?

9. **Describe the Historical Context.** We described how to analyze the history of a problem earlier in this chapter; here we emphasize a systems approach. For example, we want to know: What traditions exist in the use of sanctions (e.g., little or extensive use of intermediate sanctions)? Are there traditions of coordination among different branches of the justice system? Is there any history of litigation over criminal justice processing and sanctioning? Are there unique political factors in the history of a jurisdiction that are relevant to an understanding of current sanctioning policy?

10. **Describe Current Uses and Availability of Information.** A key factor influencing any jurisdiction's ability to engage in successful systems assessment is the quality of information resources at its disposal. In some systems, much information about processing and sanctioning is still stored in manual systems (e.g., files and folders, index cards). In other systems, some agencies have rudimentary computerized data systems. In other agencies, relatively sophisticated information systems may exist, but there is still no guarantee that agencies share information or communicate information effectively with one another. Key questions include the following: Do agencies currently share information, and to what degree? Are they willing to share information? What information is available from each source, how is it kept, and where is it?

11. **Describe Community Involvement in the Criminal Justice System.** Jurisdictions vary in the degree to which community involvement has been invited or encouraged, and the nature of that participation. For example, citizens may be involved in town watch and similar communi-

ty policing efforts. In some cases, citizens may be appointed to local criminal justice councils, police review boards and other policy groups. Lack of community involvement can create suspicion and resistance; positive involvement can be an asset to planning and policy development. Key questions include: To what degree is the community involved in any aspect of criminal justice processing and sanctioning? What are community attitudes toward existing forms of sanctions? Who are the active and vocal community leaders on criminal justice issues?

Identify Barriers to Change and Supports for Change

We have talked only a little so far about resistance to change. Even at this early stage, a decision must be made about whether to continue forward. Is the change attempt possible? Are the necessary resources and cooperation likely to be available? Before proceeding, we offer some techniques to identify potential barriers to change. These barriers or sources of resistance take many forms:

- *Physical* (e.g., the physical design of a jail prevents adequate supervision).

- *Social* (e.g., inequalities related to class, gender, race).

- *Economic* (e.g., inequalities related to income and employment).

- *Educational* (e.g., clients do not understand or know about services).

- *Legal* (e.g., criminal justice agencies are often legally obligated to do certain things and not do other things). For example, prison industry programs that could reduce the costs of incarceration are severely restricted by federal prohibitions regarding the movement and sale of prisoner-made goods.

- *Political* (some groups have more power than others to make their views heard; political processes can support or block a change).

- *Technological* (e.g., sophisticated information and communications systems may be required to implement a specific program or policy).

Consider the following example. Under the permanent provisions of the Brady Act, effective November 1998, pre-sale firearm inquiries will be made through the National Instant Criminal Background Check System (NICS). State criminal history records will be provided to the FBI through each state's central repository and the Inter-State Identification Index. The index points instantly to state-held criminal records. Although the Brady Act requires states to develop their criminal history record systems and improve their interface with the NICS, states have complained bitterly that the federal government has not provided sufficient technical or financial resources to implement the informational requirements of the Brady Act (see Chapter 5). What barriers need to be overcome, and how can this be done?

Consider a second example. A county is under court orders to reduce its jail population. Everyone agrees that a new jail is needed. However, when certain locations within the county are proposed as sites for the new jail, citizens with economic and/or political power organize community opposition to oppose the construction of a jail in their own neighborhood. Such opposition, called the "NIMBY" response ("not in my back yard")[26] may take the form of protests or even lawsuits by powerful citizens to block construction. Is it fair that some parties can more effectively resist unwanted change than others?

One particularly useful technique for analyzing sources of support and resistance is called *force field analysis*. Remember that participation and communication are keys to change, and that collaborative strategies are preferred to conflict strategies. This technique requires us to consider diverse views and to use collaborative strategies to reduce resistance and increase support for change.

The technique of force field analysis, developed by Kurt Lewin,[27] is based upon an analogy to physics: a body will remain at rest when the sum of forces operating on it is zero. When forces pushing or pulling in one direction exceed forces pushing or pulling in the opposite direction, the body will move in the direction of the greater force. In planned change, we are dealing with *social* forces rather than *physical* ones. To succeed in implementing any intervention, we want to try to reduce resistance to change.

Figure 2.3

Forces in Support   Resistance

Equal Forces = No Movement

Social change, like physical change, requires one of three options:

- increasing forces in support of change
- decreasing forces against change (usually creates less tension and leads to fewer unanticipated consequences)
- doing both in some combination

There is always resistance to change. At best, there is inertia, which the change agent must anticipate and overcome. Force field analysis is a valuable tool for doing this. Generally, we focus on reducing, rather than overcoming, resistance. Case studies at the end of this chapter provide opportunities to apply these concepts to specific examples. Three steps are involved in a force field analysis:

1. *Identify driving forces* (those supporting change) and restraining forces (those resisting change).

2. *Analyze the forces* identified in Step 1. Assess (for each):

   • *amenability to change* (how likely is it that this force can be changed?)

   • *potency* (how much impact would a reduction of this source of resistance have on moving the intervention forward?)

   • *consistency* (does this force remain stable or change over time?)

3. *Identify alternative strategies* for changing each force identified in Step 1. Focus on reducing sources of resistance.

Figure 2.4

Kurt Lewin and "Action Research"

In our travels to academic conferences, we often hear complaints by researchers that policymakers ignore the results of their research. In our consultations with policymakers, we often hear complaints that researchers use excessive jargon, that research results are inconsistent, and research rarely provides the timely and specific information needed to form a basis for decisions. Clearly, researchers and policymakers need to interact more closely to facilitate relevant research and informed policy decisions.[28] Few social scientists have taken this task more seriously than Kurt Lewin, who asserted: "Research that produces nothing but books will not suffice."[29]

Lewin coined the term "action research" to describe an intentional process of change whereby social science research intentionally and explicitly informs and shapes social action (including organizational and public policy decisions) and evaluates the results of that action. It involves fact-finding, planning, execution and evaluation. Results from action research provide new information that gives planners a chance to learn and gather new insights about the strength and weaknesses of their decisions. Lewin emphasized that action research is a dynamic and interactive process. Successful action research requires attention to the field or system in which particular decisions are made, and the identification of different "forces" (individuals, groups or agencies) pushing for and against a particular type of change.

DISCUSSION QUESTIONS

1. Define each of the following:

   (a) *change agent system*

   (b) *initiator system*

   (c) *client system*

   (d) *target system*

   (e) *action system*

2. Define: (a) *need*, and (b) *problem*.

3. Define: (a) *incidence*, and (b) *prevalence*.

4. What techniques can we use to estimate the degree and serious-ness of a problem? Describe each method of documenting the need for change: (a) key informant approach; (b) community forum; (c) community survey; and (d) social indicators.

5. What does it mean to say that a problem is "socially constructed"? Give an example.

6. (a) Define *etiology*. (b) Describe the five levels of etiology, and give an example of each.

7. Define *theory*.

8. What is a *systems analysis*? Describe four steps in a criminal justice systems analysis. Use examples to illustrate your understanding of these concepts.

9. Discuss different types of barriers to change, and give an example of each: (a) physical, (b) social, (c) economic, (d) educational, (e) political, (f) legal, and (g) technological.

10. (a) Define *force field analysis*. (b) Describe each of the three steps.

11. Define *action research*.

Case Study 2.1

Domestic Violence

Instructions: Read the following hypothetical case scenario. Break into groups (assigned by the instructor), and answer the questions that follow it. Each group member should take some notes about the discussion, but the group will appoint a spokesperson to report the group's findings to the class. Plan on preparing a five-minute summary.

A headline in a local newspaper, the *Bigtown Chronicle*, read: "Woman killed by husband in domestic dispute." Bigtown Police said that Betty Benson, age 32, died of multiple stab wounds allegedly inflicted by her husband, Bill, age 34, following a violent argument in the couple's home. Police had been called to the home four times in the previous six months in response to complaints by neighbors that "there was a lot of yelling, and she was screaming like she was being beaten." Betty Benson had declined to press charges in each instance.

The next day, there was a noisy protest in front of city hall by a local group called WASA (Women for Action against Spouse Abuse). WASA spokesperson Sarah Smith told reporters, "This kind of nonsense has been going on far too long. The police were called to that house four times before she got murdered, and they didn't do anything to help her. The police should be arresting sick people like Bill Benson and putting them away for a long time, not just talking to them and letting them go right back to beating their wives."

Police Commissioner Frank Fine responded to the criticisms by pointing out that the police don't make the laws. "WASA can complain all they want," Fine said, "but the state legislature makes the laws regarding domestic assault, and right now, the law says that police can't make an arrest unless the victim swears out a complaint. We can't arrest people like Bill Benson just because they appear to be unsavory characters."

WASA began protesting in front of the state capital and, two days later, Rep. Alan Atkinson introduced a new bill calling for sweeping changes in the laws regarding spouse abuse. The bill called for mandatory arrest and a mandatory 48-hour detention period, pending investigation, for anyone suspected of spousal assault. According to the bill, the police would use "reasonable discretion" in enforcing the law. The local chapter of the ACLU (American Civil Liberties Union) expressed outrage, arguing that the new bill would deprive suspects of their constitutional rights of due process and give the police the power to be "judge, jury and hangman."

Bob Bigheart, a spokesperson for the Bigtown Social Services Agency said that tough new laws were not the answer. Instead, he suggested, the police should train officers in family-crisis counseling so that they can mediate domestic disputes and refer couples to community agencies to help solve their problems. Police Commissioner Frank Fine says that is what the police

Case Study 2.1, *continued*

do anyway, "We are a service-oriented police department," Fine said, "and our officers are among the best-trained in the nation." Claiming that the Commissioner was "arrogant and insensitive to the rights of victims," WASA called for Fine's immediate resignation.

Questions

The governor has asked you, as members of the state planning agency, to study the problem of domestic assault and make preliminary recommendations about what to do, if anything, to deal with the problem. Include the following in your answer:

1. Is there a problem here? If so, what is it? How can you tell?

2. Identify the participants and the role that each plays.

    (a) *change agent system*

    (b) *initiator system*

    (c) *client system*

    (d) *target system*

    (e) *action system*

3. Identify the specific change being proposed, and conduct a force field analysis.

4. Who perceives the need for what kind of change? Are there differences of opinion? Whose views need to be considered, and how do you choose among competing views?

5. Do you need any additional information before you make your report to the governor? Should some kind of change proceed?

Case Study 2.2

Prison Overcrowding

Instructions: Read the hypothetical case scenario below. Then, break into groups (assigned by your instructor) and answer the questions that follow. Each group member should take some notes about the discussion, but the group will appoint a spokesperson to report the group's findings to the class. Plan on preparing a five-minute summary.

Are Parole Reductions Partly to Blame for Prison Crowding?[30]

HARRISBURG—Here's where things stand with Pennsylvania's bulging state prison system:

- There are now 32,410 inmates in a system designed to hold 20,970.

- More than 4,100 were added just last year.

At that rate, the state would need to build four prisons every year at a cost of between $200 million and $300 million just to keep up. And the system would still be over capacity.

Those were some of the sobering facts brought out yesterday at a state Senate Judiciary Committee hearing on prison crowding. Committee chairman Stewart J. Greenleaf (R., Montgomery) said the legislature needed to get a handle on the causes of crowding and possible remedies, especially with a new budget about to be negotiated.

"Opening new facilities is part of the solution, but it is not the sole answer," Greenleaf said at the start of the hearing. "Almost as soon as we open a new institution, it becomes filled." He added: "Now that we are facing a cell-space crisis as the result of increasing incarceration rates, we must consider—very carefully consider—alternatives to institutional punishment for those offenders who are judged to be good risks and who are convicted of nonviolent crimes."

Nicholas P. Muller, chairman of the Pennsylvania Board of Probation and Parole, told the committee that his agency continued to approach parole decisions cautiously, which has led to a slowdown in the release of inmates.

Paroles have dropped since the furor last year over Robert "Mudman" Simon, a convicted murderer accused of fatally shooting a New Jersey police officer. Muller said the number of paroles was moving up again, but still was not where it was before the flap over Simon, a Pennsylvania parolee.

"We are hearing reports of a tremendous, high level of frustration within the prison walls," said Angus R. Love, president of the Pennsylvania Prison Society. "Parole is the one area that I hear the most questions about. . . . What we're hearing is that inmates are very upset."

Case Study 2.2, *continued*

Muller said a backlog of cases that topped 3,000 in July was now nearly cleared out. He also said that because the agency had more personnel, cases were being reviewed more quickly.

Officials from the Pennsylvania Commission on Crime and Delinquency said other factors were contributing to crowding, including rising incarceration rates, mandatory drug sentences, life without parole, more time being served, and more parole violators being sent back to prison.

From 1985 through 1994, the number of people in state prisons for drug offenses rose 625 percent, the commission reported. In that period, the total prison population doubled.

Last year's increase of 4,108 prisoners was "the biggest one-year jump ever in the history of this state," said Dennis Buterbaugh, spokesman for the Department of Corrections, after the hearing.

The jump in the number of drug-offense inmates also has changed the racial makeup of the state system. In 1985, the number of nonwhite inmates in for drug convictions was roughly equal that of whites, and both figures were well below 500, the commission reported. By the end of 1994, the number of nonwhites rose to nearly 2,000, while the number of whites remained below 500. Critics of mandatory drug sentences have argued that they are more punitive for blacks because the laws are aimed at deterring the crack trade in the inner city.

Overall, the state's prison capacity was at 154 percent by the end of last month. But prison crowding is not merely a state problem. The commission reported similar situations in counties across Pennsylvania. Chester County was at 223 percent of capacity at the end of 1994, according to the commission. Delaware County was at 188.4 percent, Montgomery at 186.5 percent, Philadelphia at 161, and Bucks at 130.

Questions

1. Define the problem, and describe the evidence that the author provides to document the problem.

2. The article suggests several possible causes of the problem. Describe (briefly) each cause, and describe the evidence that the author provides for each cause.

3. Based upon the evidence, what are the two strongest causes of prison overcrowding? Explain, and provide evidence to support your answer.

Case Study 2.2, *continued*

4. Assume now that the following hypothetical circumstances occur:

   The governor makes an announcement that parole criteria in Pennsylvania will soon be relaxed to reduce the state's rapidly growing prison population. Be aware that the governor and state are bound by the terms of a consent decree, signed in federal court, agreeing that the state will do "everything within its power" to reduce its prison population when it exceeds capacity by more than 10 percent.

   Now, using force field analysis, do the following:

   (a) Identify *driving forces* and *restraining forces*. Try to identify at least two of each.

   (b) Analyze one of the restraining forces in Part (a) in terms of its: amenability, potency and consistency.

   (c) Describe two possible strategies to reduce this source of resistance.

Case Study 2.3

Criminal Justice System Assessment of Sacramento County[31]

Instructions: Read the case study below, then answer the questions that follow.

During the 1980s, Sacramento County experienced a 32 percent population increase, from 783,381 residents to a 1992 population of more than 1,041,219. Already the seventh largest county in California, Sacramento is expected to grow at a rate exceeding those of most other heavily populated regions of the state. This growth has brought with it public demands for additional and improved government services and an increased concern for criminal justice issues.

Sacramento County and City governments have responded to this public concern by taking a tougher stance on crime. Additional police and sheriff's officers have been hired. Their activities have included crackdowns on alcohol and other drug abuse crimes and teenage gangs. The legislature has defined new crimes, increased criminal sentences and penalties, and enacted more mandatory minimum sentences. New judicial positions have been created to handle the increasing criminal caseload.

As a result of these measures, more offenders are being incarcerated. Tougher probation conditions have increased the number of adult and juvenile offenders incarcerated for violating probation. Judges are increasingly sentencing felony and habitual misdemeanor offenders to serve time in jail, often in combination with a period of probation. This has led to an increase in the use of jail and prison sentences in felony cases from 63 percent in 1977 to 85 percent in 1990. Another major change has been an increase in the number of convicted defendants participating in the Sheriff Department's Work Program, with driving under the influence (DUI) and serious traffic offenders constituting over 75 percent of the 21,275 defendants in this program. Punishments such as fines, restitution, and treatment are being used in addition to jail sentences or juvenile hall commitment.

To house the increasing number of incarcerated offenders, county jail capacity was increased by construction of the $125 million Main Jail and an expansion of the Rio Consumnes Correctional Center (RCCC) branch facilities. The budget needed to operate these facilities now exceeds $47 million a year. These new and expanded facilities represent only part of the county's response. Studies have been conducted to identify alternatives to incarceration programs. Special case processing practices have been implemented. These programs and practices allow for earlier release of selected incarcerated inmates while still maintaining a high standard and regard for public safety.

Despite all these efforts, and a tenfold increase in spending for justice agencies in the 1980s, public confidence in the local justice system has decreased while the fear of crime has increased. Agency administrators and elected officials express concern about inadequacies in the justice system. A

Case Study 2.3, *continued*

common opinion is that the criminal justice system has undergone a costly expansion in the last decade that has not resulted in a meaningful or measurable impact on criminal conduct. It has been suggested that the system itself is facing a crisis in the 1990s.

Increases in staffing, technology, and funding have only allowed the system to keep pace with the number of arrests without allowing it to curb criminal conduct. During 1990, 61,342 adults and 7,292 juveniles were arrested in Sacramento County, representing 6.6 percent of the population. Analysis shows that the number of adult arrests is increasing at a significantly faster pace than the growth in the county's adult population. Felony adult arrests are at the highest level at any time since 1964, with serious violent crimes and drug law violations accounting for nearly one-fourth of all arrests. Adult arrest rates exceed the peak levels of the 1970s. Similar patterns are evident among juveniles.

These increasing arrest rates are overwhelming police, corrections, and judicial resources and seriously crowding the jails and juvenile hall. The Board of Corrections (BOC) 1990 rated capacity of the County's jail facilities was 2,890. Based on this standard, the average daily inmate population (ADP) in 1990 exceeded available bed space by nine percent. Projections [showed that] the jails may have a shortage of 1,059 beds in five years, requiring modifications to programs, services, and staff. These crowded conditions have also led to an increased exposure to litigation. A recently filed lawsuit, for example, alleges that crowding at the new Main Jail and RCCC has resulted in detainees having to sleep on the floor and has limited or restricted services to inmates in violation of rights established under the 8th and 14th Amendments. In response to this suit, the federal court has set a "cap" of 1,808 inmates who can be housed in the Main Jail. Other litigation issues are currently set for further judicial review.

The courts have also been affected by these work load increases. Case processing times are lengthening. The average time to dispose of a typical felony complaint from arrest to conviction was increased by 21 percent, from 126 days in 1977 to 152 days in 1990. In addition, victims, witnesses, and jurors have expressed concern about the time-consuming complexity of the process. The trial of civil court cases is adversely affected because of the expansion of criminal calendars, and there is a growing need for both improved secure facilities and expansion of courtroom space.

Public confidence has also declined because of a perception that a large number of probationers are totally unsupervised. Also, crowded jail conditions have led to a policy of releasing less dangerous pretrial misdemeanant detainees. This has created the perception of a "revolving door" that criminals are using to escape prosecution. This perception is supported by the fact that the failure-to-appear (FTA) rate for misdemeanants booked and released exceeds 60 percent. Issuance of bench warrants for these and other fugitives has caused a backlog of unserved warrants that exceeds 100,000.

Case Study 2.3, *continued*

The issue of sentencing is also being viewed with concern by the public and the judiciary itself. Sentencing practices are often seen as inconsistent and of little support to those defendants wanting to make lifestyle changes that might reduce recidivism rates. Criminal defendants have significant psychological, social, economic, family, education, and treatment needs. At this time, there appear to be no ties between the court process and the human service agencies that could address these needs. In addition, there are very few alternative punishment options available to judges. Consequently, judges have to sentence criminal defendants either to county or state institutions or return them to the community on probation. While longer periods of prison or jail confinement are seen as appropriate for most repeat offenders and probation/parole violators, incarceration may be ineffective, inappropriate, or counterproductive for certain other targeted defendants.

A further indication of an adult and juvenile justice system that is failing has been the inability to effect change in the criminal behavior of defendants. Recidivism is high and is continuing to increase. In 1983, a felony pretrial detainee in the county jail has been arrested an average of six times. By 1989, that average had increased to eight times. As a consequence of this trend, the public has felt the need to "protect itself." Housing developments are now being designed as "gated" or "walled" neighborhoods, and private security firms are flourishing.

Another important concern is the growing realization that local governments do not have the financial resources to handle the increasing criminal justice caseload. The departments within the system are burdened with divergent goals and with priorities that are not clearly defined, well communicated, or effectively coordinated. Their budget requests are often directed to the symptoms of the system's shortcomings, rather than the major problems of the system. Programs and policy changes seem to be reactive, rather than proactive, in responding to needs.

From a planning perspective, the system has not yet adopted a systematic and comprehensive approach to identifying existing and long-term requirements for law enforcement, corrections, and court agencies. The coordinated leadership necessary to establish public policies based on research, evaluation, and monitoring of previous policy decisions is lacking. The data required to determine whether the current enforcement, case processing, administrative, and sentencing practices are working have not been developed. Only limited information measuring system performance or concerning the experiences of other jurisdictions is available.

A comprehensive approach to educating the public about its unrealistic expectations of justice agencies has not been undertaken. Only minimal efforts have been made to obtain community acceptance for a more balanced range of intermediate punishments, which combine the characteristics of punishment, surveillance, and rehabilitation. Innovative corrections programs that might build confidence in local corrections policies have not been introduced to the community. The extent of the county's fiscal problems in responding to jail crowding and crime issues, and the limited role justice agencies can realistically play, have not been thoroughly explained to the public. The public's demand for "tough" criminal justice polices has discouraged system officials from undertaking such education efforts.

In recognition of the critical need to address these issues, and with the realization that the criminal justice system cannot continue to function in this manner, Sacramento County is proposing to establish a new Criminal Justice Cabinet. The Cabinet will include city and county elected officials and budget managers, and court, criminal justice, and human services department personnel. Through a coordinated planning effort, the Cabinet will review, evaluate, and make policy recommendations on common juvenile and adult justice system issues.

The Criminal Justice Cabinet brings together the various institutions that can affect the changes necessary to improve the current system. The Cabinet is a convention of delegates from the various branches of State and local government that constitute, operate, serve, fund, regulate, and otherwise affect the juvenile and criminal justice system in Sacramento County. It constitutes a voluntary association of government institutions represented by the delegates.

The Cabinet is composed of the following officials (not designees):

- Presiding Judge, Superior Court, Chairperson

- Presiding Judge, Municipal Court

- Presiding Judge, Juvenile Court

- Sacramento County State Assembly Representative

- Board of Supervisors-member (designated by Chairperson)

- Sacramento City Council-member (designated by Mayor)

- District Attorney

- Sheriff

- County Executive

- Public Defender

- Chief Probation Officer

- Health Director

- Chief, Sacramento Police Department

The mission of the Cabinet is to study the Sacramento County juvenile and criminal justice system, identify deficiencies, and formulate policy, plans, and programs for innovative change. In addition, its mission is to communi-

Case Study 2.3, *continued*

cate and present planning, financial, operational, managerial, and programmatic recommendations to the agencies represented in the Cabinet. In order to discharge its primary mission, the Criminal Justice Cabinet will be organized into three committees:

1. Juvenile Institutions and Programs Committee;

2. Intermediate Punishments Committee; and

3. Adult Facility Planning and Operations Committee.

Questions

1. Briefly describe how the Sacramento case study illustrates principles of criminal justice system assessment. Use examples to respond to at least two of the following:

    - Describe the roles and responsibilities of different levels, branches and agencies of government.

    - Describe the funding environment.

    - Describe the existing continuum of sanctions.

    - Describe the offender population.

    - Describe the policy environment.

    - Describe the historical context.

    - Describe current uses and availability of information.

    - Describe community involvement in the criminal justice system.

Endnotes

[1]   Spector, Malcolm, and John I. Kitsuse (1977). *Constructing Social Problems*. Menlo Park, CA: Cummings; Walker, Samuel (1998). *Sense and Nonsense About Crime and Drugs*. Belmont, CA: Wadsworth.

[2]   Chandler, Kathryn A., Christopher D. Chapman, Michael R. Rand, and Bruce M. Taylor (1998). *Students' Reports of School Crime: 1989 and 1995* (NCES 98-241/NCJ-169607). Washington, DC: U.S. Departments of Education and Justice.

[3]   O'Brien, Ellen (1998). "Children's Killings Defy Easy Answers." *The Philadelphia Inquirer*, 16 August 1998.

4   Sickmund, Melissa, Howard N. Snyder, and Eileen Poe-Yamagata (1997). *Juvenile Offenders and Victims: 1997 Update on Violence* (NCJ-165703). Washington, DC: U.S. Department of Justice, Office of Justice Programs, Office of Juvenile Justice and Delinquency Prevention.

5   Maguire, Kathleen, and Ann L. Pastore (eds.) (1997). *Sourcebook of Criminal Justice Statistics 1996*, p. 260. U.S. Department of Justice, Bureau of Justice Statistics. NCJ-165361. Washington, DC: U.S. Government Printing Office.

6   Maguire, Kathleen, and Ann L. Pastore (eds.) (1997). *Sourcebook of Criminal Justice Statistics 1996*, pp. 514-15. U.S. Department of Justice, Bureau of Justice Statistics. NCJ-165361. Washington, DC: U.S. Government Printing Office.

7   Maguire, Kathleen, and Ann L. Pastore (eds.) (1997). *Sourcebook of Criminal Justice Statistics 1996*, p. 214. U.S. Department of Justice, Bureau of Justice Statistics. NCJ-165361. Washington, DC: U.S. Government Printing Office.

8   Biderman, Albert D., and James P. Lynch (1991). *Understanding Crime Incidence Statistics*. New York: Springer-Verlag.

9   Reiss, Albert J., and Jeffrey A. Roth (eds.) (1993). "Appendix B: Measuring and Counting Violent Crimes and Their Consequences." *Understanding and Preventing Violence (Vol. 1)*. Washington, DC: National Academy Press, p. 404.

10   Moran, Richard (1997). "New York Story: More Luck Than Policing." *The Washington Post*, 9 February 1997, p. C03.

11   Williams, Larry (1996). "Inmate Total is Over Twice the '85 Level. The Inmate Population Reached 1.6 Million in 1995. One in Every 167 Americans was in Prison." *The Philadelphia Inquirer*, 19 August 1996, p. 1. Reprinted with permission from *The Philadelphia Inquirer*, Aug. 19, 1996.

12   Jones, Rachel L. (1996). "Sharp Rise Reported in Teenagers' Drug Use. In All, 10.9% of Youths in a Survey Admitted Using Drugs. That's a 105% Jump Since '92." *Philadelphia Inquirer*, 21 August 1996, p. 1. Reprinted with permission from *The Philadelphia Inquirer*, Aug. 21, 1996.

13   *Thurman v. City of Torrington, 595 F. Supp. 1521 (1984). Thurman v. City of Torrington, USDC. No. H-84120 (June 25, 1985)*.

14   Welsh, Wayne N., Philip Harris, and Patricia Jenkins (1996). "Reducing Overrepresentation of Minorities in Juvenile Justice: Development of Community-based Programs in Pennsylvania." *Crime & Delinquency*, 42 (1):76-98.

15   Definitions of "community" vary quite a bit: Should it refer to a small number of street blocks where regular, face-to-face interaction among residents occurs? Larger clusters of homes, businesses and places that are still recognized by residents as distinct "communities"? City-designated wards or districts? Census tracts? Areas that are demarcated by physical boundaries such as busy streets, rivers, railroad tracks, parks, and so on? We do not attempt to resolve such debates here. The change agent should be explicit, however, about which definition of "community" he/she decides to adopt and why. For more detailed discussion, see: Bursik, Robert J., Jr., and Harold Grasmick (1993). *Neighborhoods and Crime: The Dimensions of Effective Community Control*. New York: Lexington Books; and Reiss, Albert J., Jr., and Michael Tonry (eds.) (1986). "Communities and Crime." *Crime and Justice*, Vol. 8. Chicago: University of Chicago Press.

[16]   See, for example: Akers, Ronald L. (1997). *Criminological Theories: Introduction and Evaluation*, 2nd ed. Los Angeles, CA: Roxbury; Vold, George B., and Thomas J. Bernard (1986). *Theoretical Criminology*. New York: Oxford University Press.

[17]   Adapted from: Buzawa, Eve S., and Carl G. Buzawa (1990). *Domestic Violence: The Criminal Justice Response*. Newbury Park, CA: Sage.

[18]   Kettner, Peter, John M. Daley, and Ann Weaver Nichols (1985). *Initiating Change in Organizations and Communities: A Macro Practice Model*. Monterey, CA: Brooks/Cole.

[19]   Fairchild, Erika S., and Vincent J. Webb (1985). *The Politics of Crime and Criminal Justice*. Beverly Hills, CA: Sage; Gottfredson, Michael R., and Don M. Gottfredson (1988). *Decision Making in Criminal Justice: Toward the Rational Exercise of Discretion*, 2nd ed. New York: Plenum.

[20]   President's Commission on Law Enforcement and Administration of Justice (1968). *The Challenge of Crime in a Free Society*. New York: Avon Books; Rossum, Ralph A. (1978). *The Politics of the Criminal Justice System. An Organizational Analysis*. New York: Marcel Dekker.

[21]   Wellford, Charles (1998). "Changing Nature of Criminal Justice System Responses and Its Professions." In U.S. Department of Justice, *The Challenge of Crime in a Free Society: Looking Back, Looking Forward*, pp. 58-71. Symposium on the 30th Anniversary of the President's Commission on Law Enforcement and Administration of Justice. (NCJ-170029) Washington, DC: U.S. Department of Justice, Office of Justice Programs.

[22]   Burke, Peggy, Robert Cushman, and Becki Ney (1996). *Guide to a Criminal Justice System Assessment: A Work in Progress*, p. 7. Washington, DC: National Institute of Corrections.

[23]   Welsh, Wayne N. (1995). *Counties in Court: Jail Overcrowding and Court-Ordered Reform*. Philadelphia, PA: Temple University Press; Welsh, Wayne N., and Henry N. Pontell (1991). "Counties in Court: Inter-Organizational Adaptations to Jail Litigation in California." *Law and Society Review*, 25:73-101.

[24]   Parent, Dale, Terence Dunworth, Douglas McDonald, and William Rhodes (1997). *Key Legislative Issues in Criminal Justice: Mandatory Sentencing* (NCJ 161839). Washington, DC: U.S. Department of Justice, Office of Justice Programs, National Institute of Justice.

[25]   Ibid., note 21, p. 8.

[26]   Welsh, Wayne N., Matthew C. Leone, Patrick T. Kinkade, and Henry N. Pontell (1991). "The Politics of Jail Overcrowding: Public Attitudes and Official Policies." In Joel A. Thompson and G. Larry Mays (eds.) *American Jails: Public Policy Issues*. Chicago: Nelson-Hall.

[27]   Lewin, Kurt (1951). *Field Theory in Social Science*. New York: Harper and Row.

[28]   Petersilia, Joan (1991). "Policy Relevance and the Future of Criminology—The American Society of Criminology 1990 Presidential Address." *Criminology*, 29:1-15.

[29]   Lewin, Kurt (1947). "Group Decision and Social Change." In T.M. Newcomb and E.L. Hartley et al. (eds.) *Readings in Social Psychology*, pp. 202-203. New York: Holt and Company.

30   Robert Moran (1996). "Parole Reductions Are Partly to Blame for Prison Crowding. The State Can't Build Enough Prisons, The Senate Judiciary Committee Says It's Looking Into Alternatives." *The Philadelphia Inquirer*, 26 January 1996, p. B03. Reprinted with permission from *The Philadelphia Inquirer*, Jan. 26, 1996.

31   McGarry, Peggy, and Madeline M. Carter (eds.) (1993). *The Intermediate Sanctions Handbook: Experiences and Tools for Policymakers*, pp. 50-52. Washington, DC: U.S. Department of Justice, National Institute of Corrections. Reprinted with permission of the authors.

CHAPTER 3

SETTING GOALS AND OBJECTIVES

CHAPTER OUTLINE

▶ *Write goal statements* specifying the general outcome to be obtained. Consider the goals of criminal sanctions and normative values driving desired outcomes.

▶ *Write specific outcome objectives for each goal:* These should include a time frame for measuring impact, a target population, a key result intended and a specific criterion or measure of impact.

▶ *Seek participation* from different individuals and agencies in goal setting. Consider top-down versus bottom-up approaches.

▶ *Specify an impact model:* This is a description of how the intervention will act upon a specific cause so as to bring about a change in the problem.

▶ *Identify compatible and incompatible goals in the larger system:* Where do values of different stakeholders overlap or conflict?

▶ *Identify needs and opportunities for interagency collaboration:* Whose cooperation and participation is needed to achieve the goals of this program or policy?

Many interventions fail, not because they lack good ideas, but because of vague goals or disagreement about goals. Every program or policy needs a precise definition of what outcome is expected if the intervention is to be effective. Defining goals and objectives is crucial to the rest of the planning process. It is amazing how many expensive and otherwise well-designed interventions fail to define adequately the desired outcomes of the intervention. Without specific, agreed-upon criteria for success, it is impossible to determine whether any intervention works. Without specific goals, it is also likely that program staff, directors and various stakeholders will frequently disagree on the mission of the program and the type of intervention approach to use. It is impossible to measure success if *success* has not been defined.

Every intervention attempts to achieve some kind of outcome, some desired change in the problem. Both goals and objectives refer to desired outcomes, but objectives are much more specific. *Goals* are broad aims of the intervention (e.g., to reduce drug abuse); *objectives* specify explicit and measurable outcomes (e.g., in a one-year follow-up of ex-offenders who participated in a drug treatment program while in prison, researchers predict that participants will have a lower re-arrest rate than nonparticipants).

Identify Goals and Values

Goals describe desired future states, some intended change in the problem. Generally, goals are broad statements intended to provide direction for change. While goals lack the specificity needed to measure actual outcomes of the intervention, they provide some sense of mission that may be crucial to gaining political support for the intervention. For example, the goals of a shelter for abused women might be "to provide temporary shelter for victims of domestic violence and reduce spouse abuse"; the goals of a drug treatment program might be "to reduce drug dependency and help clients lead productive, drug-free lives." Goal statements should be relatively brief (one to two sentences), but at the same time they should accurately capture the intent of a particular program or policy and explain the rationale (reasons) for its creation and its particular structure.

Writing goal statements can be difficult, particularly where relevant stakeholders (individuals, groups and organizations) have widely differing viewpoints about the desired results of a proposed change. Formulating goal statements requires disclosure and discussion of personal beliefs and values. It requires officials to be clear about what they are doing and why they are doing it.

We present below a few brief examples of the most common goals of criminal sanctions and then some of the most common normative values guiding the formulation of criminal justice programs and policies. Case studies at the end of this chapter ask students to consider these issues further and apply their understanding of concepts to specific examples. The change agent and relevant stakeholders involved should seek to identify explicitly and acknowledge the goals and values that underlie any specific program or policy being considered.

The Goals of Criminal Sanctions

Often referred to as purposes of sanctioning, five different goals (retribution, rehabilitation, deterrence, incapacitation and restoration) are commonly asserted as reasons for punishing particular offenders and offenses in particular ways. Some authors[1] have suggested that American society has alternated or cycled through punitive and rehabilitative extremes over its history, while others[2] have argued that a more discrete progression from one set of goals (e.g., rehabilitation in the 1950s and 1960s) to another (e.g., incapacitation in the later 1980s and early 1990s) has occurred. Regardless of the historical perspective that one adopts, the dominance of any one goal at any one time in history is never complete. The five goals below are currently relevant and are likely to be hotly debated for some time.

Retribution

According to advocates of this position, the rightful purpose of punishment is to assign blame and punishment to the wrongdoer. No future good for society is intended, only that the balance of justice be restored by making the offender pay for his or her transgression against society. The death penalty is often justified by its advocates on such grounds.

Rehabilitation

The purpose of punishment, according to this view, is to reduce the likelihood of future offending by diagnosing and treating its causes within the individual. Implicit are theoretical notions that criminal behavior is learned and can be unlearned, and that individual deficits can be corrected. Programs may attempt to alter educational deficits or psychological factors such as anger control, social skills and problem-solving skills.

Deterrence

According to *general deterrence*, the purpose of punishment is to send a message to other potential lawbreakers that the specific offense being punished will not be tolerated. Potential lawbreakers, as a result of fearing the punishment they see inflicted on others, should be "deterred" from committing similar acts. This approach assumes that people make a rational calculation of costs and benefits associated with specific actions. Advocates contend that the "pain" (of apprehension, prosecution and punishment) outweighs the "gain" (the benefits of criminal behavior).

For *specific deterrence*, the message is not to others who might be deterred, but to the specific individual being punished. The individual is expected to learn his or her lesson and refrain from future criminal acts. Many "shock incarceration" programs such as Scared Straight and juvenile boot camps have been based on such premises.

Incapacitation

The simple purpose of incapacitation is to physically restrain offenders to prevent them from committing further crimes. The logic is simple: a person cannot commit further crimes against society during the time in which he or she is locked up or incapacitated. Long prison sentences for certain offenses are often based, at least in part, upon such notions. Less severe forms of incapacitation might include curfews, house arrest, intensive supervision, probation and day reporting centers. Advocates often believe that crime rates can be reduced by incarcerating (incapacitating) the worst offenders ("career criminals") for long periods of time.

Restoration

More recent than the other four types of goals, restoration or reparation attempts to restore the victim and/or the community to his or her (or its) prior state before the crime occurred. It is similar to retribution in the sense that crime is viewed as a disruption of the peace. However, restoration seeks to repair the harm, while retribution seeks only to apply blame and punishment. Many current programs are exploring options such as financial restitution to victims, as well as requiring offenders to perform community service work.

Normative Values

Normative values are guiding assumptions held by individuals about how the justice system *should* work. For example, Packer[3] discusses two very broad, competing value orientations of the criminal justice system. To some officials, criminal case processing is like an "assembly line," by which cases should be processed and disposed of as quickly as possible. Proponents of this view, the *crime control model*, believe that, for the most part, police, prosecutors, judges and juries make correct decisions, and the system effectively ferrets out the guilty from the innocent. In contrast, those who lean more toward the *due process model* believe that the system is imperfect, and that individual officials frequently make hasty and incorrect decisions. As a result, many safeguards are needed to protect the interests of the accused against the much greater power of the state. Criminal case processing, according to this view, is more like an obstacle course than an assembly line. We warn the reader that neither model truly represents reality. No individual should completely adopt one or the other orientations. In Packer's own words, "A person who subscribed to all of the values underlying one model to the exclusion of all of the values underlying the other would be rightly viewed as a fanatic."[4]

Criminal justice officials hold normative values about what type of change should proceed and why, how important specific goals are and what results should be expected from a specific program or policy. For example, the case study at the end of Chapter 2 (Case Study 2.2) illustrated that a value orientation toward reducing prison overcrowding was dramatically at odds with the orientation of "getting tougher" with offenders. Any potential solution had to account for at least those two tradeoffs, and perhaps others. Four broad value orientations common to criminal justice are described below.

Proportionality

Proportionality is a principle that punishment for criminal behavior should not be any more onerous, intrusive or painful than warranted by the severity of the crime. At least in theory, this principle holds that there is some logical hierarchy of crimes and a corresponding (proportional) hierarchy of appropriate punishments. One does not give the death penalty to jaywalkers, for example.

Equity

Equity is the principle that similarly situated offenders should be treated similarly. For example, those accused of committing the same criminal offense should be processed in a similar manner, unrelated to their personal or demographic characteristics (e.g., age, race, gender or income).

Parsimony

Parsimony is the principle of using the least drastic and expensive measure needed to produce a specific objective. For example, if a one-year driver's license suspension and probation term is sufficient to motivate a first-time offender to abstain from drunk driving, a three-year suspension and probation term would be overly harsh and wasteful.

Humane Treatment

Humane treatment is a principle meaning that the decision regarding appropriate punishment is guided by a desire to use the most humane method to achieve specific objectives. One attempts to avoid unnecessary humiliation, pain and discomfort. For example, incarceration and its associated deprivations of liberty would be considered appropriate punishment in and of itself. Only considerations of appropriate sentence length, security classification and perhaps rehabilitation opportunities should guide the decision about where and how the offender serves his or her sentence, and for how long. Under this principle, one would not impose additional punishment by making prison conditions as unbearable as possible (e.g., by tolerating inmate-on-inmate assaults and rapes).

What are the "Right" Goals and Values?

We do not advocate any particular set of punishment goals or values in this book; we attempt to give readers the tools they need to make such decisions feasible and explicit. We also caution that different goals and values are not necessarily mutually exclusive: it is possible that a specific program or policy could attempt to address more than one goal or value simultaneously. A considerable amount of research has been conducted to test the assumptions and expectations that underlie the goals of policies and programs. Excellent discussions of competing views and related research evidence are provided by Peter Greenwood[5] and Samuel Walker.[6] Do rehabilitation programs work sufficiently well to serve as a basis for correctional policy? Does retributive justice result in satisfaction of the victim that justice was done? Does the threat of punishment deter others from committing crimes? Consulting the body of research that addresses these questions will help to avoid unrealistic expectations and increase our capacity to make a clear identification and evaluation of the intended outcomes of our programs and policies.

It is important to understand that the pursuit of specific goals may be driven by values, in spite of past failures to achieve these goals. The goal of rehabilitation, for example, has been challenged consistently over the past two decades, and yet many of us continue to believe that people can change and that positive change can be supported by well-designed interventions.[7] Similarly, in spite of consistent evidence that capital punishment does *not* deter others from committing murder, death penalty statutes continue to be supported because of the *perceived* deterrent effect of executions.[8]

Write Specific Outcome Objectives for Each Goal

Objectives are much more specific than goals. Objectives should define clearly and concisely exactly what outcome is to be achieved by the intervention. Objectives precisely describe the intended results of the intervention in measurable terms.

An intervention should have at least one specific goal, and each goal should be accompanied by at least one specific objective. It is possible, therefore, to have more than one objective for each goal. Because goals are broadly defined, any program may have several specific objectives. For example, the goal of a new drug treatment program is "to help clients lead drug-free lives." Two objectives are possible:

- Objective #1: Six months after leaving the program, fewer clients will have been re-arrested on drug charges, compared to those who did not go through the program.

- Objective #2: After six months, treated clients will score higher (on average) on a "personal and family responsibility" scale.

Objectives, therefore, must always be measurable and specific. Objectives should include four major components:

1. A *time frame:* date by which objectives will be completed.

2. A *target population:* who will evidence the intended change?

3. A *result:* the key outcome intended; a specific change in the problem.

4. A *criterion:* a standard for measuring successful achievement of the result.

Example 3.1

Four Components of an Objective: The Minneapolis Domestic Violence Experiment

In the Minneapolis Domestic Violence Experiment,[9] researchers reviewed major studies of police response to domestic violence. In various jurisdictions, they found a rather low rate of arrest out of all calls reported to the police. Other frequently used police responses included: separation (ordering the offender to leave the house for a cooling-off period, often overnight) and mediation (encouraging a couple to resolve the conflict).

The researchers hypothesized that, due to greater deterrent effects, mandatory arrest for misdemeanor domestic assault would result in fewer repeat offenses (recidivism) than either separation (order the suspect to leave for at least eight hours) or mediation (try to restore peace, informally

Example 3.1, *continued*

solve the conflict). Researchers convinced police to randomly assign all mis-demeanor domestic violence cases in two precincts to one of these three interventions. Six months later, researchers predicted, there would be a lower rate of repeat incidents of domestic assault for cases in which manda-tory arrest was used. We can summarize the four components of the objec-tive as follows:

1. *Time frame:* six months.

2. *Target population:* the experiment included only misdemeanor assaults, for which police were empowered (but not required) to make arrests under a new state law. Police had to have prob-able cause, and felonies (e.g., obvious or serious injury) were excluded (i.e., felony suspects were always arrested). Two precincts with the highest density of domestic violence were selected for the study.

3. *Result:* fewer repeat incidents of domestic abuse.

4. *Criteria:* Two measures were used: (1) police arrest records (incident reports over a six-month period), and (2) victim self-reports (follow-up interviews were conducted with victims every two weeks for 24 weeks, asking about frequency and seriousness of any victimization).

Note that these four components could have been quite different depending upon the results of the problem analysis. First, a different *time frame* could have been specified (e.g., one year? two years? three years?). Second, a different *target population* could have been specified (e.g., differ-ent demographic and income groups could have been studied in different neighborhoods). Third, a different *result* could have been specified (e.g., victim satisfaction with the police response they received). Finally, different *criteria* (measures) could have been used (e.g., hospital records of injuries, incidents reported to social service agencies or crisis lines). Any change agent should define the four components of an objective and explain the reasoning behind these specifications.

Another distinction is sometimes made between process and out-come objectives. *Process objectives* refer to short-term tasks that must be completed in order to implement a program (e.g., within 30 days all police agencies will hold orientation sessions to acquaint officers with a new domestic violence policy). Strictly speaking, these are not objectives at all, because they do not define any specific change in the problem. We note this distinction only because it is likely to arise as one reads pub-lished reports of interventions, and one should be aware of the differ-ence. We are concerned here with *outcome objectives* (specific, measur-able changes in the problem).

Seek Participation in Goal Setting

Is it necessary that everyone agree on the same goals for a specific program or policy? What are the implications if they do not? At the most basic level, the implications are that different individuals (stakeholders) perceive that they are each working toward some specific end point. They may believe, correctly or incorrectly, that they are working toward the same desired end. The problem is that if they have not articulated or discussed their own goals and values with each other, they may find out after considerable expenditure of energy and resources that they are working toward very different ends. Certainly no effective program or policy can be constructed if those responsible for designing the program or policy hold widely disparate or conflicting goals. Participants need some basic agreement about what is they are trying to achieve and why. Not every stakeholder needs to agree on the final goals, but those responsible for implementing the program or policy must be held accountable for articulating what it is they are doing and why.

Once again, we stress the virtues of participation in program planning. Having the relevant stakeholders involved in setting program goals is crucial to gaining the support and cooperation necessary to make the intervention work. The first step, if it has not already been accomplished (see Chapter 2), is to identify relevant participants for inclusion in the goal-setting and objective-setting phase.

The change agent (e.g., the person responsible for coordinating the program planning effort) should involve various participants in the planning process, not just agency administrators. Participants might include program staff, potential clients, citizens in the surrounding community, representatives from justice and social service agencies, schools, and so on. This requires patience and negotiating skills, as there are likely to be different assumptions and opinions regarding the problem, its causes and the type of intervention needed.

Targets and clients are often overlooked at this stage: what should they expect from this planned change? A major question to ask at this point is whether goal setting should proceed from a top-down or bottom-up approach.

Typically, change follows a top-down format. This is often the case because the change agent is likely to be working for—or contracted by— the agency that is funding the intervention, and the change agent has some obligation to weight the agency's definitions of goals more heavily. There may be advantages to this situation, as well as costs. It may be the case that those in the higher levels of the organization have the most experience with interventions of this type, and they might indeed be in the best position to state realistic, feasible outcomes to be expected. They might also be best equipped to formulate goals that can garner widespread political support for the program (e.g., support from other stakeholders). However, there is a very real danger in ignoring the views of program staff and clients. The danger is that the goals handed down from above may be unrealistic to program staff or irrelevant to the clients. In either case, the impact of the intervention could be severely compromised: the goals might prove unrealistic, in which case the program would be held accountable for unreachable goals, or clients and program staff might refuse to provide information to program evaluators or might provide incomplete or inaccurate information. Regardless of which approach is used to formulate initial goals, therefore, it is crucial that all stakeholders eventually have some input into defining program goals. These issues are examined in more detail in Case Study 3.1 at the end of this chapter.

Definitions

Goal Setting: Top-Down versus Bottom-Up Approaches

Top-Down: The change agent begins by getting goal definitions from top officials at the administrative level of his or her organization (e.g., the Chief of County Probation, the Chief of Police, the Director of Social Services, etc.), and then getting responses from lower levels of the organization—perhaps first from agency supervisors, then program staff and eventually potential clients. Thus, those at the top of the organizational hierarchy have more "say" in defining the program's goals, because their definition is the first one. It carries more weight and more power as subordinates and clients are asked to respond to it.

Bottom-Up: The change agent begins by seeking goal definitions at the client or staff level. In contrast to the top-down approach, in this approach the change agent first gets definitions from clients and staff about what the program goals are or should be. The change agent then gets responses to these goal definitions from successively higher levels of the agency responsible for implementing the intervention, as well as the agency that is funding the intervention. Other stakeholders to consult may include agency supervisors, administrators and government representatives. The views of clients and program staff are given more priority using this format; their definitions guide subsequent responses. Obviously, this approach is favored when it is viewed that so-called "experts" are out of touch and that front-line program staff and/or clients are in a better position to state the needs and goals of the target population. Many "grassroots" organizations follow this format.

Specify an Impact Model

We discussed causes and theories in Chapter 2. Examination of theories helps us to formulate what is called an *intervention hypothesis* or an *impact model*—a prediction that a particular intervention will bring about a specific change in the problem. Formulating such a model forces us to answer several important questions: What is the intervention? Why would a proposed intervention work? Which causes will it address? In other words, through what process will change occur, and why? What outcome (a change in the problem) is expected? We can now illustrate how the impact model is made up of three key elements we have discussed: (1) the *intervention* (policies and programs), (2) the *cause(s)* to be addressed by the intervention (theories about what causes the problem), and (3) some specific *outcome*, a desired change in the problem (goals and objectives). We can analyze an intervention by working backward, that is, first specifying the intervention, then the problem it addresses and then the causes of that problem. Program planning proceeds from problem analysis to causal analysis to formulation of goals and objectives. Analysis of an existing program simply reverses the process, even though it requires going through the same three crucial steps.

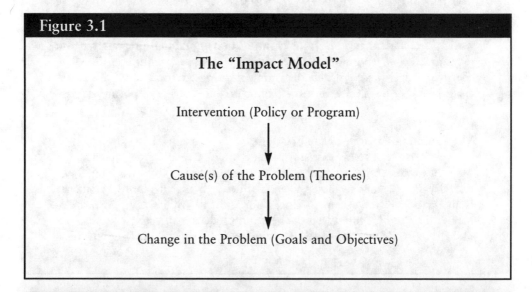

Figure 3.1

The "Impact Model"

Intervention (Policy or Program)

Cause(s) of the Problem (Theories)

Change in the Problem (Goals and Objectives)

Example 3.2

An Impact Model for a Halfway House Program

The Program:
A halfway house program for ex-offenders provides housing and training aimed at helping ex-offenders make a successful transition back into society. The intervention consists of monitoring ex-offenders in a minimum-security, residential facility and administering a system of behavioral contracting (described below under "causes"). Staff, composed primarily of trained social workers, provides counseling and assistance to each inmate based upon an individual behavior contract formulated with the participation of the inmate.

Example 3.2, *continued*

The Cause(s):

The major cause of the problem (recidivism) is seen to be learned behaviors that impede an inmate's successful transition. Herein lies the rationale for the treatment approach. According to behavioral theory, as espoused by B.F. Skinner and others, one's behavior over time is shaped by the repeated performance of certain behaviors (or even the observance of others performing behaviors) and the differential experience of rewards and punishments by an individual. Based upon behavioral theory, an individualized contract is developed for each inmate, in an attempt to reward certain behaviors conducive to success as well as punish behaviors likely to lead to failure. Specific behaviors might include prohibition of the use of alcohol or drugs, or specifying certain rules for maintaining a 9:00 – 5:00 retail job (e.g., being on time for work, dressing appropriately, being respectful to customers). Sanctions (rewards or punishments) might include granting (or removing) greater freedom and privileges in the halfway house. For example, if a person successfully maintains stable employment for three weeks, a reward may consist of granting that individual greater freedom (e.g., a later curfew, more privileges, etc.). Similarly, failure to complete specified behaviors results in the imposition of sanctions (e.g., an earlier curfew, loss of privileges, or returning to prison if terms of parole are violated).

The Intended Change in the Problem:

In a one-year follow-up study comparing halfway house clients with offenders who served out their entire sentence in prison, two specific objectives are stated: halfway house clients will have a higher rate of abstinence from alcohol or drug use, and halfway house clients will have a higher rate of maintaining stable employment. These objectives are directly related to the causal theory (behavioral theory). Ultimately, if these two presumed causal

Identify Compatible and Incompatible Goals in the Larger System

As we discussed in Chapter 2, criminal justice problems and policies are shaped by the interactive actions of various decisionmakers and agencies in any jurisdiction. We argued that a "systems assessment" provides a common language to describe and evaluate the present state of affairs (i.e., "the problem"), to shape a common vision for the future and to make that vision a reality.

It is the notion of shaping a common vision that is relevant to this chapter. Based upon information collected in Stage 1 (*problem analysis*), we should be able to identify and describe the competing interests of different individuals and agencies. We try to determine where agreement and disagreement about goals exists, and attempt to get stakeholders to articulate and discuss their desired goals for any specific program or policy.

In Case Study 2.3 (Criminal Justice System Assessment of Sacramento County), for example, we saw that initiatives to get tough on crime resulted in dramatic increases in criminal caseloads and severe jail overcrowding. A new jail was constructed at a cost of $125 million, and annual operating budgets soared to more than $47 million a year. However, crime rates remained unchanged, public confidence in the justice system dwindled, and federal courts imposed population caps on the jails and ordered county officials to remedy unconstitutional conditions of confinement upon threat of contempt of court and heavy fines. The Criminal Justice Cabinet, composed of various city and county elected officials, budget managers as well as court, criminal justice and human services personnel, was formed to identify system deficiencies and formulate plans for change. In addition to gathering specific information about criminal justice system processing, officials also needed to identify and discuss the competing goals that had given rise to problems of overcrowding and court orders. Part of their purpose was to articulate shared goals clearly in order to guide future planning efforts.

In another example, contracting out prison operations to private companies (i.e., privatization of prison operations) is often seen by elected officials as a benefit due to assumed cost savings. Other stakeholders disagree about whether cost savings are likely and whether cost savings should be the goal at all. Several major objections to privatization have emerged.[10]

- Correctional officers have initiated lawsuits alleging violation of their collective bargaining agreements. Privatization, they argue, is designed to drive down wages and benefits that were won through hard-fought, legitimate union negotiations.

- Inmate advocates and attorneys, concerned with civil rights, argue that turning over the power to punish from government to the private sector is absolutely unethical. Private corporations are motivated to make profits, not to rehabilitate prisoners, protect public safety or provide constitutionally mandated, humane conditions of confinement.

- Private interests, many argue, will attempt to use inmates as a source of cheap labor or, worse, indentured slavery. Such conditions would mark a return to the barbaric days of inmate exploitation and abuse prior to court intervention.

- Cost-cutting motivations, it is feared, will lead to lapses in prison security that threaten public safety (e.g., higher inmate-to-guard staffing ratios).

The change agent, consultant or analyst guiding the change effort should constantly carry a systems perspective throughout the seven-stage planned change process. A systems perspective is no less important at the goal-setting stage than at any other stage, and is perhaps more so, because the fundamental assumptions developed at this stage will critically shape the design and structure of the entire program or policy. Case Study 3.2 at the end of this chapter further examines these issues, using mandatory sentencing as a context for analysis.

We offer six guidelines to identify compatible and incompatible goals or values in the larger system:

1. Have the appropriate stakeholders been identified via a thorough problem analysis (see Chapter 2)?

2. Review the five goals and four values described earlier in this chapter. Do different stakeholders disagree over specific goals and values? Have their assumptions about the problem, its possible causes and possible solutions been described?

3. Do individuals within the same agency agree or disagree about the goals or values of the proposed change? Where?

4. Do individuals within different agencies agree or disagree about the goals or values of the proposed change? Where?

5. Has a systems analysis been conducted to provide stakeholders with relevant information about criminal case processing in this jurisdiction? Is all the information needed to make decisions about goals available, or does some information need to be developed?

6. Do any group mechanisms (e.g., a Criminal Justice Cabinet) exist for bringing stakeholders together to discuss the goals of a proposed change? Is it necessary to create or further develop such a group before proceeding?

Identify Needs and Opportunities for Interagency Collaboration

It is highly likely that any criminal justice intervention will at some point require the cooperation of other agencies to achieve its goals. To be successful, many criminal justice interventions require the participation of police, courts and corrections to carry out their program plans. Other public agencies such as schools or social service agencies may also be called upon, depending upon the problem to be addressed (e.g., juvenile violence) and the type of intervention to be attempted. The change agent, as part of the planning process, needs to consider his or her program's and/or agency's external environment when attempting any kind of change. Different types of collaboration or support may be required:

political support, shared information, exchange of services, joint client intake or assessment and perhaps even cross-referrals of clients among different agencies.[11] Such forms of cooperation, obviously, must be negotiated and agreed upon. Each agency must perceive tangible benefits from undertaking such cooperation.

Interagency cooperation is not always possible or even desirable, however. Political relationships and administrative structures occasionally preclude opportunities for collaboration.

Example 3.3

Agency Politics: Roadblocks to Collaboration?

In a recent project, we found that the juvenile court, part of a state agency, was resistant to participating in the development of an information system that would benefit a group of city agencies. The purpose of the information system project was to create an integrated system that would link the databases of the juvenile court, the department of human services, the police, the district attorney, the public defender and the school district. Sharing information electronically was viewed as a primary means of supporting effective decisions and avoiding fragmented planning for individual youths and families. The juvenile court resisted involvement because pre-existing political conflicts with other agencies had not been resolved and because of its stated desire to protect confidential court data from misuse by other agencies.

Under some circumstances, planning partnerships may not be desirable. Kevin Wright, for example, argues that a complex justice system in a complex society cannot and should not have any common set of goals and values.[12] There is (and should be) a certain tension between different criminal justice agencies, because they do not (and should not) all have the same goals. For example, prosecutors tend to emphasize goals of crime control, while defense attorneys emphasize goals of due process. Such goal "tension" helps protect the competing interests of victims and suspects. Moreover, distinctions need to be made between goal conflicts and agency conflicts. Opposition on specific goals does not imply that agencies cannot work together under all circumstances. There will be many situations in which collaboration will serve the purposes of agencies that represent different interests. Plea bargaining between prosecutors and defense attorneys is a classic example of such exchange relations.

Example 3.4

Goal Conflict in Criminal Justice: Roadblocks or Speedbumps for Interagency Collaboration?

According to Wright, there are at least three reasons why goal conflict within the criminal justice system is desirable: (1) reflective diversity, (2) mediation of interests and system adaptation, and (3) efficient offender processing.

1. **Reflective Diversity:** Fragmentation and lack of integration allow different interests to be incorporated into the system. Conflict may be necessary to mediate among conflicting interests in the community, including competing demands for crime prevention, public order, justice, due process, efficiency and accountability.

2. **Mediation of Interests and System Adaptation:** Conflicting goals promote a system of checks and balances. No single component of the system can dominate others, nor can any unitary interest be overemphasized. Conflict establishes and maintains a balance of power within the structure of the system [e.g., a prosecutor gives an overly stiff sentence in reaction to public sentiment, but corrections (parole) may modify that sentence and balance out the fairness (and vice versa)].

3. **Offender Processing:** Conflict and fragmentation may actually promote and support rather than hinder the processing of offenders. Prosecution, for example, may be smoother and more efficient precisely because police officers *do* consider decisions about prosecution, and that tension reduces the likelihood that prosecutors will need to void illegal, improper or weak arrests.

The concept of *loose coupling* further illustrates the need for interagency cooperation in criminal justice. Loose coupling refers to agencies that are responsive to one another, yet maintain independent identities.[13] In such systems, "structural elements are only loosely linked to one another and to activities, rules are often violated, decisions often go unimplemented, or if implemented have uncertain consequences, and techniques are often subverted or rendered so vague as to provide little coordination."[14] In other words, the criminal justice "system" has been called a "nonsystem" due to its decentralized and fragmented nature.[15] Different agencies interact with one another, but only rarely do different agencies cooperate effectively or efficiently to process criminal cases.

For example, narcotics enforcement and white-collar crime prosecution require a departure from the loose coupling that dominates criminal justice organizations.[16] While reactive police work based on loosely coupled processes is the norm, proactive policing requires more tightly coupled interagency relations. Narcotics work requires police to use more controversial tactics to obtain evidence, including undercover work, entrapment and informants.[17] Police officers are more dependent upon prosecutors for feedback on the legal permissibility of evidence, and prosecutors are more dependent upon police officers for extensive information and cooperation in the preparation of cases. Such information exchange influences charging decisions and plea bargains engineered to develop cooperation from informants and codefendants. Hagan argues that the proactive prosecution of white-collar criminals requires similar leverage to "turn witnesses." Judges must participate in these decisions as well, because their approval is necessary to implement charge reductions or negotiated sentences.

Using loose coupling as an explanatory concept, Hagan describes how sudden changes in the external environment of an organization (e.g., a riot, a murder committed by an escaped prisoner, court orders to reduce jail overcrowding) create demands for tighter coupling.[18] The distinction between *proactive* and *reactive* problem solving is crucial. For example, proactive policing or prosecution implies that officials actively target certain problems for attention. Proactive problem solving, however, requires a departure from the norm of "loose coupling": it necessitates cooperation and planning from multiple agencies and actors. In an analysis of urban riots in Los Angeles and Detroit, Balbus[19] suggested that black suspects were rounded up en masse, at least initially, to serve an ostensible order maintenance function ("clearing the streets"). This initial increase in restrictiveness was followed by "uncharacteristic leniency" as bail release became much more frequent than usual ("clearing the jails"). This shift from "normal" court operations required a tightening of the relations between the police, prosecutorial and judicial subsystems, so that bail decisions became less variable.

Similarly, local jails operated by cities or counties interact extensively with law enforcement agencies, courts, probation departments and local government.[20] Court orders against jails represent sudden changes that put pressure on entire criminal justice systems to adapt by altering the routine processing of accused and convicted offenders. Police book arrestees into jail, the courts try them, jails house them and probation provides alternative programming for both pretrial and sentenced offenders. County government (e.g., the county board of supervisors) is responsible for financial and personnel allocations to these agencies. The implications of this interagency perspective are illustrated in Example 3.5.

Example 3.5

Identifying Needs and Opportunities for Interagency Collaboration: Jail Reform in California

In an analysis of interagency adaptations to jail litigation in three California counties, Welsh and Pontell[21] reported that court orders against county officials for jail overcrowding and other unconstitutional conditions of confinement facilitated shifts toward tighter coupling in each county. The "impact model" looks like this:

Intervention: Court-ordered reform

↓

Cause(s): "loose coupling"

↓

Problem: Jail overcrowding and other unconstitutional conditions of confinement

Court orders initially created unexpected or latent effects as agencies resisted the court's demands for greater interagency coordination and planning. For example, the Santa Clara County sheriff resisted attempts by the probation agency to screen inmates for eligibility to participate in alternatives to incarceration (e.g., county parole), while the Orange County sheriff accused local judges of not doing their part to help deal with overcrowding (e.g., not considering current levels of jail crowding when sentencing convicted offenders).

Interagency conflict and power struggles developed in response to court orders. In Santa Clara, the county Board of Supervisors accused the sheriff of attempting to use the lawsuit to demand greater human and institutional resources from the county budget. Resource competition constrained interagency cooperation in each county. Some agencies (e.g., the District Attorney, County Probation) perceived resource shortages because, they believed, scarce county funds were being diverted to jails. Counties in California are indeed financially strapped, due largely to tax reforms of the 1980s.[22] As the Supreme Court indicated, however, a lack of finances is never an acceptable excuse for the violation of inmates' constitutional rights[23] and jails have thus obtained a grudging priority in county budgets.

Tightened coupling and more proactive responses eventually emerged in each county. Judges, especially in Santa Clara, attempted to engineer broad cooperation between county agencies to solve their own problems. Proactive responses included the creation of jail overcrowding committees and interagency task forces. In addition, new programs that required interagency coordination to reduce jail populations were created in response to court orders (e.g., early screening programs to divert weak cases from prosecution, pretrial release programs, electronic surveillance and county parole).

Example 3.5, *continued*

The leadership styles and attitudes of key actors were influential.[24] In Santa Clara, for example, personal acrimony and political struggles between the sheriff and the county executive hampered interagency solutions to jail problems. In Orange County, a powerful sheriff largely insulated himself from the influence of the board of supervisors. In Contra Costa, the sheriff actively cultivated interagency cooperation. Criminal justice subsystems certainly do not constitute rational forms of bureaucracy in the Weberian sense,[25] but creative leadership from one or more officials may enhance tight coupling and expedite proactive solutions. Conversely, lack of vision among leaders[26] may contribute to loose coupling as well as reactive, rather than proactive, agency responses.

Demands created by court orders tightened the loose coupling that normally characterizes criminal justice agencies. Court orders sparked proactive reforms, but they also fueled conflict by requiring involuntary, increased coordination among agencies that typically deal with problems in an autonomous, reactive manner. Conflict, however, may be necessary before organizational reform is possible.[27]

Conclusion

Failure to make a clear identification of the goals, values and expectations guiding the development of an intervention can spell certain failure. At best, continued disagreement over intended goals and outcomes can be expected long after the program or policy is implemented. While discussion between stakeholders of competing goals and values can initially heighten conflict, it may also direct us toward eventual compromise or collaboration, more effective planning, and achievement of our intended goals.

DISCUSSION QUESTIONS

1. At the end of Chapter 1, you were asked to write a short essay describing one possible intervention addressing a specific problem in criminal justice. You are also likely to be doing one of the following in this course: (a) writing about a specific problem and/or intervention as a class assignment, or (b) participating in the development of a specific program or policy within the agency for which you work. Briefly describe a specific criminal justice program or policy, then describe one goal and one objective for this intervention.

2. (a) Define the terms: *goal* and *objective*. (b) Describe the difference between the two.

3. Describe the four components of an objective.

4. Some argue that goal setting should proceed from the bottom up; others argue it should proceed from the top down. (a) Describe each of these positions. (b) Which position do you agree with? Why?

5. Describe five common goals of punishment.

6. Describe four common value orientations in criminal justice.

7. Describe an example of *incompatible goals* within the criminal justice system, and explain why it is important.

8. Discuss advantages and disadvantages of interagency collaboration. Give specific examples.

9. Describe the concept of *loose coupling* and explain why it is important, using a specific example.

Case Study 3.1

Top-Down versus Bottom-Up Goal Setting: Reducing Minority Overrepresentation in Juvenile Justice

Instructions: Read the case study below, then answer the questions that follow.

Recall the previous discussion of Pennsylvania's initiative to reduce minority overrepresentation in juvenile justice (see Examples 1.5 and 2.5). After identifying jurisdictions with the highest rates of minority juvenile arrests, the Pennsylvania Commission on Crime and Delinquency (PCCD) funded five community-based delinquency prevention programs in Harrisburg in 1991; four Philadelphia programs were added in 1992.

The first goals defined were clearly "top-down." All programs, as requirements of receiving PCCD funding, were given two mandated goals: (1) to reduce future involvement with the juvenile justice system, and (2) to improve school behavior and performance. PCCD used these goals to evaluate funding proposals received from various programs. All programs understood that they would be held accountable for achieving these outcomes. However, program directors were upset when preliminary evaluation results were presented a year later. The results focused too heavily, they thought, on recidivism and academic performance only. What about all the other short-term goals that are part of the process to prevent delinquency, they asked? Why were there no measures of individual client change, such as attitudes (e.g., self-esteem) and behavior (e.g., social skills)? Clearly, program staff and directors wanted more of a say in defining what program goals and objectives should be: they wanted a bottom-up approach to goal setting.

Following the first year of evaluation, researchers from Temple University assumed responsibility for program evaluation. One of their first tasks was to use a process called *evaluability assessment* to create program models (i.e., descriptions of program content and intended objectives), based upon the views of program staff and directors.

The nine programs varied in the types of services they provided. All programs stressed the value of supervised activities to keep youths out of trouble; all provided some form of life skills training, which often included service delivery in areas such as problem-solving skills, conflict resolution, and cultural diversity and awareness training; eight provided homework or tutoring assistance; eight provided structured recreation and/or field trips; six stressed some form of career development or vocational training; four included some community service component; three provided some kind of retreat or camp experience to encourage self-reflection and build teamwork; one focused heavily on the role of adult mentors who provided support and counseling for youths.

Researchers identified common objectives across programs and later selected appropriate outcome measures of each.[28] As Table 3.1 indicates, program staff and directors identified many different objectives that had not

Case Study 3.1, *continued*

been considered by PCCD or previous evaluators. In addition to the two major objectives previously mandated by the funding agency, PCCD, we developed a research plan to assess the other major objectives identified by program staff and directors. Two major benefits resulted from this process. First, the process helped establish evaluators' credibility with program personnel and gain necessary cooperation from program personnel in the evaluation process (e.g., collecting outcome data). Second, staff and directors were more satisfied that their views of the programs' mission had been fairly represented. The outcomes for which programs were held accountable were not simply handed down from above (i.e., by the funding source, PCCD); program staff and directors themselves had input into defining what those outcomes should be.

Table 3.1
Outcome Objectives: Philadelphia and Harrisburg Programs[29]

1. Camp Curtain YMCA
2. Boys Club of Harrisburg
3. Project Connect
4. Hispanic Center
5. Girls Inc. of Harrisburg

6. Impact Checkmate Program
7. Project Youthlead
8. CUNAD
9. Youth Self-Empowerment Project

	1	2	3	4	5	6	7	8	9
Program Participation									
• Attendance	X	X	X	X	X	X	X	X	X
• Create Commitment to Program	X	X	X	X	X	X	X	X	X
• Create Trusting Relationships	X	X	X	X	X	X	X	X	X
• Screen for Level of Need				X		X			X
Education									
• Improved School Attendance						X	X		
• Increased Committment to School		X		X	X		X		
• Improved Study Habits				X		X			
• Improved Basic Skills	X		X		X			X	X
• Improved Behavior at School				X		X	X	X	
• Improved Academic Performance	X	X	X	X		X	X	X	X
• Increase High School Completion							X		
• Increase College Attendance	X				X		X		
• Reduce Number of At-Risk Students			X						
• Involvement in School Activities			X						
• Positive Rel'ns w/School Personnel			X						

Case Study 3.1, *continued*

Table 3.1, *continued*

	1	2	3	4	5	6	7	8	9
Employment									
• Develop Job Skills		X			X	X			
• Develop Career Goals		X			X		X	X	
• Provide Role Models							X	X	X
• Increased Employment							X		
• Learn to Enjoy/Value Work		X			X				
• Learn to Respond to Authority		X							
• Develop Business Skills					X				
Delinquency									
• Reduced Recidivism	X	X	X	X	X	X	X	X	X
• Reduced Drug Use	X				X		X	X	
Family									
• Build Commitment to Program			X			X			
• Improve Parenting Skills						X			
• Encourage Parental Involvement			X			X		X	X
• Provide Support for Parents						X		X	X
• Strengthen Family Relationships	X								
Individual Development									
• Increase Self-awareness			X		X	X	X	X	X
• Improved Self-esteem	X		X	X	X	X		X	X
• Learn Problem-Solving Skills	X	X		X		X			
• Increased Self Control			X				X		
• Establish Individual Goals						X	X	X	
• Positive Use of Free Time	X						X		
• Develop Responsibility			X		X		X		X
• Provide Mutual Support			X		X		X		X
• Develop Possibility/Vision				X	X		X		
• Reinforce Achievement			X				X		
• Define Values, Moral Principles	X	X							
• Develop Creative Expression				X					
Physical Development									
• Improved Motor Skills						X			
• Improved Physical Fitness	X					X			X
• Improved Health Awareness	X								

Case Study 3.1, *continued*

Table 3.1, *continued*

	1	2	3	4	5	6	7	8	9
Interpersonal Skills									
• Improved Communication Skills		X				X		X	X
• Develop Leadership Skills		X			X	X		X	
• Develop Teamwork		X			X	X		X	
• Increased Respect for Others		X				X			
• Resolve Disputes Peacefully						X		X	X
• Less Aggression Toward Others					X	X		X	X
• Dealing with Peer Pressure								X	
• Make Friends		X							
Other									
• Increased Cultural Awareness		X		X		X		X	X
• Increased Awareness of Diversity				X		X			X
• Monitor Youth Activities						X			
• Develop Pride in Community			X		X		X	X	X
• Awareness of Environmental Issues								X	
• Awareness of Community Resources								X	
• Increased Resources: Youth/Family			X						

Questions

1. Did the original goal setting in this example proceed from the top down or the bottom up? Explain and give evidence to support your answer.

2. Should the change agent be concerned because people disagree about the goals of this intervention? Why or why not? Make an argument. Explain and give evidence to support your position.

3. What, if anything, could have been done differently in this example to reduce disagreement about goals? Be specific, using concepts discussed in this chapter.

Case Study 3.2

The Goals of Mandatory Sentencing[30]

Instructions: Read the case study below, then answer the questions that follow.

By 1994, all 50 states had enacted one or more mandatory sentencing laws,[1] and Congress had enacted numerous mandatory sentencing laws for Federal offenders. Furthermore, many State officials have recently considered proposals to enhance sentencing for adults and juveniles convicted of violent crimes, usually by mandating longer prison terms for violent offenders who have a record of serious crimes. Three-strikes laws (and, in some jurisdictions, two-strikes laws) are the most prominent examples of such sentencing enhancements.

Three-strikes laws impose longer prison terms than earlier mandatory minimum sentencing laws. For example, California's three-strikes law requires that offenders who are convicted of a violent crime, and who have had two prior convictions, serve a minimum of 25 years; the law also doubles prison terms for offenders convicted of a second violent felony.[2] Three-strikes laws vary in breadth. For example, some stipulate that both of the prior convictions and the current offense be violent felonies; others require only that the prior felonies be violent. Some three-strikes laws count only prior adult violent felony convictions, while others permit consideration of juvenile adjudications for violent crimes.

A second frequently mentioned mandatory sentencing enhancement is "truth-in-sentencing," provisions for which are in the Violent Crime Control and Law Enforcement Act of 1994. States that wish to qualify for Federal aid under the Act are required to amend their laws so that imprisoned offenders serve at least 85 percent of their sentences.

Rationale for mandatory sentencing

Mandatory sentences are based on two goals— deterrence and incapacitation. The primary purposes of modest mandatory prison terms (e.g., 3 years for armed robbery) are specific deterrence, which applies to already sanctioned offenders, and general deterrence, which aims to deter prospective offenders. If the law successfully increases the imprisonment rate, the effects of incapacitation also will grow because fewer offenders will be free to victimize the population at large. The intent of three-strikes (and even two-strikes) is to incapacitate selected violent offenders for very long terms— 25 years or even life. They have no specific deterrent effect if those confined will never be released, but their general deterrent effect could, in theory, be substantial.

By passing mandatory sentencing laws, legislators convey the message that certain crimes are deemed especially grave and that people who commit them deserve, and may expect, harsh sanctions. These laws are a rapid and visible response to public outcries following heinous or well-publicized crimes. The high long-term costs of mandatory sentencing are deferred because the difficult funding choices implicit in this policy can be delayed or even avoided.

Impact of mandatory sentencing laws

Mandatory sentencing has had significant consequences that deserve close attention, among them its impact on crime and the operations of the criminal justice system. The possible differential consequences for certain groups of people also bear examination.

Crime. Evaluations of mandatory sentencing have focused on two types of crimes—those committed with handguns and those related to drugs (the offenses most commonly subjected to mandatory minimum penalties in State and Federal courts). An evaluation of the Massachusetts law that imposed mandatory jail terms for possession of an unlicensed handgun concluded that the law was an effective deterrent of gun crime,[3] at least in the short term.

However, studies of similar laws in Michigan[4] and Florida[5] found no evidence that crimes committed with firearms had been prevented. An evaluation of mandatory gun-use sentencing enhancements in six large cities (Detroit, Jacksonville, Tampa, Miami, Philadelphia, and Pittsburgh) indicated that the laws deterred homicide but not other violent crimes.[6] An assessment of New York's Rockefeller drug laws was unable to support the claim for their efficacy as a deterrent to drug crime in New York City.[7] None of the studies examined the incapacitation effects of these laws.

The criminal justice system. The criminal courts rely on a high rate of guilty pleas to speed case processing and thus avoid logjams. Officials can offer inducements to defendants to obtain these pleas. If only in the short term, mandatory sentencing laws may disrupt established plea-bargaining patterns by preventing a prosecutor from offering a short prison term (less than the new minimum) in exchange for a guilty plea. However, unless policymakers enact long-term mandatory sentences that apply to many related categories of crimes, prosecutors usually can shift strategies and bargain on charges rather than on sentences.

The findings of research on the impact of mandatory sentencing laws on the criminal justice system have been summarized by a prominent scholar.[8] He found that officials make earlier and more selective arrest, charging, and diversion decisions; they also tend to bargain less and to bring more cases to trial. Specifically, he found that:

- Criminal justice officials and practitioners (police, lawyers, and judges) exercise discretion to avoid application of laws they consider unduly harsh.

- Arrest rates for target crimes decline soon after mandatory sentencing laws take effect.

Case Study 3.2, *continued*

- Dismissal and diversion rates increase at early stages of case processing after mandatory sentencing laws take effect.

- For defendants whose cases are not dismissed, plea-bargain rates decline and trial rates increase.

- For convicted defendants, sentencing delays increase.

- Enactment of mandatory sentencing laws has little impact on the probability that offenders will be imprisoned (when the effects of declining arrests, indictments, and convictions are taken into account).

- Sentences become longer and more severe.

The research review concluded that mandatory sentencing laws:

- Do not achieve certainty and predictability because officials circumvent them if they believe the results are unduly harsh.

- Are redundant with respect to proscribing probation for serious cases because such cases generally are sentenced to imprisonment anyway.

- Are arbitrary for minor cases.

- May occasionally result in an unduly harsh punishment for a marginal offender.[9]

Racial and ethnic minorities. One issue that has received considerable attention in recent years is whether racial or ethnic minorities are treated unfairly in the courts' application of mandatory minimum sentences. The question cannot be answered simply by comparing the proportion of minority offenders sentenced before and after introduction of, or changes in, mandatory sentencing laws. If, for example, it is objectively determined that minorities are more likely than the general population to commit offenses that carry mandatory sentences, an equitable application of the law would result in an increase in the proportion of imprisoned minorities—and probably in the lengths of their average sentences.

Consequently, the central question is whether criminal justice officials' discretionary choices in the application of mandatory sentencing laws are made in a racially neutral manner.

Results of particular studies are relevant. In one study involving cases of Federal offenders sentenced for crimes subject to mandatory minimums, the researcher examined whether sentencing severity varied by amount and type of drugs involved in the current crime, weapons, offense record, role in offense, history of drug use, age, gender, and race.[10] She found sentencing differences associated with the offender's race, even after accounting for dif-

Case Study 3.2, *continued*

ferences associated with these other characteristics. However, the magnitude of this difference was small.

The U.S. Sentencing Commission expanded this study and found significant differences in the proportion of whites (54 percent), Hispanics (57 percent), and African Americans (68 percent) who received mandatory minimum sentences for the most serious offense charged against them.[11] A reanalysis of the U.S. Sentencing Commission data drew different conclusions, however.[12] The reanalysis showed that when legally relevant case-processing factors were considered, a defendant's race/ethnicity was unrelated to the sentence. Also examined in the reanalysis was why more than 40 percent of the cases apparently eligible for mandatory sentences did not receive them. Reasonable explanations include evidentiary problems and instances in which defendants provided substantial assistance to prosecutors in preparing cases against others.

In an analysis of the Federal sentencing guidelines, other researchers found that African Americans received longer sentences than whites, not because of differential treatment by judges but because they constituted the large majority of those convicted of trafficking in crack cocaine— a crime Congress had singled out for especially harsh mandatory penalties.[13] This pattern can be seen as constituting a "disparity in results" and, partly for this reason, the U.S. Sentencing Commission recommended to Congress that it eliminate the legal distinction between crack and regular cocaine for purposes of sentencing (a recommendation Congress rejected).

Three-strikes laws. The recent wave of three-strikes laws has not yet been evaluated, but the costs and benefits of California's three-strikes law have been simulated.[14] Assuming that the law would produce incapacitation effects but not deterrent effects, the researchers projected it would:

- Triple California's prison population over the next 25 years, creating a prison population about equal in size to that of the entire U.S. prison population in 1980.

- Cost an average of $5.5 billion more each year for the next 25 years than the previous law, for a cumulative additional cost of $137.5 billion.

- Reduce serious crime by 28 percent, at a total correctional cost of about $16,300 for each crime averted.

The researchers found that California's three-strikes law would avert crimes inefficiently because many offenders would be confined for long periods after their criminal activity became negligible because of the effects of aging. They calculated that if the law were limited to offenders whose current crime and both of the two prior offenses were violent, serious crime could be cut 18 percent, at a total correctional cost of $12,000 per averted crime.

Case Study 3.2, *continued*

The effects on future California budgets of funding the three-strikes law were estimated. In their calculations, the researchers assumed that health and welfare costs would not increase (an assumption they labeled as unlikely) and that educational spending for grades K-12 would increase only as a direct result of foreseeable demographic changes. They found that corrections would consume 18 percent of State spending by the year 2002—double the 1994 percentage. Together, corrections, health and welfare, and K-12 education would consume 99 percent of the State's budget by 2002, leaving just 1 percent to fund everything else.

Future issues

In the interviews conducted for this review of mandatory sentencing, State policymakers expressed the need to respond to the public's fear of crime and call for tougher sanctions, but also recognized the need to rein in spiraling costs of corrections. If the costs of government are cut, spending more on prisons means spending less on other public purposes. The fiscal analysis of California's three-strikes law, for example, has implications for that State's future.

In a major study of sentencing policy, Michael Tonry of the University of Minnesota suggested that States consider the following options:[15]

- Pursue presumptive rather than mandatory sentences.

Presumptive sentences, which are developed by sentencing commissions and set forth as guidelines, can shift overall sentencing patterns in ways acceptable to policymakers. For example, they can seek to imprison more violent offenders and fewer property offenders. A sentencing commission can help maintain sentencing policy while still preserving ultimate legislative control. Presumptive sentences have generally achieved their intended goals, and research shows high rates of conformity to the sentences by judges.

In the rare instance in which a presumptive sentence is inappropriate (i.e., either too harsh or too lenient, given the facts of the case), judges can depart from the guidelines by providing in writing reasons that can be reviewed by higher courts. If legislatures so instruct sentencing commissions, they can craft the guidelines to control future costs and, at the same time, toughen sentences for repeat violent offenders.

- Include sunset provisions to require periodic reconsideration of the propriety of the laws, if mandatory sentencing laws are enacted.

- Limit the duration and scope of mandatory sentencing laws.

Crime is, quite literally, an activity of young men. As the study of the California law emphasized, extremely long mandatory sentences (e.g., 25 years to life) are inefficient because they confine offenders for long periods (at great cost) after they would have "aged out" of crime. Sentencing could be mandated for only a few especially serious crimes. If such laws are aimed at repeat serious offenders, they could include a requirement that only particularly serious prior and current convictions trigger them.

- Conduct some form of periodic administrative review to determine if continued confinement of the offender is required, in the event mandatory sentences are imposed.

- Closely link sentencing and fiscal policy decisions to enhance the legislative process. Legislatures could ensure that they know the financial impact of proposed sentencing legislation and, where substantial long-term costs will be incurred, a funding plan might be a required provision of the enabling law. This would prevent today's legislature from avoiding the fiscal implications of its sentencing policies.

Cultivating alternative sanctions

Legislatures also may want to develop policy that makes more effective and systematic use of intermediate sanctions, if the twin objectives of punishment and lower correctional costs are to be achieved. Such policy might specify goals for each particular sanction, locate each category of intermediate sanctions along the continuum between standard probation and total confinement, and define target populations for each category. For example, it could specify which confined offenders will be considered for early release, which sanctions should enhance standard probation, and which offenders need treatment or services.

In addition, States may want to develop a financial structure to steer development of intermediate sanctions in intended directions. This could be a variant of current community corrections acts, for which a central State agency sets standards for local programs and administers performance-based financial aid to local governments. For intermediate sanctions, the State could provide greater support to jurisdictions whose program met or exceeded the performance objectives specified by the agency.

Finally, States that make greater use of intermediate sanctions may want to develop policies that govern their use in individual cases. Examples are the development of presumptive guidelines for non-confinement as well as confinement sanctions. Such policies could be designed to ensure that overall use of nonconfinement sanctions is consistent with goals established by the legislature and broad principles that govern sentencing generally (e.g., proportionality, uniformity, and neutrality). In particular, guidelines could limit additive use of sanctions (imposing two or three nonconfinement sanctions on a particular offender) and control revocation decisions in order to minimize needless confinement for minor rule violations.

Case Study 3.2, *continued*

Notes

1. Tonry, M. (1995). *Sentencing Matters*, Oxford, England: Oxford University Press.

2. In mid-1996, the California Supreme Court ruled the State's three-strikes law an undue intrusion on judges' sentencing discretion. State legislative leaders immediately announced plans to introduce legislation that would reinstate the law.

3. Pierce, G.L., and W.J. Bowers (1981). "The Bartley-Fox Gun Law's Short-Term Impact on Crime in Boston." *Annals of the American Academy of Political and Social Science,* 455:120-132.

4. Loftin, C., M. Heumann, and D. McDowall (1983). "Mandatory Sentencing and Firearms Violence: Evaluating an Alternative to Gun Control." *Law and Society Review,* 17:287-318.

5. Loftin, C., and D. McDowall (1984). "The Deterrent Effects of the Florida Felony Firearm Law." *Journal of Criminal Law and Criminology,* 75:250-259.

6. McDowall, D., C. Loftin, and B. Wiersema (1992). "A Comparative Study of the Preventive Effects of Mandatory Sentencing Laws for Gun Crimes." *Journal of Criminal Law and Criminology,* 83:378-394.

7. Joint Committee on New York Drug Law Evaluation (1978). *The Nation's Toughest Drug Law: Evaluating the New York Experience.* A project of the Association of the Bar of the City of New York, the City of New York and the Drug Abuse Council, Inc. Washington, DC: U.S. Government Printing Office.

8. Tonry, M. (1987). *Sentencing Reform Impacts.* Washington, D.C.: U.S. Department of Justice, National Institute of Justice.

9. Ibid.

10. Meierhoefer, B.S. (1992). *General Effect of Mandatory Minimum Prison Terms.* Washington, DC: Federal Judicial Center; Meierhoefer, B.S. (1992). "Role of Offense and Offender Characteristics in Federal Sentencing." *Southern California Law Review,* 66:367-404; and Meierhoefer, B.S. (1992). *General Effect of Mandatory Minimum Prison Terms: A Longitudinal Study of Federal Sentences Imposed.* Washington, DC: Federal Judicial Center.

11. U.S. Sentencing Commission (1991). *Federal Sentencing Guidelines: A Report on the Operation of the Guidelines System and Short-Term Impacts on Disparity in Sentencing, Use of Incarceration, and Prosecutorial Discretion and Plea Bargaining.* Washington, DC: U.S. Sentencing Commission.

12. Langan, P. (1992). *Federal Prosecutor Application of Mandatory Sentencing Laws: Racially Disparate? Widely Evaded?* Washington, DC: U.S. Department of Justice, Bureau of Justice Statistics.

13. McDonald, D.C., and K.E. Carlson (1993). *Sentencing in the Courts: Does Race Matter? The Transition to Sentencing Guidelines, 1986-90.* Washington, DC: U.S. Department of Justice, Bureau of Justice Statistics.

Case Study 3.2, *continued*

14. Greenwood, P.W., et al. (1994). *Three Strikes and You're Out: Estimated Benefits and Costs of California's New Mandatory-Sentencing Law*. Santa Monica, California: RAND Corporation.

15. Tonry, *Sentencing Matters*.

Questions

1. What goals and normative values guided the creation of "three strikes" policies? Explain and give evidence.

2. Identify and describe any incompatible goals or values of different stakeholders.

3. Describe one objective that could be used to evaluate the effectiveness of "three strikes" policies. Pay careful attention to the four components of an objective discussed in Chapter 3.

Endnotes

1   Rothman, David J. (1980). *Conscience and Convenience. The Asylum and its Alternatives in Progressive America*. Boston: Little, Brown.

2   Von Hirsch, Andrew (1985). *Past or Future Crimes: Deservedness and Dangerousness in the Sentencing of Criminals*. New Brunswick, NJ: Rutgers University Press.

3   Packer, Herbert L. (1968). *The Limits of the Criminal Sanction*. Stanford, CA: Stanford University Press.

4   Packer, note 3, p. 154.

5   Greenwood, Peter W. (1982). "The Violent Offender in the Criminal Justice System." In Marvin E. Wolfgang and Neil Alan Weiner (eds.) *Criminal Violence*. Beverly Hills, CA: Sage.

6   Walker, Samuel (1998). *Sense and Nonsense About Crime and Drugs*. Belmont, CA: Wadsworth.

7   Andrews, Donald, Ivan Zinger, Robert D. Hoge, James Bonta, Paul Gendreau, and Francis T. Cullen (1990). "Does Correctional Treatment Work? A Clinically Relevant and Psychologically Informed Meta-Analysis." *Criminology*, 28:369-404.

8   Ibid, notes 5 and 6.

9   Sherman, Lawrence W., and Richard A. Berk (1984). "The Specific Deterrent Effects of Arrest for Domestic Assault." *American Sociological Review*, 49: 261-272.

10   Shichor, David (1995). *Punishment for Profit: Private Prisons/Public Concerns*. Thousand Oaks, CA: Sage.

[11] Rossi, Robert J, Kevin J. Gilmartin, and Charles W. Dayton (1982). *Agencies Working Together. A Guide to Coordination and Planning.* Beverly Hills: Sage.

[12] Wright, Kevin N. (1994). "The Desirability of Goal Conflict Within the Criminal Justice System." In Stan Stojkovic, John Klofas, and David Kalinich (eds.) *The Administration and Management of Criminal Justice Organizations,* 2nd ed., pp. 19-31. Prospect Heights, IL: Waveland.

[13] Cohen, Michael D., James G. March, and Johan P. Olsen (1972). "A Garbage Can Model Of Organizational Choice." *Administrative Science Quarterly,* 17:1-25; Hagan, John (1989). "Why Is There So Little Criminal Justice Theory? Neglected Macro- and Micro-Level Links Between Organization and Power." *Journal of Research in Crime and Delinquency,* 26:116-135; Weick, Karl (1976). "Educational Organizations as Loosely Coupled Systems." *Administrative Science Quarterly,* 21:1-19.

[14] See Hagan, note 13, P. 119.

[15] Eisenstein, James, and Herbert Jacob (1977). *Felony Justice: An Organizational Analysis of Criminal Courts.* Boston: Little, Brown; Feeley, Malcolm (1983). *Court Reform on Trial: Why Simple Solutions Fail.* New York: Basic Books; Forst, Martin L. (1977). "To What Extent Should the Criminal Justice System be a 'System'?" *Crime & Delinquency,* 23:403-416; Gibbs, Jack (1986). "Punishment And Deterrence: Theory, Research, and Penal Policy." In Leon Lipson, and Stanton Wheeler (eds.) *Law and the Social Sciences.* New York: Russell Sage; President's Commission on Law Enforcement and Administration of Justice (1967). *The Challenge of Crime in a Free Society.* New York: Avon Books; Reiss, Albert (1971). *The Police and the Public.* New Haven, CT: Yale University Press; Rossum, Ralph A. (1978). *The Politics of the Criminal Justice System. An Organizational Analysis.* New York: Marcel Dekker.

[16] See Hagan, note 13.

[17] Skolnick, Jerome (1966). *Justice Without Trial.* New York: John Wiley.

[18] See Hagan, note 13.

[19] Balbus, Isaac (1973). *The Dialectics of Legal Repression.* New York: Russell Sage.

[20] Hall, Andy (1985). *Alleviating Jail Overcrowding: A Systems Perspective.* Washington, DC: U.S. Department of Justice, National Institute of Justice, Office of Development, Testing, and Dissemination.

[21] Welsh, Wayne N., and Henry N. Pontell (1991). "Counties In Court: Interorganizational Adaptations to Jail Litigation in California." *Law and Society Review,* 25:73-101.

[22] Koehler, Cortus T. (1983). *Managing California Counties: Serving People, Solving Problems.* Sacramento, CA: County Supervisors Association of California.

[23] *Gates v. Collier,* 501 F. 2d 1291 (5th Cir. 1974); *Miller v. Carson,* 401 F. Supp. 835 (M.D. Fla. 1975).

[24] Stogdill, Ralph M. (1974). *Handbook of Leadership.* New York: Free Press.

[25] Feeley, Malcolm (1973). "Two Models of the Criminal Justice System: An Organizational Perspective." *Law and Society Review,* 7:407-425.

[26]   Bennis, Warren (1976). "Leadership: A Beleaguered Species?" *Organizational Dynamics,* 5:3.

[27]   Brager, George and Stephen Holloway (1978). *Changing Human Service Organizations: Politics and Practice.* New York: Free Press; Coleman, James S. (1957). *Community Conflict.* New York: Free Press.

[28]   See: Welsh, Wayne N., Philip W. Harris, and Patricia H. Jenkins (1995a). *Evaluation of Minority Overrepresentation Programs. Report 2: Evaluability Assessment and Process Evaluation.* Philadelphia, PA: Temple University, Department of Criminal Justice; and Welsh, Wayne N., Philip W. Harris, and Patricia H. Jenkins (1995b). *Evaluation of Minority Overrepresentation Programs. Appendix to Report 2: Individual Program Reports.* Philadelphia, PA: Temple University, Department of Criminal Justice.

[29]   Welsh et al., see note 28.

[30]   Excerpted from: Parent, Dale, Terence Dunworth, Douglas McDonald, and William Rhodes (1997). *Key Legislative Issues in Criminal Justice: Mandatory Sentencing* (NCJ-161839). Washington, DC: U.S. Department of Justice, Office of Justice Programs, National Institute of Justice.

CHAPTER 4

DESIGNING THE PROGRAM OR POLICY

tten objectives (handwritten annotation)

CHAPTER OUTLINE

▶ *Choosing an intervention approach* involves integrating the information assembled in previous stages. How can the information collected at previous stages be used to decide what the substance of an intervention will be? How will a specific goal be accomplished?

▶ *Major activities for program design* include the following. (1) Define the target population: at whom is the intervention aimed? (2) Define target selection and intake procedures: how are targets selected and recruited for the intervention? (3) Define program components: the precise nature, amount and sequence of activities provided must be specified. Who does what to whom, in what order, and how much? (4) Write job descriptions of staff, and define the skills and training required.

▶ *Major activities for policy design* include the following. (1) Define the target population of the policy. Which persons or groups are included, and which are not? (2) Identify the responsible authority. Who is required to carry out the policy, and what will their responsibilities be? (3) Define the provisions and procedures of the policy. Provisions specify the sanctions or services that will be delivered, and the conditions that must be met in order for the policy to be carried out. Individuals responsible for implementing a specific set of rules must also clearly understand the specific sequence of actions to be taken (procedures) to ensure that the policy is carried out consistently.

Stage 4 involves specifying all of the program's activities or the policy's rules and procedures. Although planning for programs and policies shares many common features (e.g., analyzing the problem, setting goals and objectives), the two types of intervention are quite different in substance (design). This chapter will treat *program design* and *policy design* separately in order to distinguish these two intervention approaches from one another.

Choosing an Intervention Approach

Choosing an intervention approach involves integrating the information assembled in previous stages. For example, your goal might be to reduce juvenile violence, but how will that goal be accomplished? What will be the substance of the intervention—creating a boot camp, enforcing a curfew, developing community recreation programs, applying tougher punishment, or something else? How do you decide? Up to this point, you have collected and analyzed data, you have an idea of the intervention options that fit the problem or need, and your goals and objectives have been established. Your *force field analysis* (see Chapter 2) has revealed critical sources of resistance and support, and your *systems analysis* (Chapter 2) has identified important characteristics of the organizational environment in which the change effort will take place. These data should be used to make informed choices about which intervention approach to choose.

Another critical ingredient is the cost of the option selected.[1] At this point, our interest is in broad cost questions. For example, is capital punishment really cheaper than a life sentence? Common wisdom would tell us "yes"—after all, maintenance costs end when a person dies—but experience tells us that a system of capital punishment is considerably more expensive. Jury selection, complex appeals and incarceration on death row add tremendous costs to case processing.[2]

In selecting an approach, past experience is an important guide: we can learn about the potential costs of an option by examining its use in other settings. In the case in which the policy results in the creation of a new agency, the costs can be very high. The Juvenile Justice and Delinquency Prevention Act of 1974 was developed to improve state-level planning for combating juvenile crime and to halt the practice of confining status offenders with delinquents. One of the Act's provisions was the creation of the Office of Juvenile Justice and Delinquency Prevention within the Department of Justice. Between 1974 and 1980, Congress increased funding for this act from 25 million to 100 million.

Program and policy options are often weighed in terms of cost. One option is compared to another in terms of its expected benefits in relation to its costs as well as its costs in relation to available resources. Joan Petersilia, for example, listed the typical annual costs of different types of intermediate sanctions and treatment approaches to assist the California Department of Corrections in making its choices. These costs were as follows:[3]

Figure 4.1	
OPTION	COST
State Prison	$21,000
County Jail	19,700
Boot Camps (121 days prison plus 244 days intensive probation)	11,700
House arrest with electronic monitoring	3,500-8,500
Parole	4,000
Routine probation/parole supervision	200-2,000
Substance abuse treatment programs	
Residential	22,400
Social model (drug-free home)	12,500
Outpatient	2,900
Methadone maintenance	2,500

Some people are surprised to learn that a residential treatment program can be more costly than imprisonment or that an in-home drug treatment program can cost more than a boot camp. Similarly, many states have chosen to invest in developing community-based correctional programs to reduce dependency on costly prisons. However, these community programs, if run well, can be costly, too. Are offenders in these programs expected to work or go to school? If so, will it be necessary to purchase training, assist with job searches, monitor their behavior on the job or intervene when conflicts occur at the place of employment? Programs that include treatment are considerably more expensive than those that do not, and yet treatment improves the effectiveness of intensive probation programs.[4] These are facts that must be known in order to avoid wasteful planning or eventual program failure because of inadequate resources.

Designing a Program

In general, in designing a program we must answer the following questions as specifically as possible: who does what to whom, in what order, how much, and how often? How will the program be set up? How are targets selected? What activities are delivered, and how? What training and qualifications are required for staff? By the time you reach this stage of analysis, you should have information about:

- the problem or need to be addressed
- etiology and theory
- possible interventions
- potential barriers to change
- goals and objectives

Now the change agent's task is to design the "nuts and bolts" of the new program. If you are acting as a program analyst (or if perhaps you are writing a paper for this course), you would look at an existing program and specify in detail exactly what it does. The goals and objectives that have previously been specified must now be translated into specific tasks and activities, and the appropriate sequencing and timing of each activity must be defined. A complete example is provided in Case Study 4.1 at the end of this chapter.

Define the Target Population of the Program

Who is to be targeted, or changed? This process often involves specifying some level of need on the part of potential targets (e.g., level of drug involvement) and the characteristics of the intended target population (e.g., age, gender, geographic residence, type of offense, prior criminal record, etc.). First, we must clarify the intervention approach to be used. In Chapter 2, recall that we discussed five levels of causality. We now need to clarify exactly who or what is the target of change. Are we trying to change:

- individuals? (e.g., via counseling, teaching problem-solving skills)
- a group or groups? (e.g., via support groups, peer groups, family counseling)
- an organization? (e.g., via police training)
- a community? (e.g., via community policing, neighborhood watch, community service)
- social/structural conditions? (e.g., via welfare reform, job training, employment assistance)

Once we are clear about the intervention approach, we need to specify the target population. Usually, two major steps are required: defining eligibility and specifying numbers to be served.

1. *Define Eligibility*: Who is eligible for the program? For what kind of individuals is the program intended, and which targets are best suited to the intervention approach? Eligibility is often based on

age, residence, income, gender, ethnicity or other demographic variables. It is also based on level of need: What is the appropriate population to be targeted, in terms of their level of need?

2. *Specify Numbers to be Served*: Given scarce resources, how are program funds most wisely spent? How many resources are available to serve how many people? How many individuals can the program accommodate over a time period of six months? One year?

Assessing Risk and Needs

One of the most common tools for defining a target population and matching individual needs with appropriate programming is a *risk/needs assessment*. *Risk* typically refers to the likelihood of a negative outcome, like re-arrest, while *needs* pertain to the treatment-relevant issues and problems that an individual brings to the program. The risk/needs assessment tools most commonly used are empirically based; that is, they were developed from research on actual individuals from the targeted population. Among the most widely used of these tools are the MMPI-based Inmate Typology,[5] the Wisconsin Juvenile Probation and Aftercare Risk Instrument,[6] and the Youth Level of Service Inventory, developed by Don Andrews and his colleagues.[7]

Define Target Selection and Intake Procedures

Now that we know who the targets of change are, the next question is: How are targets recruited and selected for the intervention? Given that targeted individuals and potential referral sources (e.g., police, courts, schools, probation, social services, etc.) are initially unaware of the program (or perhaps hostile toward it), how will we make them aware of this program, and how will we encourage them to use it? For example, boot camp programs are often intended for first-time, nonviolent offenders. A list of eligible offenders might be obtained from court records; an application from the individual may be required; an interview and screening process may be required to determine the applicant's suitability for the program. The following five issues should be considered when defining target selection.

1. *Access:* How are targets "recruited" (i.e., how do they become aware of the program)? How are they informed of program operations and activities? Are referrals made to the program by any outside agencies? If so, by whom and for what reasons?

2. *Screening:* How are targets screened for eligibility? Is some kind of needs assessment or other format used? Are application procedures required? How do they work? How is it decided who will be admitted to the program and who will be excluded?

3. *Intake:* Is an intake form used to record basic information when an individual is referred to the program, such as name, age, source of referral, reason for referral, etc.?

4. *Individual Records:* Is information to be recorded or stored throughout an individual's participation in the program? What kinds of information are needed for agency reporting purposes? For feedback to the individual? For treatment planning?

5. *Retention:* How long are targets to be retained in the program? What procedures will encourage them to complete the program?

[handwritten: how long]

[handwritten: who will be responsible]

Define Program Components

The precise nature, amount, and sequence of activities provided by a program must be specified. *Service delivery* refers to all those parts of the program that involve the delivery of "services" or program operations (counseling, training, intensive supervision, etc.) to targets. Who does what to whom, in what order, how often, and how much? What is the sequence of activities?

A boot camp program, for example, might contain several components: rigid military style drills and physical training, academic or vocational education, life skills or problem-solving training, drug awareness education, social skills training, and so on. We need to describe how frequently each activity is provided (e.g., how many times a week?) and how much (e.g., one hour per week?). We need to specify which staff will be responsible for providing each activity and exactly how it will be done (e.g., how are "life skills" taught? what approach is used: text, lectures, speakers, films, role plays, individual or group counseling?). We need to describe the sequence of activities: what happens when an individual is first admitted? What order of activities is followed: upon admission? in a daily routine? on a weekly basis? How long does the program last (e.g., six weeks? six months?). How are targets "graduated" from the program?

Output refers to criteria for defining when the program has been completed (some unit of intervention provided to a specific individual). For example: 10 counseling sessions; eight weeks of boot camp; 12 problem-solving skills training sessions; and so on.

When reviewing applications for funding, general program descriptions or even academic articles, we are often surprised by the vagueness of the actual activities specified by the program. For example, we are told only that a program offers "counseling for battered women." We ask: How are women referred to this program? By whom? How is eligibility determined? Who delivers counseling? How? What kind of counseling (e.g., psychotherapy? behavior modification? cognitive restructuring?) How often is counseling given? For how long? In what setting (inpatient vs. outpatient?). Obviously, the simple information that "counseling" is provided is, by itself, insufficient for understanding anything about the program's service delivery.

Write Job Descriptions of Staff and Define the Skills and Training Required

How many and what kinds of staff are required to operate the program? What specific duties will they carry out? What kind of qualifications do they need to possess, and what further training will be necessary? How much money is needed for staff salaries and training? *Service tasks* are job descriptions of all program staff, their qualifications and training, and the major activities that are completed by program staff.

Designing a Policy

Policies differ from programs in that policies are rules, principles or guidelines that govern actions, while programs are social structures created to address specific needs or problems of a target population (see Chapter 1). Often programs are created to carry out large-scale policies. For example, the policy of requiring drug-abusing defendants in criminal court to participate in drug treatment has produced both new drug treatment programs and, more recently, drug courts.[8] Drug courts possess more specialized knowledge of drug addiction and are better equipped to address the unique problems of the addicted defendant.

Policies are never designed by individuals working alone. Instead, because the decisions of a great many people will be affected, policy design occurs within a legislative process. Elected legislators of government bodies typically vote on policies designed by subcommittees. In private organizations, a similar process occurs through the board of directors. In other words, the creation of rules is usually the business of a legitimate body of rule makers.

In Chapter 1, we noted that policies vary in terms of their complexity. For example, a policy states that visitors to the offices of a program must sign a visitors' log. This is not a rule that typically requires discussion by a legislative body. Instead, these lower-level policies are handled at an administrative level. We will concern ourselves here, however, with broader polices created to address significant criminal justice problems.

The design of a policy involves specifying in detail the elements of the policy that make it possible for others to use it appropriately. In other words, if the provisions and procedures of the policy are not laid out clearly, actions may be taken that are inconsistent with the intent of the policymakers. In addition, if elements of the policy are missing, then incomplete implementation may result.

For example, in the early 1980s, Philadelphia's Municipal Court initiated a new policy for handling drunk drivers. The idea was that small amounts of punishment combined with education and treatment would be more effective than punishment alone. Consequently, new penalties that included jail sentences of only a few days were created, requirements were added that the offender would be tested for alcohol abuse problems immediately after sentencing, and contracts were established with private programs to provide alcohol abuse treatment and education. However, a critical piece was missing. No one was made responsible to see that the sentence was carried out and no record of participation was maintained. Over time, offenders learned that if they ignored the sentence, nothing would happen. Ironically, the more times an offender was sentenced, the less likely it was that the sentence was completed.[9]

In designing a policy, the change agent typically identifies:

- The target population, or who will be affected by the policy.

- The decision authority, or who has the authority to carry out the policy.

- The provisions of the policy (what members of the target population will receive) and the steps that must be followed (procedures).

Define the Target Population of the Policy

Policies affect people. Much like programs, they are intended to benefit or punish specific groups of people through the actions of decision-makers. A policy that certain juveniles will be automatically tried as adults ("direct file" or "automatic exclusion") must clearly specify the characteristics of individuals and their offenses that will make them eligible for trial in criminal court. How old must they be? What offenses are included? Do they need to have a record of prior offenses? Must the prior offenses be serious? Is there any way that these juveniles can be tried in juvenile court?

For other types of policies, the question is often one of selection: whether the rule applies to everyone or whether only certain persons or groups are being targeted. Recent research has shown that serious juvenile crimes occur at specific times of day. Many cities have instituted curfews in order to reduce crimes that occur between 11:00 P.M. and 6:00 A.M. This type of policy applies to all persons within a specific age range. In a South Carolina study, however, researchers found that most violent crimes occur around 3:00 P.M., right after school. This information implies that more after-school programming is needed.[10]

Identify the Responsible Authority

Who is to carry out the policy, and what will the responsibilities of those persons be? Many states, for example, have implemented sentencing guidelines that limit the ranges of sentences that judges can give to offenders, depending on current and prior offense information. Judges are required to stay within the specified reasons or to provide written justification for giving a sentence that is outside the range. In this case, the judge is the responsible authority, and the judge must consult the guidelines before assigning the sentence. This assignment of responsibility to an organizational unit or to persons occupying a specific role in an organization is important to the policy's success. It assures that relevant knowledge, credibility and lines of authority are consistent with other policies.

In some cases, a new policy results in the creation of new agencies. In the case of sentencing guidelines, many states have created commissions that monitor implementation of the guidelines, including training judges, prosecutors, defenders and others who need to know the new rules. Importantly, these sentencing commissions monitor use of the guidelines and thus learn how to improve them. For example, if judges routinely make exceptions to the guidelines in cases involving use of a weapon or drug addiction, then the commission needs to review the guidelines to see if changes are needed. It may be that the justifications provided by judges are consistent and convincing, and that the guidelines should reflect the values and beliefs being expressed by these judges. This example shows how important it is to assign responsibility for carrying out a policy to the right persons. Not only will implementation be more effective, but the policy itself has a better chance of being improved.

Specify Policy Provisions and Procedures

In order for a set of principles or rules to be implemented well, individuals responsible for carrying them out must understand what is to be done (provisions) and the steps that must be taken (procedures) so that the policy is carried out consistently. In the case of a curfew for juveniles, the rule about "who gets what and in what order" is clear. In other cases, however, the policy statement must be more detailed. It is critical that provisions and procedures be developed and stated clearly in order to ensure consistency, fairness and control of costs associated with the policy's implementation. Typically the policy identifies:

- What is to be done: the goods, services, opportunities or interventions that will be delivered to members of the target population (provisions).

- The steps that need to be followed and the conditions that must be met to apply the policy (procedures).

For example, state Community Corrections Acts (CCAs) are policies that specify how community correctional programs should be developed to control the growth of prison populations. The provisions of state CCAs vary in at least four dimensions:[11]

1. *The degree of decentralization* of authority from state to local levels (e.g., administrative control granted to city/county networks versus state-run programs).

2. *The nature of citizen participation* in the design, governance and operation of community corrections programs (e.g., citizen advisory board, role in case screening).

3. *The relative emphasis on deinstitutionalization of offenders* (the degree to which reductions in local or state prison populations are explicitly mandated or funding incentives or disincentives are tied to prison populations).

4. *The nature and scope* of *individualized sanctions and services* to be offered (e.g., relative emphasis on rehabilitation, reintegration, restitution, restoration or control).

We see that provisions may overlap to some degree with decision authority and target identification. The decision authority who chooses to keep some prison-bound offenders in the community may be bound by strict criteria for target selection that include the type of crime the offender committed, the offender's prior court history and family or employment situations. In another setting, the policy may specify a requirement (provision) that a certain proportion of prison-bound offenders must stay in the community. How these offenders are selected may or may not be left to the discretion of a group of decisionmakers.

When specifying the provisions of a policy, it is also important to specify the specific steps or procedures to be followed. For example, emergency release acts are controversial policy options that require a local or state correctional agency to release certain prisoners in order to bring the population down to an acceptable level. Obviously, such a policy is not popular with everyone. Letting prisoners out before their sentence is completed may be regarded as cheating. After all, the judge handed down a sentence that seemed fair. The fact that the prison is crowded does not change the appropriateness of the sentence. The fact is, however, that criminal justice agencies are not given infinite resources. They must do the best that they can with limited resources. In designing an emergency release policy, then, it is important to state clearly the sequence of actions (procedures) that must be taken when the prison population reaches a specified level:

- Prison populations are to be monitored daily.

- Projections are made about immediate crowding problems.

- Responsible persons are designated to make release decisions.

- The governor's office must be consulted in specific cases.

- Orders must be signed by specific persons of authority.

- Arrangements must be made for those inmates about to be released.

- Notification to other agencies (e.g., law enforcement) may be required.

These steps are especially important when the rights of individuals are affected, eligibility might be challenged, resources are limited and/or public objections are likely. Clear procedures help to ensure consistency and fairness in the application of a policy.

Conclusion

Once the intervention approach is chosen, it is necessary to specify clearly and in detail the design of the program or policy. Vague descriptions are not sufficient. Not all boot camps provide the same programming, for example, nor do all mandatory sentencing policies contain the same provisions. We want to know, in detail, who does what to whom in what order, how much and how often (see the summary table below). Only when the program or policy design has been clearly defined are we ready to move to the next stage of planning or analysis.

Figure 4.2

Critical Elements of Program and Policy Design

	Program Design	Policy Design
who (does)	staff	decision authority
what	"service delivery" (program components and activities)	provisions
to whom	target population	target population
in what order	"service delivery" (program components and activities)	procedures
how much	"service delivery" (program components and activities)	provisions
how often	"service delivery" (program components and activities)	procedures

DISCUSSION QUESTIONS

1. (a) Briefly describe the design of a program that we have discussed in class, or use one that you have found while doing library research for your class paper. (b) Do you have enough published material to do this analysis? If not, what information do you need, and how might you get it?

2. What factors should you consider in choosing an intervention approach? Give a brief example to illustrate your answer.

3. What is meant by the term *service tasks*? Describe the different aspects that need to be specified.

4. What is meant by the term *service delivery*? Describe the different aspects that need to be specified.

5. What is meant by *policy provisions*? Give an example.

6. What kinds of factors are considered in defining the target population?

7. Identify a criminal justice policy and outline its major components, including its target population, provisions, responsible authority and procedures.

8. Describe each of the following concepts:

   - *Access*
   - *Screening*
   - *Needs/risk assessment*
   - *Intake*
   - *Client records*
   - *Retention*
   - *Direct file*
   - *Emergency release acts*

Case Study 4.1

Program Design: The Checkmate Program

Instructions: Read the case study below, then answer the question at the end of the material.

The Checkmate Program was one of four community-based delinquency prevention programs funded by the state of Pennsylvania under its initiative to reduce minority overrepresentation in juvenile justice (see previous Examples 1.5, 2.5 and Case Study 3.1). The following program description was excerpted from an evaluation report to the state.

Target population and target selection

At its inception in the fall of 1992, the program was intended to serve the 25th Police District through a close cooperative relationship with Stetson Middle School. Because the Alternative School next door to Stetson received disciplinary transfers from the rest of the school system, including Stetson, youths from the Alternative School were also eligible to attend the Checkmate Program. Inclusion criteria included truancy and disruptive behavior in school. Program staff stated that the only reason for exclusion was if "youths are too much to handle."

Programs were mandated, as a condition of PCCD [Pennsylvania Commission on Crime and Delinquency] funding, to select at least half of their clients from youths having had prior contact with the justice system. While these criteria were originally interpreted to mean "at least one prior arrest," this literal interpretation proved too restrictive and not enough eligible clients at Stetson could be found. Thus, early in 1993, after discussions with PCCD staff, eligibility criteria were broadened. "Police contact" was no longer limited to an arrest, it could include a warning from the police or being questioned by the police. Also, if information was available to suggest that a youth was in a gang, he/she would be eligible. Following these changes in target selection, Checkmate achieved the mandated criteria.

Intake, exit, and follow-up procedures

Stetson Middle School was the major source of referrals when the program began. Police made a couple of referrals; a few clients were residents of Hancock Manor (self-referrals or referrals from parents living in the building where the Checkmate Program was located); a small number came from word of mouth. A mailing was sent to all potential referral sources explaining the purpose of the program and services provided for youths.

About two-thirds of the referrals came from schools. Program staff also had "House Meetings" (meetings with teachers at each grade level) in 1992 to recruit students. These efforts were so successful that by 1993 the program had received a surplus of referrals but had already admitted the maximum number of clients they could serve. As a result, there were no House Meetings in 1993. School referrals came mostly from the vice principal, counselors and teachers. Reasons for referral included truancy, cutting classes, inappropriate behavior, and causing trouble in class.

The demand for services proved quite high. By late fall of 1992, the Checkmate Program had already received 100 applications. By April of 1993, they had received about 200 applications, with room for only 50 clients at one time. Part of the reason for high demand was that Checkmate staff were very visible in schools. This was necessary, according to staff, to maintain good relations with the school and with students.

After the referral was received, there was an intake interview by a member of the staff (all staff conducted interviews). At the interview, the benefits of the program were explained. Youths were also advised of their obligations if they chose to enroll in the program. After the intake interviews, the interviewer met with the rest of the staff to discuss the applicant's suitability for the program. At the case conference, staff discussed whether there was a "good fit" between the youth's needs and the program. If the youth had no real problems, he/she was excluded from the program. Once a decision was made, each applicant was given a verbal orientation of the rules and regulations of the program.

While youths could be terminated from the program for poor attendance and/or failure to participate, the program preferred to encourage good attendance and participation by providing incentives, which included: field trips (i.e., aquarium, ball games), recreation and after-school homework assistance. Rewards were contingent upon fulfilling obligations. For example, if a youth completed his/her homework, he/she was allowed to participate in recreation activities.

General program goals and intervention philosophy

In its original program proposal, the Checkmate Program provided the following goal statement: "The intent of the Impact Checkmate Program is to establish an accountability system for youth with school activities, supplemental education services, evening and weekend personal development and leadership training activities, and other services that will result in positive behaviors in school and in the community." A cornerstone of the program has been its emphasis on the "Four As": attendance, academics, athletics and attitude.

Definitions of program success and failure, as provided by staff, were modest but clear. For example, staff stated that just getting youths to attend school is a major achievement. Staff also expected progress in each youth's attitude and behavior, physical fitness and academic performance. The most crucial factors needed for program success, according to staff, were consistent leadership and meaningful interaction with the clients.

Perceived obstacles to program success included a lot of attrition due to the transitional nature of the neighborhood and the age of the youths. Staff felt that there was too much of a "revolving door" policy regarding attendance. Efforts were made to contact youths, and encourage attendance. Unfor-

Case Study 4.1, *continued*

tunately, parents were sometimes a part of the problem. Program staff were limited by lack of resources in their ability to reach out to parents who resisted or did not seek assistance.

The school setting (Stetson) provided serious obstacles as well as support. For example, original target selection procedures were not successful. "Block Rostering" of students (i.e., identifying eligible students; scheduling classes to enable program clients to attend Checkmate activities) never happened. There were also problems in classroom scheduling (Checkmate originally offered its life skills classes at Stetson). Often, neither staff nor students knew in advance which classroom they were going to be in, creating delays and confusion.

Security and safety at the school was an issue. For example, random searches with metal detectors during the 1993-94 school year and fire alarms that were frequently set off by students caused disruption. Also, program staff reported that about six to eight serious incidents had occurred since the beginning of the school year, and there was inadequate protection for students. "Two trained counselors cannot provide effective service delivery to the school population of approximately 1,000 students." In addition, transportation from the Alternative School was stopped because of discipline problems on the bus, and this created an important gap.

At the conclusion of the 1992-93 school year, Checkmate maintained its relations with the school but began providing services to youth in a different physical setting (Hancock Manor). Checkmate staff members began visiting the schools at least three times per week to provide support for participants and recruit clients. There was a strong relationship with school staff.

Program content (service delivery)

Program activities and objectives are diagrammed in Figure 4.1. The program offered two weekend retreats (2½ days) as part of its regular programming. In 1992, the first retreat was a general orientation and introduction to the program that allowed the staff to assess individual strengths and weaknesses and encouraged youths to develop a sense of teamwork. Orientation at the beginning of the program was important for setting expectations about the program. A lot of youths had no experience with sharing or teamwork. Now, the orientation was provided only for new clients. Participants eventually recognized their own commitment toward progress and learning. They worked through goal setting, participated in "trust" activities, had several sporting activities and attended several presentations (i.e., life skills, group norms). Although both retreats were intensive, the second retreat was aimed at furthering individual and group development, including leadership skills.

The Checkmate Program emphasized truancy reduction and follow-up. Program staff telephoned the school to make sure that youths attended school, and followed up if students did not attend (phone calls, neighborhood "roundup," home visits). Over time, limited resources (i.e., too few program

Case Study 4.1, *continued*

staff and inconsistent police assistance) resulted in less intensive truancy follow-up, although school attendance was still closely monitored.

Regular life skills classes were offered by the Checkmate Program. These classes discussed a variety of issues, such as dealing with anger and communicating effectively. The program's staff had a very well-organized curriculum, including lesson plans and discussion questions. In 1992-93, a "Homework Club" was originally scheduled for one hour each day after school. Staff members encouraged clients to do their homework and provide assistance. It was very difficult to get students to do homework, however, and limited resources resulted in this component being offered mainly on a voluntary basis. To develop the desire to learn, the staff provided educational activities and games. Staff members found that they needed to focus on very basic skills. During 1993-94, the educational component was less intensive because there was no educational coordinator. On Monday, Wednesday and Friday, life skills were taught, and on Tuesday and Thursday homework/academic work was stressed. Activities not only included homework assistance, but also games, discussions and other activities. Those youths that did not have homework were allowed to participate in a game (i.e., chess), read, draw or do other activities.

The evening recreation program was provided eight to 12 hours per week and two hours on Saturday. Structured activities (i.e., basketball, games) and supervision were provided. In 1992, the "Four As" were stressed: attendance, attitude, athletics and academics. The "Four As" were not emphasized as much in 1993-94. Physical activities were seen as a means to specific objectives: increased sense of teamwork, increased self-esteem, improved motor skills and development of leadership skills. Games like chess also teach an important process, according to the Program Director: chess teaches rules, self-discipline and thinking skills.

The Computer Learning Center, located at Hancock Manor, provided computer resources and training. Assistance in developing basic skills (math, science and reading) was offered. Staff stated that they were working on new plans to get more clients involved and were setting up some software. Unfortunately, the computers were frequently in need of repair. An educational coordinator was subsequently hired, and the educational program was reorganized.

Field trips to museums and cultural and sporting events included attending a conference on Multicultural Disabilities, workshops on cultural awareness, and a school fair (college and career options).

In 1992-93 program staff originally stated that they provided mediation and counseling for clients but later agreed in discussions with evaluators that this component was really only an occasional part of their job descriptions (i.e., regular interaction with youth) and not a structured service.

The Police-Community Interracial Task Force provided Nonviolent Conflict Resolution Training on a contract basis. The basic curriculum was a 30-hour package including presentations, discussions and assignments.

Case Study 4.1, *continued*

A group "rap session" in which youths regularly met and discussed their goals, problems and progress was originally planned and implemented, but this was no longer being done because of problems with poor attendance and high client turnover. Five "subgroups" were planned (i.e., Rooks, Bishops, etc.). Each group was supposed to have a weekly rap session. In place of rap sessions, staff provide more one-on-one counseling.

One-to-one mentoring with adults was also intended in the original program proposal, but this component did not fully materialize due to limited resources. The program made increasing use of "student mentors" over time, however. Volunteers from local high schools and colleges assisted with program supervision and helped monitor the program's clients. The program intended to increase the number of mentors to one for each client and began more intensive recruiting of volunteers from sources such as high schools (community service program), colleges, the United Way, St. Christopher's Church and Temple University.

A parent support group was also intended in the original proposal, but this got off to a very slow start due to lack of interest by parents. Participation increased gradually, however, due to persistence by staff. A handful of parents (six or seven) met regularly once a month to discuss their children's progress (in the program, at school, at home) and strategies to facilitate progress and provide support for each other. Other activities included life skills workshops, guest speakers and parenting skills. A stress reduction clinic and a session on parents' rights were also offered.

Youths were provided with some assistance in the area of career development. George C., who was acting director until he left in mid-1993, was using an assessment tool called "The Self-Directed Search (Form E)." His goal was to assess needs and skills of both youths and mentors, then match up pairs with similar interests and talents. George also used the "Career Directions Series" available at the Philadelphia Free Library to provide information about careers and facilitate planning with youth. The objectives were to assist staff and support youth in their progress toward their goals. A monthly "mentors" meeting was held; about 12 volunteers attended regularly.

Program goals

The primary program goals were as follows:

- improve attendance and achievement at school

- increase self-awareness and self-esteem

- improve problem-solving skills

- improve communication skills

- increase respect for others

- improve school performance

Case Study 4.1, *continued*

- improve basic skills (i.e., reading, writing)

- widen the range of experiences and opportunities

- develop life skills (i.e., job skills)

- encourage less aggressive behavior toward others

- increase cultural sensitivity

- learn to resolve disputes peacefully

Program staffing

In April 1993, Mike M., the Program Director, carried out administrative, coordinating and monitoring duties. The Project Coordinator, George C., planned program activities, supervised project staff, recruited and supervised volunteers, maintained program records and completed required reports (i.e., funding). He supervised the evening recreation program, taught life skills at the Alternative School (Mondays, Wednesdays and Thursdays) and provided counseling. Lela B. was the Educational Coordinator and Administrator: she served as a liaison with teachers and helped with truancy reduction, homework and counseling. Yvette S., the Youth Vocational Counselor, taught life skills, provided liaison with parents and assisted with truancy reduction efforts. She also provided counseling and referral services, maintained case notes and other pertinent information in youth files and met with school personnel to review youths' academic performance. An Evening Recreation Director, McKinley W., was added in March of 1994. Katia V. was a part-time clerical assistant, and Darren C. was a part-time recreational assistant.

Questions

1. Review the program description and chart in Case Study 4.1, and critically evaluate it. How well is the design of this program described? Is there any other information about the program design that should be included? What questions might you ask to gain more information about the program design?

Case Study 4.1, *continued*

Figure 4.1
Checkmate Program Model

✳ Activities ⚐	Goals
Two Weekend Retreats (2½ days each)	• Assess individual needs and strengths
Life Skills Training (90 minutes weekly)	• Improve self-esteem • Improve communications skills • Increase respect for others • Learn problem-solving skills
Truancy Reduction and Follow-up (Daily checks with school)	• Reduce truancy
After-School Club (3:30 - 5:00 P.M., Monday - Friday)	• Improve school behavior and performance • Provide homework assistance
Evening Recreation: Organized Sports and Games (6:00 P.M. - 9:00 P.M., Monday - Friday; and 10:00 A.M. - 2:00 P.M. Saturday)	• Develop leadership skills • Develop teamwork • Improve self-esteem
Field Trips (1 - 2 per month)	• Increase cultural awareness • Increase awareness of diversity • Practice life skills in the field
Computer Learning (optional)	• Improve basic skills in math and reading
Nonviolent Conflict Resolution (30 hr. curriculum)	• Learn to resolve disputes peacefully • Encourage less aggressive behavior toward others • Increase cultural sensitivity
Youth Mentoring	• Assist staff in evening program and support youths.
Career Development	• Provide information about careers and facilitate planning with youth.
Date: June 1994	

Case Study 4.2

Getting Tough with Juvenile Offenders

Instructions: Read the material below, then answer the questions at the end of the case study.

One area in criminal justice that has seen dramatic change in recent years is the processing of juvenile cases by the courts. The experience of Pennsylvania illustrates these changes well. In 1994, the state's District Attorney's Association asked the legislature to change the Juvenile Act. The recommended change was to give prosecutors the option of filing criminal charges directly in adult court when the offense was serious, violent or if the offender was at least 16 and a chronic offender. Armed with factual evidence of increasing youth violence and arguments that the juvenile justice system was not equipped to deal with the problem, they pressed their case even harder when a new governor was elected in November of 1994.

The juvenile court judges of the state strongly opposed this proposed change. Instead, the judges proposed enhancements of the juvenile justice system that would support a comprehensive, community-focused effort to control violent juvenile delinquency. With greater resources and continued control over the decision to transfer juveniles to the adult system, the judges believed that youth violence could be reduced.

These initiatives were addressed aggressively by the new governor, Tom Ridge, when he came into office in January of 1995. Within a year, new legislation had been passed that changed the purpose of the juvenile court from one of rehabilitation to one of "balanced attention to the protection of the community, the imposition of accountability for offenses committed and the development of competencies to enable children to become responsible and productive members of the community." Importantly, this legislation shifted the status of beneficiary from the child to the community.

Other major changes also were brought into law:

- The police are authorized to fingerprint and photograph any child alleged to have committed a misdemeanor or felony.

- Parents can be required to participate in summary offense hearings.

- Schools and the police must be notified of the disposition of a case.

- Juvenile records of former juvenile offenders can be used at bail hearings.

- Juvenile hearings are open to the public in cases in which the juvenile is charged with a felony.

The District Attorney's Association also got what it wanted: a number of offenses were excluded from juvenile court jurisdiction, thus enabling prosecutors to try these cases in adult court. The excluded offenses, which apply only to youths 15 and older, are: rape, involuntary sexual intercourse, aggravated assault, robbery, robbery of a motor vehicle, aggravated indecent assault, kidnapping, voluntary manslaughter and attempt to commit murder. If the juvenile can demonstrate that a trial in juvenile court would be better for the public, then the criminal court can choose to transfer the case back to juvenile court. In addition, juvenile court judges are to consider primarily the public interest when deciding to transfer other cases. Again, it is the public, not the juvenile, that now is seen as the beneficiary of the law.

Obviously, each of the provisions listed above requires judges, administrators, prosecutors and probation staff to follow detailed procedures. Consider the direct file provision known as Act 33. This act not only specifies what offenses are excluded from juvenile court jurisdiction, but it defines in detail each offense so that fairness can be achieved. For example, aggravated assault includes an intentional attempt to cause bodily harm to a public official, an attempt to cause bodily harm with a deadly weapon or an attempt to cause bodily harm to a teacher or student while they are engaged in school activities.

Missing from this new law, however, are two important procedures:

- What rules apply to detaining a juvenile who is charged as an adult? Juveniles cannot be detained in a place where adults are detained. However, if the trial will occur in adult court, do the rules pertaining to juveniles still apply?

- What happens if the initial charge is for an excluded offense and then later the charge is reduced?

These and other procedural questions are being added as they arise.

Important cost issues have been created by this new legislation. With all of these new procedures, training of judges, prosecutors, defense counsel, probation officers and the police is necessary. There is much for them to learn in order for the system to function smoothly. Moreover, the adult courts may need new resources for detaining and processing juveniles. For example, is the court obligated to provide educational programs? Further, where will the system place those youths who are sentenced to prison? In Pennsylvania, new institutional facilities have been proposed for housing youths who have been sentenced as adults.

Case Study 4.2, *continued*

QUESTIONS

1. Review the policy description given in Case Study 4.2 and critically evaluate it. Is the policy design (as described here) adequate? Why or why not? Is anything missing?

2. Consider what decision issues are raised by shifting the emphasis of the juvenile justice system from "the best interests of the child" to "the protection of the community," and what cost considerations should be addressed.

3. For Pennsylvania's new Juvenile Act, what is the law's target population? What are its provisions? Who is the authority responsible for carrying it out? What procedures have been provided, and what procedures still need to be addressed?

Endnotes

[1]   We discuss cost and resource planning in further detail in Chapter 5. In Chapter 8, we examine cost-benefit and cost-effectiveness evaluation.

[2]   See: Baldus, David C., George G. Woodworth, and Charles A. Pulaski, Jr. (1990). *Equal Justice and the Death Penalty: A Legal and Empirical Analysis* Boston: Northeastern University Press; Bohm, Robert M. (1989). "Humanism and the Death Penalty, with Special Emphasis on the Post-Furman Experience." *Justice Quarterly,* 6:173-195; Zimring, Franklin, and Gordon Hawkins (1986). *Capital Punishment and the American Agenda*. Cambridge: Cambridge University Press.

[3]   Petersilia, Joan (1997). "Diverting Nonviolent Prisoners to Intermediate Sanctions: The Impact of California Prison Admissions and Corrections Costs." *Corrections Management*, vol. 1, no. (1):10.

[4]   Petersilia, Joan, and Susan Turner (1993). "Intensive Probation and Parole." In Michael Tonry (ed.) *Crime and Justice: A Review of Research*. Vol. 17. Chicago: University of Chicago Press.

[5]   Megargee, E.I., and M.J. Bohn, Jr. with J. Myer and F. Sink (1979). *Classifying Criminal Offenders*. Beverly Hills, CA: Sage Publications.

[6]   Baird, S., Storrs, G., and Connolly, H. (1984). *Classification and Case Management for Juvenile Offenders: A Model Systems Approach*. Washington, DC: A.D. Little.

[7]   Andrews, D., Kiessling, J., Robinson, D., and Mickus, S. (1986). "The Risk Principle of Case Classification: An Outcome Evaluation with Young Adult Probationers." *Canadian Journal of Criminology*, 28:377-384.

[8]   See: Goldkamp, John (1994). "Miami's Treatment Drug Court for Felony Defendants: Some Implications of Assessment Findings." *The Prison Journal*, 74:110-166.

[9]   Rourke, Nancy E. and Philip W. Harris (1988). "Evaluating Your DUI System: It Can be Sobering." *Judicature*, 27(2):14-18, 45-49.

[10]   February/March, 1996. *Juvenile Justice Update*, vol. 2, (1):5.

[11]   Harris, M. Kay (1996). "Key Differences Among Community Corrections Acts in the United States: An Overview." *The Prison Journal*, 76:192-238.

[12]   Welsh, Wayne N., Philip W. Harris, and Patricia H. Jenkins (1995b). *Evaluation of Minority Overrepresentation Programs. Appendix to Report 2: Individual Program Reports*. Philadelphia, PA: Temple University, Department of Criminal Justice.

CHAPTER 5

DEVELOPING
AN ACTION PLAN

By now, you have the program or policy design specified; now it is time to develop a plan to put it into motion. An *action plan* is like the blueprint for building a house: in addition to the description of the house (e.g., a four-bedroom, two-story, brick house with a deck, modern kitchen and landscaped yard), you need a blueprint that specifies all the necessary materials, supplies and tools required, what goes where, and how things are supposed to fit together. Without the blueprint, you cannot even begin. We find out how good the blueprint is when we actually put it into action step-by-step. Alas, though, the blueprint didn't just fall out of the sky into our waiting hands; someone (the architect) put considerable thought and effort into explaining how to translate his or her vision of a house into reality. In a sense, developing an action plan is like writing a blueprint.

Here is another analogy: developing an action plan is like writing the instructions on how to assemble a new stereo or computer system. Most of us know how frustrating instructions for so-called "easy to assemble" products can be. Let's say you've assembled a complex system of electronic equipment by carefully following all the manufacturer's instructions. You have all the necessary components laid out in front of you, you hook up all the wires and cords according to the instructions, and you hook up the power supply. Now it is time to turn on the switch. The question is: Will it run? Will it run effectively and efficiently? What do you do if it doesn't? Simply having all the components does not do much good unless the instructions effectively explain what is needed to get the thing going. One needs a plan for putting the system into operation and making sure that it is working properly.

Interventions are similar. You have the program or policy design on paper (i.e., descriptions of target selection procedures, job descriptions and qualifications of staff and all the program/policy components or services to be delivered), but that is not sufficient for implementing program or policy operations. You need to develop an action plan, a blueprint that methodically specifies the sequence of tasks that need to be completed in order to successfully launch or implement the program or policy. These include technical and interpersonal tasks (e.g., identifying and acquiring the necessary resources for the program or policy, locating office space and/or meeting space, hiring and training staff, designing client intake and reporting forms, purchasing equipment and supplies, setting dates and assigning responsibility for the completion of specific tasks).

Definition

Action Planning: Charting the entire sequence of activities and completion dates required to implement the program or policy design. It involves specifying, in clear and concise detail, the steps required to implement the program or policy design. It is, in essence, a "blueprint" explaining how to translate a vision of the program or policy into reality.

Naturally, as with the hypothetical computer system, you want the thing to run properly after you've spent so much of your money (and energy) on it. If you have planned carefully, you will minimize (but not eliminate) unanticipated problems that can surface when the program or policy actually begins operations.

Identify the Needed Resources and Make Cost Projections

We need to identify all the specific resources that will be necessary to implement an intervention. In real life, this is extremely important. One cannot launch any program or policy without the fiscal and personal resources needed to translate a vision into reality. One must start by developing a *resource plan,* which enumerates all the specific costs associated with each program or policy component, including staff salaries, benefits, training, supplies, physical space, and so on.

Definition

Resource Plan: A comprehensive statement of the specific fiscal, material and social resources required to implement an intervention. All program or policy costs are estimated, including personnel, training, equipment, supplies, facilities, travel, etc.

A resource plan attempts to achieve the following goals:

- It matches resources to objectives: in other words, one must carefully ensure that all the resources necessary to achieve the program's or policy's objectives are in place. It forces us to impose a test of feasibility: either resources must rise to the level needed to achieve the stated objectives of the program or policy, or the objectives must be downscaled to match the level of resources available.

- It identifies the availability of current resources, as well as those still needed to implement the program or policy design.

- It attempts to control expenditures over a specified period of time, usually by specifying how much money is to be spent over specific periods of time, such as each quarter (a three-month period).

- It provides data for monitoring fiscal aspects of the program or policy and provides feedback to funding sources and other stakeholders (e.g., annual reports or quarterly grant reports).

We offer a few simple guidelines for developing the resource plan. We emphasize that one need not be a financial wizard, an economist or an accountant to understand and use basic principles of resource planning. We will not be discussing professional budgeting models such as incremental models, performance-based budgeting, program budgeting or zero-based budgeting. The interested reader can find ample discussions on these specialized techniques elsewhere.[1] Suffice it to say we believe firmly in the principles of *program-based budgeting* (also called *functional budgeting*). We present two basic principles of resource planning. First, we identify the kinds of resources needed. Second, we estimate cost projections for each type of resource needed.

First, list the different categories of resources that are needed to achieve each program or policy objective. Work closely from the program or policy design (see Chapter 4). Your list should include everything that will cost anything. For example:

- Staff: how many? with what qualifications?

- Staff training: what kind, and how much will be needed?

- Supplies: paper, printing and copying, office supplies?

- Advertising: brochures, flyers, public service announcements?

- Equipment: computers, telephones, copiers?

- Rental costs for office space, meeting space and other specialized space, if required (e.g., private interviewing rooms?).

- Telephone, electrical and water bills?

Some types of costs can be anticipated and calculated fairly precisely (e.g., salaries, rent); others may vary a great deal (e.g., telephone, xeroxing, supplies). How do you know? Ask around; do some research on similar programs or policies. Consult directors of other programs and agencies; see if it is possible to look at proposals that other agencies have prepared. Contact potential funding sources (e.g., state or federal government) to see if they will allow you to look at selected proposals they have funded in the past (probably with confidential financial information such as individual salaries removed but with basic categories of costs such as personnel costs intact).

Those involved with the day-to-day operations of the program or the implementation of the policy (e.g., program or agency staff, coordinators and directors) should have some input into what fiscal and social resources are needed to run the program or administer the policy effectively. Too often, especially in applications to government agencies for funding, we see resource plans that were developed entirely by professional grant writers outside of the agency. The problem is that those grant writers have had little or no contact with the daily operations of the program or agency, and their estimates of resources needed may not correspond very closely with the experience of the staff or the clients. Again, we emphasize the value of participation: do not exclude the input of staff persons who have valuable experience to aid resource planning.

Next, we ask how much of each kind of resource is needed? It is very important to be realistic about cost estimates. If you estimate too little, the program or policy is likely to fail. If you estimate too much, the proposal may not get funded, or the agency may face accusations of wastage. A good budget will not only describe all estimated costs, but will provide a clear justification for each expenditure item.

In general, we are attempting to estimate all the costs involved with processing all clients or targets through all phases of the program or policy over a specific period of time (e.g., one year). As we are trying to estimate these costs associated with each program or policy design component, we try to be as thorough as possible. In addition to paying staff salaries, how much will it cost to train staff? How much will it cost to print and duplicate the client intake forms and other record-keeping forms needed? How much will it cost to acquire the supplies needed to deliver specific services (e.g., textbooks, learning aids, computer software, etc.)? How much will it cost to pay electrical, telephone and water bills for the rooms or offices that are to be used?

Again, we recommend working closely from the program or policy design. Estimate the costs involved for each program or policy design component. For example, tutoring is one of several program components in an after-school delinquency prevention program. How much staff time will be needed for each student over a specific time period, and how much will that staff time cost? Case Study 5.1 provides an example of these estimation procedures.

Some will complain that in this era of scarce resources and shrinking budgets, funding agencies expect programs to do everything for nothing, that is, provide comprehensive, intensive services on a shoestring budget. How, they will ask, can you tell us to make program-based estimates like those in Case Study 5.1, when doing so will inflate our already overstretched budgets? Program directors may complain that they are already committed to providing services far beyond what their meager budgets actually cover. But how can they provide more services than what their budgets allow? By overworking and burning out their most motivated staff persons, by pushing untrained staff to provide specialized services (e.g., life-skills training, conflict resolution training), by constantly training and recruiting new staff to replace the ones who left, by working hard to provide the impression (a "front") that the program is really "working" and by actively covering up any negative information that might threaten the program's survival. Such a situation is untenable. A good resource plan would never allow such a fiasco.

Plan to Acquire or Reallocate Resources

The task of obtaining funds to implement the program or policy requires a combination of experience, dedication, persistence and patience. In most cases, the change agent or another specifically appointed individual (e.g., the program director or the agency's executive director) will scour the grant announcements of government, private and nonprofit agencies, attempting to find some match between the interests of potential funding providers and the type of services the program is designed to provide. The interests of funding providers are usually clearly spelled out in annual program announcements, grant announcements or solicitation for proposals. In other cases, the change agent will lobby to find individuals or agencies interested in putting up funding for the program, arguing that it addresses a compelling problem or need within the mission of the funding provider. This task takes some skill, dedication and persistence. Figure 5.1 lists some funding sources that might be considered.

Figure 5.1

Potential Funding Sources

- *Local, state or federal government agencies:* Does the program or policy address a compelling need or problem that lies within the mission statement and jurisdiction of a government agency? Federal agencies are most likely to have specific grant announcements; local (city or county) agencies are most likely to fund specific programs that address their mission.

- *Governmental funds designated for special purposes:* Find out if city, state or federal agencies have designated specific funds for certain programming areas (e.g., crime prevention, drug awareness education, violence prevention, etc.). Funding priorities or targeted programming areas change from year to year, so one must stay up-to-date with each agency's funding priorities.

- *User fees:* In some cases, nominal fees may be charged to the clients, although these fees are usually far less than actual program costs. In many criminal justice programs, such "user fees" are not popular, but we have seen more creative user fees in recent years (e.g., an intensive supervision probation program charges a daily fee to all participants to help offset program costs. The incentive to pay such fees resides in an offender's desire to be supervised in the community rather than prison, to begin full-time employment and to be closer to his or her family).

Figure 5.1, *continued*

- *Private and nonprofit agencies* (e.g., the MacArthur Foundation, the United Way and the Pugh Foundation): These agencies often provide funding for programs that address their mission statements.

- *Donations from businesses:* Many large corporations and even many small community businesses have become increasingly involved in providing support or resources for programs or policies that address community needs. In addition to "giving something back to the community" by being good citizens, many business people may qualify for valuable tax breaks by making donations of equipment, goods, services or money.

- *Volunteers:* Many programs and agencies make extensive use of volunteers to provide some services (e.g., tutoring and mentoring in after-school delinquency prevention programs). Of course, volunteers need to be qualified and trained to provide specific services, and the program or agency must be prepared to support its volunteers.

- *Fund-raising projects:* Special projects may occasionally be undertaken to raise money for the program's services.

Acquiring the necessary resources to implement the program may involve any or all of a combination of activities: writing a formal funding application to a government or nonprofit agency; lobbying local, state or federal politicians for funding; making informal inquiries, presentations and solicitations to various agencies; and familiarizing oneself with the entire funding terrain of potential funding sources.

Make Adjustments to the Resource Plan

Unfortunately, one may find that potential funding providers cannot fully fund the proposed budget, or one might discover that adjustments to the budget become necessary later on if resources prove inadequate. Commonly, a potential funding source receives the application for funding, favorably reviews it, then asks the proposal writer to cut program or policy expenses by, say, 25 to 30 percent. The change agent and/or the program manager/director must be ready to make adjustments. Four options for adjusting resources are possible if resources prove inadequate for implementation of the intended program or policy design.

Figure 5.2

Making Adjustments to the Resource Plan: Four Options

1. *Redefine target selection and/or eligibility criteria:* This might involve restricting the eligibility of clients (e.g., to those most in need) or lowering the number of clients to be served (e.g., perhaps only 30 high-risk youth can be effectively served by an after-school delinquency prevention program, rather than the originally intended 50).

2. *Reduce or modify program objectives* (e.g., lower the outcome expected): Perhaps a 10 percent reduction in recidivism can be realistically achieved rather than a 50 percent reduction.

3. *Modify the program design* (e.g., eliminate one or more program components, beginning with the least essential components of the program).

4. *Try to increase funding to cover costs:* Multiple funding sources may be required to fund the program's expenses. Maybe more than one grant will be needed. Sometimes funding providers will ask the agency applying for funds to match the provider's contribution, with the requirement that no award will be made until the applying agency comes up with matching funds.

Example 5.1

A Gantt Chart for a Delinquency Prevention Program

Recall Example 1.4 from Chapter 1. We examined an excerpt from a funding proposal submitted by a community-based delinquency prevention program applying for state funds. Major program components included: a seven-day challenge course in which juveniles are encouraged to examine their lives and set goals, one-to-one mentoring of youths by adult "committed partners," and weekly "follow-through" meetings of all mentors and clients. The proposal spelled out, in considerable detail, exactly who was responsible for completing numerous activities required to launch the program. Specific job titles and descriptions were provided in Example 1.4. Activities included training, travel, site costs, seven-day course costs and follow-through costs. Included here is the time line (Gantt chart) they submitted with their proposal. While specific completion dates are not shown here, the time line clearly indicates a time period for beginning and ending each task; it indicates clearly the sequence of activities to be accomplished (and by whom) in implementing the program. Note that the "consultants" referred to are subcontractors, trainers from a well-established national youth program called "Youth At Risk." Note also that additional technical tasks (e.g., acquiring office space, meeting space, etc.), while not shown, could easily be specified in such a chart.

Example 5.1, *continued*

Activity	Person Responsible	1	2	3	4	5	6	7	8	9	10	11	12
1. Hire Program Coordinator.	Consultant	▮											
2. Project Coordinator training and coaching.	Consultant	▮											
3. Recruit and train volunteers (Youth Enrollment Coaches, Outreach, Facilitators).	Three trainers provided by consultant.	▮											
4. Market the program.	Project Coordinator; Outreach volunteers.	▮	▮	▮									
5. Youth enrollment training.	Youth Enrollment Coaches.		▮										
6. Recruit and orient youth participants.	Project Coordinator; Youth Enrollment Coaches.	▮	▮										
7. Conduct pre-course volunteer orientation.	Three trainers provided by consultant.			▮									
8. Conduct youth violence clearance, medical exams.	Specialists, professionals provided by consultant.		▮										
9. Conduct 10-day intensive curriculum.	Facilitators, Coaches, Course Production Team, Situation Intervention Team, Security.			▮									
10. Conduct parents' orientation.	Project Coordinator.			▮									
11. Assign Committed Partners and introduce to their youth partners.	Project Coordinator.		▮	▮									
12. Conduct monthly Committed Partner coaching sessions.	Project Coordinator.				▮	▮	▮	▮	▮	▮	▮	▮	▮
13. Conduct monthly youth and partner follow-through sessions.	Project Coordinator; two Workshop Leaders provided by consultant				▮	▮	▮	▮	▮	▮	▮	▮	▮
14. Manage weekly youth/partner communications.	Project Coordinator.				▮	▮	▮	▮	▮	▮	▮	▮	▮
15. Provide life skills counseling, educational and job training, referral and placement.	Project Coordinator; Committed Partners.				▮	▮	▮	▮	▮	▮	▮	▮	▮

Time Schedule (in months)

Specify Dates by Which Implementation Tasks Will Be Accomplished

The next task, probably the most important one at this stage, is to develop a program or policy time line, sometimes called a *Gantt chart* (see Example 5.1), which specifies three elements: (1) all the specific implementation activities that need to be accomplished, (2) assignment of responsibility for each specific task to one or more individuals, and (3) a specific date by which each task is to be completed. This process may seem tedious, but it is a far more effective alternative than merely "winging it" or improvising program/policy implementation. Without a specific plan that incorporates all three elements listed above, the program or policy is likely to experience difficulty (or even mortality) before it even gets off the ground. A Gantt chart is a blueprint for putting all the program or policy elements into operation: step-by-step instructions explaining how to implement the program.

Develop Mechanisms of Self-Regulation

Orienting Participants

Everyone involved in the program or policy, including staff and clients, should understand their role. Expectations for what kind of behavior is expected should be clearly spelled out, along with specific rewards and punishments. The program or agency director or coordinator should communicate a clear message about the rationale, values and intent of the change effort. Prior to beginning intake of clients, for example, it is particularly important to clarify job descriptions and expectations about the program or policy and allow program or agency staff to ask questions.

Coordinating Activities

Like the director of an orchestra, the change agent must coordinate the activities of several different individuals and groups. For the after-school delinquency prevention programs that we have described in several examples, there are various people and program parts that need to be monitored and managed on a regular basis. Program managers must hire and train their staff, they must build good relations with potential referral sources (police, schools, probation), they must train staff to use required intake forms and keep client records, they must build good relations with citizens and businesses in the neighborhood, and they must provide regular reports of program progress to their funding providers. Three guidelines help ensure smooth coordination.

Figure 5.3

Three Guidelines for Coordinating Activities

1. *Maintain consistency:* Make sure that the actual job duties of staff are consistent with their job descriptions. Develop reward systems and incentives for good performance, and communicate to staff what these rewards are. Poor program or agency managers tend to wait until something goes wrong, then blame (and punish) their staff. Good managers find that better performance results from communicating clear expectations and rewards. Such rewards include not just money, but privileges, responsibilities and access to resources. For example, most staff are interested in professional development, and a paid trip to a local or national conference would be a substantial, appreciated reward. Staff development activities are usually permissible budget items, if someone has the forethought to include them in a grant proposal.

2. *Maintain clear and frequent communication* among staff members and between staff and supervisors. Various means can be used: staff meetings, memos, conferences, informal conversations and performance evaluations. Such attempts need to be made explicitly, though, and must be done on a regular basis. Staff must also feel that their opinions count. The program or agency director should encourage honest opinions and reporting of difficulties as well as successes. Some of the worst programs we have seen are those in which the director communicates a "don't rock the boat" philosophy, with the result that staff are afraid to report any problems until they reach crisis proportions.

3. *Keep an eye on the time line:* Make sure that activities required for successful progression from one step to the next are carried out on time (e.g., make sure that staff are hired and trained by the dates specified in the action plan, that all record-keeping forms are printed and that procedures are clearly understood by staff). Imagine if 100 clients had to be turned away because a program was not ready to begin as scheduled. Perhaps a required staff position was not filled, the office space or meeting space was not ready, or the referring agency had specific reporting requirements that were not met by the program. Such events, although relatively rare, are tragic. The program suffers damage to the credibility and reputation that it worked so hard to build.

Managing Resistance and Conflict

Some resistance is inevitable with the start-up of any new program or policy. Resistance may come from any of the participants involved: clients, targets, even the program or agency's own staff (i.e., the action system). Any kind of change threatens people because it creates uncertainty. Change challenges long-standing values and views of the world; it introduces risk. If participants have had input into the planning process, resistance can be anticipated and perhaps minimized (review force field analysis in Chapter 2). However, resistance that appears should be dealt with fairly and seriously.

Conflict is not something to be avoided at all costs. It may provide the opportunity to identify and resolve misunderstandings, and it may also point out difficulties in implementation that truly deserve attention. Four general guidelines for conflict resolution are helpful.

Figure 5.4

Four Guidelines for Conflict Resolution

1. *Avoid the use of force or coercion:* Using force is not often very effective, even when one has legitimate power and authority. Attempts to stifle opposition often create or increase resistance, produce unintended side effects and lead to intentional subversion of the program's long-term goals.

2. *Try to work for a "win-win" solution, not a "win-lose" outcome:* Look for common ground, if possible. There may be options based on a principle of exchange (i.e., each party gives up something in order to get something) that would reduce resistance at little cost.

3. *Generate alternatives and options to deal with problems* (i.e., brainstorming): Identify all possible options before evaluating them. Only after a list of options is developed should parties begin discussing costs and benefits of specific strategies or negotiating outcomes (e.g., brainstorming).

4. *Use principled negotiations:* There are four basic rules for negotiating fairly.[2] First, separate the people from the problem (don't take it personally). Second, focus on interests, not positions: each party should identify and communicate their needs, preferences, values or concerns. Each party should understand what elements need to be included in a reasonable solution. Third, invent options for mutual gain: generate new options that are based on shared interests or an exchange of divergent interests. Finally, insist on objective criteria: both parties should agree on what criteria will be used to evaluate possible solutions.

Specify a Plan to Build and Maintain Support

With all the different interests represented by stakeholders and participants, one can expect that some public relations work goes with managing any program or policy, especially criminal justice interventions. The program or agency director is always trying to strengthen sources of support for the program or policy: within the staff, the community, across other agencies with which the program links, with his or her superiors, with the funding agency and with clients. Time for support-building needs to be built into one's schedule, and the person responsible for doing it needs to make sure that different stakeholders are contacted on a regular basis throughout the year.

Conclusion

The program or policy in action will never perfectly match the program or policy on paper (i.e., the program design). Developing a good "blueprint," or action plan, however, should markedly reduce subsequent problems with program or policy implementation and will help launch an effective intervention. So does looking for implementation difficulties, as we will see in the next chapter.

DISCUSSION QUESTIONS

1. Define and describe the following terms: (a) *action planning*, and (b) *resource plan*.

2. Describe the purposes (goals) of a resource plan.

3. What does it mean to "estimate the costs involved for each program component"? How does one do this?

4. What options are possible when resources prove to be inadequate?

5. What is a *time line* or *Gantt chart*? What does it attempt to do?

6. Describe three guidelines for coordinating activities.

7. Describe four guidelines for conflict resolution.

Case Study 5.1

Estimating Costs of Program Components: After-School Tutoring

Instructions: Read the material below, and check the calculations with a hand calculator. Then answer the questions at the end of the case study.

Look back at the description of the Checkmate Program (Case Study 4.1). We will try to estimate the costs for the tutoring component of the program only, which lasts for 40 weeks. The program has a maximum enrollment of 50 clients. Children in grades 6 through 8 attend the program after school five days a week for ninety minutes each day (3:30 - 5:00 P.M.). The first 60 minutes of each day are spent on homework and tutoring.

How many program staff persons are needed to effectively supervise and tutor 50 students for 60 minutes? If each student received only five minutes of personal instruction per day (50 x 5), exactly 250 staff minutes are required each day. How many staff positions do you need? Divide 250 staff minutes by 60 minutes (the length of the homework and tutoring period) and we come up with 4.16 staff persons. We will be conservative and say we need at least four staff persons to supervise 50 children effectively for this 60-minute time period.

Now, what about staff members' qualifications? Do they have any teaching experience or any familiarity with the math, spelling, science or social studies homework that the students will be bringing in? The program design describes only one position, that of education specialist. We assume that person will have at least a B.A. degree and some teaching experience. What about the other four staff members? Even if we require only a high school education, those staff will surely need some training before they can tutor children effectively. We do some research to find out what other programs pay for similar positions and experience. We come up with the following estimates:

- one education specialist @15.00/hr. x 5 hours
  per week x 40 weeks: 3,000.00

- four staff assistants @9.00/hr. x 5 hours
  per week x 40 weeks: 7,200.00

- eight hours of staff training (all four staff members
  trained at the same time) x 15.00/hr. for trainer's salary: 480.00

- Estimated annual costs for supplies
  (paper, pencils, pens, five calculators)   500.00

Total:	11,180.00

Our annual program costs, just for the tutoring component of the program, are $11,180. Now we would undertake similar estimates for each component of the program (see Figure 4.1). Note that labor laws generally

Case Study 5.1, *continued*

require that an employee be paid for at least three hours for each day they are called in to work. We do not want to overcomplicate our example right now, but when we have completed the entire resource plan and have costed out each program component, we will have to determine whether the same staff persons can fulfill multiple roles. For example, it is quite likely that the four assistants can also help supervise evening recreation. Because the after-school program ends at 5:00 and the evening program begins at 6:00, staff would have one hour to prepare for the evening program. That time could also be spent contacting parents to find out the whereabouts of any children who failed to show up that day. The time could also be profitably spent dealing with any specific problems individual children might be experiencing.

If the budget total begins to get too high (e.g., beyond the limit of available grants), we may have to cut back on the program's activities and/or its objectives. Better to cut back now than to find out later that we simply did not have the necessary resources to implement our intended program design. If the program fails to achieve its stated objectives, nobody is interested in hearing the excuse that, "We just didn't have enough resources." That is tantamount to saying, "We didn't know what we were doing when we did our budget." Such excuses do not inspire confidence in funding providers.

Question

1. Review the types of resources identified for the tutoring component. Try to identify at least one additional resource that would improve the tutoring component. Describe this resource, explain why you think it is important, and provide cost projections.

Case Study 5.2

The Brady Act: Why Action Planning is Needed[3]

Instructions: Read the material below, then answer the questions at the end of this case study.

Following seven years of congressional battles and NRA opposition, the Brady Handgun Violence Prevention Act[4] was enacted in November 1993 and became effective on February 28, 1994. The interim provisions of the act required that licensed firearm dealers request a presale check on all potential handgun purchasers from the Chief Law Enforcement Officer (CLEO) in the jurisdiction where the prospective purchaser resides. The CLEO must make a "reasonable effort" to determine if the purchaser is prohibited from receiving or possessing a handgun. The federal firearms licensee must wait five business days before transferring the handgun to the buyer, unless earlier approval is received from the CLEO.

The "interim provisions" also permit states to follow a variety of alternatives to the five-day waiting period. These alternatives include states that issue firearm permits, perform "instant checks" or conduct "point-of-sale" checks. To qualify under these alternatives, state law requires that before any licensee completes the transfer of a handgun to a nonlicensee, a government official must verify that possession of a handgun by the transferee would not be a violation of law. Examples of Brady-alternative states include California ("point-of-sale check"), Virginia ("instant check") and Missouri (permit).

This interim system remained in effect until November 30, 1998, when an instant background check became mandatory for purchasers of all firearms. Under the "permanent provisions" of the Brady Act, presale inquiries are made through the National Instant Criminal Background Check System (NICS). The background check will determine, based on available records, whether an individual is prohibited under the Federal Gun Control Act or state law from receiving or possessing firearms. The act required that the NICS, operated by the FBI, would be established no later than November 1998. At that time the procedures related to the waiting period of the interim system were to be eliminated.

Under the FBI's proposed NICS configuration, state criminal history records are provided through each state's central repository and the Interstate Identification Index. This index, maintained by the FBI, points instantly to criminal records that states hold. In addition, the FBI provides records of federal offenses, federally maintained state data, and federal data on nonfelony disqualifications. States responding to NICS inquiries for nonfelony prohibitions will provide their records directly.

The National Criminal History Improvement Program (NCHIP)

To ensure availability of complete and accurate state records, the Brady Act established a grant program authorized at $200 million. The program was intended to assist states in developing criminal history record systems and improving their interface with the NICS.

A major goal of the grant program is the interstate availability of complete state records when the NICS was implemented. Toward this goal, more than $112 million was awarded in direct awards to states during fiscal years 1995 and 1996. NCHIP program funds have also supported direct technical assistance to states, evaluation and related research.

Firearm Inquiry Statistics Program (FIST)

The FIST program was established under the NCHIP to develop data on the impact of presale firearm checks on the identification of prohibited firearm purchasers. Information requested for the survey does not include data traceable to an applicant, and the computer program that some agencies use to collect FIST data transmits only the appropriately aggregated or categorized responses. The computer program also assists agencies in purging records after the delay times specified by law. An initial report describing state background check procedures[5] was released in May 1996. Data summarizing the number of inquiries, rejections and reasons for rejections will be summarized and released semiannually by the U.S. Bureau of Justice Statistics.

Implementation of the Brady Act

Controversies surrounding the Brady Act extended far beyond arguments about the desirability of tougher handgun regulation (a fine debate topic in its own right). Disagreement about exactly how states and localities would meet the informational requirements of the act ensued: Who was going to pay, local law enforcement agencies wanted to know, to update and automate local criminal records information systems to comply with provisions of the Brady Act? Was the Brady Act another example, many local officials asked, of the "feds" dumping the expense of a new federal policy on the states, while federal politicians claimed political rewards (i.e., perceptions by voters that federal lawmakers were getting serious about reducing gun-related violence). This is a major reason why the NICS program described above was created. NICS was an excellent example of "action planning." Without the $112 million enabling legislation, problems in gaining initial state compliance with the new act would have been considerable. Similarly, the FIST program was needed to monitor implementation of the act over time.

The Bureau of Alcohol, Tobacco and Firearms (ATF) received even more questions about the act following its implementation in February 1994. The volume of questions and complaints received from local law enforcement agencies probably exceeded anyone's wildest expectations, and certainly surpassed the expectations (or concerns) of the federal politicians who passed the act. By December 1995, the ATF issued an informational release addressing no less than 44 specific questions about who was responsible for doing exactly what under the new provisions of the act.[6] Three of the questions are provided below.

Case Study 5.2, *continued*

1. Q. *Who must comply with the 5-day waiting period requirement imposed by the Brady Act?*

   A. Federally licensed firearms importers, manufacturers, and dealers must comply with the requirement prior to the sale, transfer, or delivery of a handgun to a nonlicensed individual.

2. Q. *How does the Brady Act affect a Federal firearms licensee?*

   A. The waiting period provisions of the law make it unlawful for any Federal firearms licensee to sell a handgun to a nonlicensee unless the licensee:

      (1) obtains a statement from the purchaser (Brady form) containing the purchaser's name, address, and date of birth appearing on a valid photo identification, and a statement that the purchaser is not a felon, under indictment, or otherwise prohibited from receiving or possessing the firearm under the law;

      (2) verifies the identity of the transferee by examining an identification document presented;

      (3) within 1 day after the purchaser furnishes the statement, contacts (by telephone or otherwise) the chief law enforcement officer (CLEO) of the place of the residence of the purchaser and advises such officer of the contents of the statement;

      (4) within 1 day after the purchaser furnishes the statement, provides to the chief law enforcement officer of the place of residence of the purchaser a copy of the statement and the officer makes a reasonable effort to determine whether the purchaser is prohibited from possessing the particular handgun(s) sought to be purchased; and

      (5) the licensee waits 5 business days from the date the licensee furnished notice of the contents of the statement before transferring the handgun to the purchaser (during which period the licensee has not received information from the chief Law enforcement officer that possession of the handgun by the purchaser would be in violation of the law) OR the licensee receives notice from the chief law enforcement officer of the place of the residence of the purchaser that possession of the handgun by the purchaser does not violate the law.

Case Study 5.2, *continued*

3. Q.   *Are there any exceptions to the 5-day waiting period require-ment?*

   A.   Licensees need not comply with the waiting period require-ments in 4 situations. These include handgun transfers (a) pur-suant to an official's written statement of the buyer's need for a handgun based upon a threat to life; (b) to buyers having a State permit or whose records have been checked and in either case an official has verified eligibility to possess firearms; (c) of National Firearms Act weapons approved by ATF; and (d) cer-tified by ATF as exempt because compliance with the waiting period is impractical.

In spite of the detailed planning undertaken to introduce this new policy (i.e., NCIS, FIST, Questions and Answers about the Brady Act), the long-term viability of the Brady Act remains questionable. In a close 5-4 decision on June 27, 1997, the U.S. Supreme Court ruled that the federal government cannot require local police to conduct background checks on people who want to buy handguns.[7] In general, Justice Antonin Scalia noted that the fed-eral government cannot force states to enact or administer a federal regula-tory program (a controversy known as federalism). However, the five-day waiting period specified by the act was ruled constitutional, as long as the states retain the discretion to perform the background checks or not. They cannot be made mandatory.[8]

Questions

1. Look at the three specific questions and answers about the Brady Act prepared by ATF. (a) Discuss how the Q & A format illustrates concepts discussed in this chapter (see Developing Mechanisms of Self-Regulation and Managing Resistance and Conflict). (b) Analyze how adequately the answers provided by ATF address the three questions. Is anything still unclear? Should further dif-ficulties in implementing the new act be anticipated? Why or why not?

2. Read one of the dissenting opinions of the four Supreme Court Justices who opposed the majority decision in *Printz v. United States.* The dissenting and concurring opinions can be found on the Internet at:

   http://supct.law.cornell.edu/supct/html/95-1478.ZS.html

   (a) Identify the judge who wrote the opinion, and summarize his or her argu-ments in your own words. (b) Do you agree or disagree with those argu-ments? Why or why not? Provide evidence to support your position.

Endnotes

1   For a summary, see: Kettner, Peter M., John M. Daley, and Ann Weaver Nichols (1985). *Initiating Change in Organizations and Communities*, pp. 179-182. Monterey, CA: Brooks/Cole.

2   Fisher, R., and W. Ury (1981). *Getting to Yes: Negotiating Agreement Without Giving In*. Boston: Houghton Mifflin.

3   Adapted from: Manson, Don, and Gene Lauver (1997). *Presale Firearm Checks* (NCJ-162787). Washington, DC: U.S. Department of Justice, Office of Justice Programs, Bureau of Justice Statistics.

4   *Brady Handgun Violence Prevention Act* (Brady Act), PL 103-159.

5   Regional Justice Information Service, St. Louis, Missouri (1996). *Survey Of State Procedures Related To Firearm Sales* (NCJ-160763). Washington, DC: US Department of Justice, Office of Justice Programs, Bureau of Justice Statistics.

6   The full text of 44 questions and answers can be found at: http://www.atf.treas.gov/core/firearms/information/brady/oq&abrady.htm

7   *Printz, Sheriff/Coroner, Ravalli County, Montana v. United States*, 117 S.Ct 2365, 138 L.Ed.2d 914 (1997).

8   For additional information regarding Brady Act design and implementation, go to the Bureau of Alcohol, Tobacco and Firearms web site (http://www.atf.treas.gov). Choose "Search" from the menu, and enter the words "Brady Act." You will find a wealth of relevant information about the Brady Act.

CHAPTER 6

DEVELOPING A PLAN FOR MONITORING IMPLEMENTATION

At a designated point in time, as specified in the action plan, it will be time to begin program or policy operations by following the sequence of steps specified in the action plan. Now, before continuing the planning process, we need to develop a strategy to observe the program or policy in action. History has taught us well that good intentions alone are insufficient: we cannot assume that everything planned will actually be done. The example below illustrates this all-too-frequent gap between intentions and actions. How could an expensive and popular new law such as "three strikes" legislation be so poorly implemented? What went wrong in the planning stage of this policy?

Example 6.1

The Gap Between Writing Laws and Using Them

Survey: "Three strikes" laws aren't affecting crime. The federal government and states aren't hastening to use them. California is the notable exception.[1]

WASHINGTON—Two years ago, politicians of every stripe were clamoring for "three-strikes-and-you're-out" laws—to put bad guys away forever, cut down on crime, and make the streets safe again.

But the first national survey of such laws shows they're not having much impact.

At the federal level, where "three strikes" was included in the 1994 crime bill, the law has been used on only nine occasions, according to a report being released today by the Campaign for an Effective Crime Policy, a Washington-based coalition of criminal-justice and elected officials. Twenty-four other federal cases are pending.

And the statutes simply aren't being used in many of the 22 states—including Pennsylvania and New Jersey—that passed similar laws, which typically impose a life sentence for a third felony conviction, the study shows.

"We have a serious crime problem in this country," said Walter Dickey, the University of Wisconsin law professor who wrote the report. "We are sold this as a solution. It gets all kinds of energy and attention, and yet it is relatively ineffectual."

Only in California has the law been applied broadly—15,000 offenders have been sentenced for second or third offenses, many of them nonviolent—and the experience has raised questions of equity, the study says.

The "three-strikes" laws were enacted as an answer to tackle repetitive, serious criminal behavior. Sentencing and parole eligibility vary from state to state, with some calling for third-time offenders to receive life without parole. In others, prisoners are eligible for parole after 30 or 40 years.

At the federal level, the long-term impact is minimal because less than 2 percent of violent felonies are resolved in federal courts.

Example 6.1, *continued*

With the exception of California, state third-strike laws have rarely been used. Tennessee, New Mexico, Colorado and North Carolina have not used them at all. Wisconsin has applied its law only once. Georgia has had five life sentences, and Indiana has had 10 convictions.

Washington, the first state to pass such a law in 1993, has had more than 60 convictions, but the state's corrections director says those criminals would have faced stiff sentences anyway under existing laws.

"This camouflages the real problems," said Chase Riveland, secretary of Washington's Department of Corrections. "This is almost a placebo. The public thinks something is happening that will make me feel safer. But that keeps us from looking at the real issues, such as dealing with drugs in our society."

Like prosecutors in Washington, those in other states have avoided the "three strikes" laws because they see little need for them with existing sentencing laws, the study concludes. Another reason is that some laws were narrowly written, making them harder to apply.

California is serving as a laboratory. There, about 1,300 offenders have been imprisoned on third-strike felonies and more than 14,000 criminals for "second-strike" felonies. California's law calls for a doubling of the prison sentence for a second felony and for a sentence of 25 years to life for a third conviction.

The California law was written to cover 500 felonies, including many nonviolent offenses. Some of the felonies include petty theft, attempted assault and burglary. Thus, about 85 percent of all those sentenced under the "three-strikes" laws were involved in nonviolent crimes, the study says.

For instance, 192 marijuana possessors have been sentenced for second and third strikes, compared with 40 murderers, 25 rapists and 24 kidnappers, the study says.

A California study cited in this survey says that blacks are sent to prison under the "three-strikes" law 13 times as often as whites. Forty-three percent of the third-strike inmates in California are African American, although they make up 7 percent of the state's population and 20 percent of its felony arrests.

Steve Telliano, press secretary for California Attorney General Dan Lungren, defended the law, saying the state's crime rate has dropped dramatically since its passage in March 1994.

The law also is having a huge effect on California's court backlog because many defendants are choosing to go to trial, rather than plea bargain, in the face of such sentences.

The report says the California law also has created a need to build 15 new prisons in the next five years, costing $4.5 billion. California's prison population is expected to grow by 70 percent by 1999, resulting in a 256 percent capacity rate, meaning that without new prisons, three inmates would be housed in space for one.

Before we continue it is useful to distinguish implementation from monitoring.

Definition

Implementation: The initiation, management and administration of the action plan (see Chapter 5). Once the program or policy actually begins, we want to minimize discrepancies between what was planned (i.e., the program or policy design) and what was actually done (i.e., the program or policy in action).

Definition

Monitoring: An attempt to determine whether program or policy implementation is proceeding as planned. Monitoring is a process that attempts to identify any gaps between the program or policy on paper (design) and the program or policy in action (implementation).

Previously, in the design stage (Chapter 4), we talked about identifying "who does what to whom in what order, how much, and how often?" Now at the monitoring stage, we are concerned with finding out whether the intended design has been properly implemented. How do we measure whether implementation succeeded? Monitoring, as we will see shortly, requires ongoing data collection throughout the life of the program or policy.

At the monitoring stage, then, we attempt to find out if the program or policy was implemented properly. Sometimes referred to as "process evaluation," *monitoring* refers to the collection of information to determine to what degree the design or blueprint (the program or policy on paper) is being carried out as planned. Data (e.g., observations, surveys, interviews) are collected to find out what is actually being delivered to clients (the program or policy in action). Adjustments will then need to be made to revise either the design of the intervention (e.g., either service delivery or policy provisions) or to make what is currently being done conform to the intended design.

Outline the Major Questions for Monitoring

Monitoring relates directly back to the design stage (Chapter 4). How do we measure whether the critical elements of program or policy design have been implemented properly? We can specify all the key questions for monitoring in terms of their corresponding program or policy design features.

Figure 6.1

Target Population

- What are the characteristics of the actual persons targeted by the program or policy? Are appropriate targets being selected?

- Is the program or policy meeting its specified criteria in terms of client eligibility (e.g., age, sex, income, region, etc.) as well as numbers to be served?

- Are proper target recruiting, referral, screening and intake procedures being followed? How are target selection decisions made?

Figure 6.2

Program Components or Policy Provisions

- *Who did what to whom in what order, how much, and how often?* We need some unit of measuring what was done. In a drug treatment program, for example, one way of measuring services delivered to clients is to record the total hours of counseling that are actually delivered to clients. We could also measure the number of clients admitted, attendance at regular program sessions (e.g., group meetings) and the number of clients who successfully completed a program. For "three strikes" laws, in addition to describing the rules for charging and processing suspects, we could count the number of people charged and convicted.

- *Were there variations in how program services or policy provisions were delivered?* In a program, for example, did one client receive different amounts or types of services than another (e.g., frequency or quality of treatment)? Was there more than one site or location where a program or policy was carried out, and, if so, were services administered consistently across different sites? Within a state, for example, were courts in some cities or counties more active than others in charging under "three strikes" provisions?

Figure 6.3

Program Staff or Individuals Designated to Implement the Policy

- *For a program:* Are proper staff being selected and trained? Do they fit the specified job descriptions? Do staff understand their duties and perform them as expected? Do different program staff provide services in a different manner?

- *For a policy:* Have the individuals responsible for carrying out a policy been clearly identified? Do they understand the policy and their specific responsibilities? Are proper procedures for implementing a specific policy being consistently followed by the designated authorities? Do different policy authorities implement the same rule differently?

We can illustrate the correlation between program or policy design and monitoring by referring to the chart in Figure 6.4, and we can easily see what kinds of questions we need to ask. In Column 1, we summarize all the key design features in terms of targets, staff or responsible authority, and program components or policy provisions. We should have all this information available from our previous assessment of program or policy design (Chapter 4). Then, as Column 2 indicates, we need some method of collecting data (to be discussed shortly) to find out whether intended design features were properly implemented. In Column 3, we report the results of monitoring: how was the program or policy actually implemented? Finally, in Column 4, we summarize any gaps detected between program or policy design and implementation (compare Column 1 with Column 3). Information collected from monitoring analysis is vital for modifying the program or policy to correct any implementation gaps detected.

Design Instruments to Collect Data

There are four major data collection techniques for monitoring:[2] (1) observational data, (2) service records (documents), (3) service provider data (staff), and (4) participant data (targets). Wherever possible, it is best to use more than one technique; depending on the time and resources available, use as many as possible. Each has its advantages and limitations.

Figure 6.4 Monitoring Analysis

	1. What was intended? (i.e., the program or policy on paper, the design of the program or policy).	2. How was monitoring done? (i.e., which of the four data collection methods were used?)	3. What were the results of monitoring? (i.e., how was the program or policy actually implemented?)	3. What gaps were found between the program or policy on paper (design) and the program or policy in action (implementation)?
Targets (e.g., eligibility, numbers to be served, access, screening, intake).				
Program Staff or Individuals Responsible for Implementing the Program or Policy (e.g., selection, training, duties).				
Program Components or Policy Provisions (e.g., specific goods, services, opportunities, or interventions to be delivered).				

Observational Data

Observational data may provide a rich and detailed source of information about program activities and policy provisions. By observational data, we mean data collected by evaluators and/or trained observers actually participating in or observing the program or policy in operation. For example, in the Minneapolis Domestic Violence Experiment,[3] trained observers rode along in police cars to observe how police handled domestic violence calls and to determine whether they followed agreed-upon procedures for administering one of three interventions (arrest, mediation or separation). Good observational data, however, is rarely obtained simply by "hanging out" at the program or policy site. Observers must be trained in how to make observations and how to record their observations. We need a systematic method for making and recording observations. Three main observational techniques are possible: (1) the narrative method, (2) the data guide method, and (3) the structured rating scheme.[4]

Narrative Method

When using the narrative method, an observer records events, in detail, in the order in which they occur. This is very much like a diary. It is the least structured of the three observational methods, but it may provide rich detail on implementation. The observer describes what services were provided, how the clients reacted, how the staff acted, and so on.

Data Guide Method

In the data guide method, the evaluator or change agent gives observers specific questions that they are required to answer from their observations. This technique is more structured than the narrative method, but less structured than the structured rating scheme. For example, observers may go out with police to observe DUI stops. Observers are given a list of questions that they attempt to answer for each stop:

- How did police officers select the vehicle for a DUI check?
- How many people were in the car?
- What kind of car was it (model, year)?
- Describe the driver (age, sex, race).
- Was the suspect: respectful? cooperative?
- Was the officer respectful? Did the officer explain the purpose of the stop?
- What police action was taken? (e.g., sobriety test, Breathalyzer, warning, other?)
- Did anything unusual or significant happen during this stop?

Structured Rating Scheme

This is the most structured of the three observational methods. We can ask observers to rate some kind of behavior on a standardized scale or checklist. Using the same example as above, where observers accompany police on DUI stops, the observer may be given a checklist that he or she completes for every police stop. The checklist may contain items such as the following:

Figure 6.5

Observer Checklist For DUI Stops

Name of observer: _____

Date and time of DUI stop: _____

Type of vehicle: _____

Observer Instructions: Rate the behavior of the suspect and the police officer on the five-point scales provided below. Circle the number that best fits your perception of what happened.

1. The suspect was: 1 2 3 4 5
                                polite   abusive

2. The police officer was: 1 2 3 4 5
                                polite   abusive

3. The police instructions were: 1 2 3 4 5
                                clear   vague

4. Action taken (check one):

____ field sobriety test

____ Breathalyzer

____ warning

____ no action taken

____ other (Please specify: _____)

In general, the major advantage of observational methods lies in the first-hand description of program activities that observers can provide. The major problem with these techniques is that the presence of observers may actually alter the behavior of program personnel or participants. Would police officers, for example, be more guarded in their speech and actions when they know they are being watched by a civilian observer? A less frequent, but not unusual problem is that observers may not report or record information consistently or accurately. The less structured the observational scheme (e.g., the narrative method), the greater the concerns with observer reliability and subjectivity.

Service Record Data

Service record data includes written, typed or computerized records that are kept by staff. Many programs require staff to collect certain information on program clients, service delivery and staff duties. One simple example is program attendance data: staff may be required to record whether clients are absent or present for scheduled meetings, or they may be required to record the total number of hours each client participates in the program. As a graduate student, the first author once worked at a federal forensic prison in Canada. This facility provided psychological assessments for the courts and treatment services for convicted offenders. Because the facility is an accredited hospital, as well as a prison, medical records must be kept. Staff (e.g., psychiatric nurses, psychologists, psychiatrists and research staff) must make an entry in a medical records binder every time they see a prisoner, describing the purpose of the visit, the length of the visit, what happened, the client's state of mind and any action taken with that client. In general, for many programs, we could ask program staff to make regular entries in a logbook describing what they did with each client, how much time they spent on different activities, and so on. These records may provide a good source of monitoring information, depending on how complex and how reliable these records are.

Service record data have at least two advantages: such data is (1) inexpensive, and (2) easily obtainable. However, service record data also present two common disadvantages: (1) program records may not contain sufficient information needed to monitor clients and services adequately, and (2) staff may not record this information consistently, accurately or completely. There may be sizable gaps in the information that is recorded. There are three possible solutions to these problems: (1) seek participation by staff in developing monitoring instruments, (2) train staff in how to use these instruments, and (3) conduct regular quality-control checks to make sure that records are being kept properly. There are three key guidelines for using service record data:

1. It is better to gather a few items of data consistently and reliably than to gather a lot of data poorly.

2. Recording forms should be structured as checklists whenever possible to simplify usage by program staff.

3. Service records should be checked immediately after completion for consistency and accuracy. These checks should be conducted on a regular basis, and corrective feedback should be given to staff as needed.

Service Provider Data

Service provider data refers to information that the evaluator or change agent obtains from program or agency staff members directly. As opposed to service records, for example, we could ask staff about the specific activities and services being provided. We could ask them whether client participation was high or low, how much time was spent on different activities, how clients responded, and so on. We could use either relatively informal or more structured interviews to obtain staff perceptions, or we could use questionnaires or surveys. The major advantage of this technique is that program or agency staff have regular involvement in the intervention, and they can often provide detailed, first-hand experience and knowledge. The major problem is potential subjectivity: program staff or policy authorities may answer questions so as to make themselves or the program or policy look good. In addition, staff may dislike the extra time or work required by this method (e.g., more paperwork), so the researcher or change agent must make sure that the information provided by staff is not incomplete or inaccurate.

Participant Data

Participant data refers to information that the evaluator or change agent obtains from clients or targets directly. Too often, client perceptions of interventions are ignored. It is important to get clients' perceptions not only of what services were actually delivered, but also their degree of satisfaction with program services or policy provisions. In asking about services provided by a DARE (Drug Awareness Resistance Education) program, for example, we might ask participants whether the information they received was understood and whether the information was utilized (e.g., were students rendered less likely to use drugs as a result of participating in the program?). Evidence has suggested that information provided by DARE programs may be well understood but rarely utilized.[5] As was the case with measuring staff perceptions of program services, we can assess client perceptions by using questionnaires and/or interviews. The advantages of obtaining client perceptions are that clients have abundant first-hand experience with program or policy services, and they are the only ones who can provide the perspective of the intended targets of change. Potential disadvantages to be considered are subjectivity (clients or targets may want to make the intervention look either "good" or "bad" depending on their personal experience) and mistrust of unfamiliar evaluators or "outsiders." It takes some skill to get valid responses from participants, but these problems are by no means insurmountable.

Designate Responsibility to Collect, Store and Analyze Data

We emphasize that monitoring requires collecting information. This usually means more work for program or agency staff, on top of their service delivery duties. Such information is indispensable, however, and no program or agency can survive or grow without it. For example, all programs need to record some basic information for accountability purposes. Examples might include the number of contacts made with clients in an intensive supervision probation program, the number of hours of participation in an after-school delinquency prevention program and weekly attendance at group counseling sessions in a substance abuse program.

In our work with nonprofit groups and with criminal justice agencies (e.g., probation departments), we have often found that funding agencies or program supervisors do not always clearly communicate or emphasize the information-reporting requirements for programs, and we have found that staff who have been assigned the responsibility of collecting monitoring data often lack the training, skills and time needed to fulfill such tasks. These are not excuses. The program manager or director bears full responsibility for making sure that certain information is recorded consistently and accurately. Expect that stakeholders will want regular reports on the numbers and characteristics of clients served, their level of need, their progress and participation in the program and, eventually, their outcomes. Someone must take responsibility for making sure the job gets done. If the program manager assigns responsibility to staff to undertake these tasks, he or she is also responsible for making sure that it gets done. If there is any ambiguity at all about what information is to be collected, who is responsible for collecting it or how it is to be collected, recorded and stored, the program manager must make sure such ambiguities are cleared up before the program or policy begins operations. If such gaps are detected afterwards, they must be filled. The risk of not taking such "mundane" considerations seriously is the potential death of the program or policy when those funding it or authorizing it lose faith in it.

Develop Information System Capacities

Definition
Information Systems: Ongoing methods of collecting data about clients, staff and program or policy activities. Information systems may consist of written forms and records that are filed, or may be fully computerized data entry and storage systems.

A good information system can serve several purposes. First and foremost, a good information system can demonstrate accountability to funding agents, the community and other stakeholders who may provide either critical support or resistance. A good information system is also useful for planning: it allows program managers or policy authorities to see how well plans are going and what problems emerge, and to make decisions about adjustments. A useful information system allows for continuous monitoring over time: it is sensitive to both intended and unintended changes in program or policy design.

Several guidelines should facilitate the development of a useful information system. First, it is vital to gain staff acceptance. Extra paperwork is unwelcome unless you can show that it provides meaningful and useful information. For example, staff may be more receptive to doing the work if they find out that they receive useful feedback about client performance, program services and their own performance. Cost is another consideration: even printing new forms can be expensive for a small, nonprofit agency. Certainly purchasing new computers or setting up a coordinated computer network can get very expensive. The bigger the agency, and the greater the number of clients, the greater the likelihood that more sophisticated information storage systems are needed. Greater needs are also implied by detailed and regular client assessment and reassessment procedures (e.g., risk and needs classification of ex-offenders in a halfway house) and sophisticated, multiple services provided to a diverse clientele. We should also consider compatibility: what information is already being collected? Can current information systems be modified somewhat, rather than designing a brand new information system? Safeguarding of information is important. In a delinquency prevention program, for example, staff need to protect the identity of the juvenile. To adequately assess a juvenile's needs, however, the program needs sensitive information about the juvenile's previous criminal record and his or her current school performance. Strict procedures must be developed for handling, using and storing such information. In general, training of staff is essential if good information is to be collected. One should never just give staff a package of forms and explain that "instructions are enclosed." Make sure that staff understand what is being asked of them.

Develop Mechanisms to Provide Feedback to Stakeholders

Finally, make plans for how monitoring information is to be used. Identify the appropriate audiences (e.g., program clients, staff or stakeholders), and schedule individual and/or group meetings to communicate results. Some reporting, particularly to funding agencies, will come in the form of program reports or research reports. Wherever gaps are detected, corrective action should be discussed and implemented. The bottom line is that any effective organization, private, public or nonprofit, requires monitoring information on a regular basis to figure out how well it is doing. Can you imagine an effective business that examines its sales only once a year? A stock market that reports transactions only once a month? A television network that examines ratings only at the end of the season? Ignoring monitoring is not good business. In extreme cases of inattention, it is likely to be fatal to the program or policy.

Conclusion

Monitoring is a process that attempts to identify any gaps between the program or policy on paper (design) and the program or policy in action (implementation). We can specify all the key questions for monitoring in terms of corresponding program or policy design features: what was intended in terms of targets, staff and program/policy services? Second, how do we collect data to determine the degree to which these design features are actually being implemented? Third, where are any gaps between the program or policy on paper and the program or policy in action? Where gaps are found, adjustments must be made: either the design (the program or policy on paper) must change or the way the program or policy is being implemented (the program or policy in action) must change.

The purpose of monitoring is not necessarily to ensure compliance with the original program or policy design. There is always some drift between the original design and actual implementation of any program or policy: over time, as conditions in the environment change, and as unanticipated difficulties emerge, modifications to the original design are inevitably made. Leadership changes, staff come and go, and services are altered. Sometimes these changes are necessary and for the better. What we are seeking, after all, is better programs and policies, not blind obedience to a piece of paper. If monitoring is timely and consistent, we can observe these changes in program or policy design and make explicit decisions about whether to adopt certain changes.

Consider this example. An inpatient drug treatment program's funding from the county is in jeopardy because it is serving too few clients with serious drug abuse problems. Monitoring data has indicated that the staff persons responsible for client intake have been turning away seriously addicted clients because they are too disruptive. Different options are possible. First, less stringent client eligibility criteria might be adopted to maintain funding levels. Alternatively, the program may seek funding from a different sponsor that will be more sympathetic to the existing client selection and treatment procedures. In the first case, changes in client selection (e.g., more clients with more serious drug abuse problems) will also necessitate changes in program design (e.g., type of counseling and total hours of counseling needed for seriously addicted clients). In the second case, changes in program funding may affect the program's entire mission and goals. What is important to stress is that deviations from the original program or policy design should be consciously intended, explicit and visible. Monitoring facilitates deliberate decisions about program or policy design and helps prevent unintended or invisible "drift."

Monitoring provides essential, continuous information that can be used to satisfy accountability requirements, improve program services or policy implementation on a regular basis, and move toward desired outcomes. As we will see in the next chapter, thorough monitoring should precede and accompany any valid evaluation of a program or policy. Though the two are closely linked, monitoring more closely emphasizes process; evaluation emphasizes outcome.

DISCUSSION QUESTIONS

1. (a) What is meant by the term *monitoring*? (b) What is the purpose of monitoring?

2. What questions do we need to ask about a program or policy at the monitoring stage? Be specific, and give examples to illustrate your answer.

3. Describe each of the four methods that can be used to collect data for monitoring. Discuss the strengths and weaknesses of each.

   (a) *observational methods*
   (b) *service records*
   (c) *service provider data*
   (d) *program participant data*

4. What are the purposes of an information system? Describe three major guidelines for developing such a system.

EXERCISE 6.1

Read Maxfield and Baumer's[6] article about electronic surveillance, or read a different one assigned by your instructor. Complete a monitoring analysis by using the monitoring analysis chart as a guide (see Figure 6.1).

Case Study 6.1

Program Monitoring: The Correctional Program Assessment Inventory (CPAI)

Instructions: Read the case study below, then answer the questions at the end of the selection.

Professors Don Andrews and Paul Gendreau have inquired extensively into the characteristics of effective correctional treatment programs and how those characteristics can effectively be shaped to improve treatment outcomes. Naturally, such an approach assumes that rehabilitation is sometimes effective, at least with certain offenders under certain circumstances. These researchers have provided ample empirical evidence to support their claims. Following a large review of relevant outcome literature, and using a technique called meta-analysis, they examined the average "effect size" produced by different programs with different characteristics. In short, they asked, what are the characteristics of "effective" programs (i.e., intervention programs that have produced larger-than-average decreases in reoffending)?

Their argument is simple but convincing: there are identifiable characteristics of effective programs that can be assessed and adjusted so as to improve the achievement of program outcomes (e.g., reduction of recidivism). As you read, think of the basic elements of program design and monitoring we discussed in Chapters 4 and 6, and note how the Correctional Program Assessment Inventory (CPAI) assesses critical features of program design.

In general, according to Andrews, et al., effective programs evidence the principles of risk, need and responsivity.[7]

1. *Risk.* Effective programs clearly differentiate between low-risk and high-risk clients. The largest effects on recidivism are likely to be achieved by targeting high-risk rather than low-risk offenders. High-risk cases should receive high levels of intervention and services; low-risk cases should receive minimal intervention.

2. *Needs.* Criminogenic needs are dynamic (i.e., changing) risk factors that are predictive of recidivism (e.g., antisocial cognitions and emotional states, association with antisocial peers, substance abuse, weak self-control and problem-solving skills). Programs that effectively target and reduce such individual needs result in larger decreases in reoffending.

3. *Responsivity.* In general, programs that *appropriately* target the specific needs and learning styles of their clients are more effective. For example, clients who are interpersonally and cognitively immature require more structured services, but more mature clients benefit from more flexible approaches. Andrews, et al. argue that the most effective styles of treatment have been cognitive-behavioral and social learning strategies that focused on skill development in a variety of areas. Conversely, programs that incorrect-

ly target the criminogenic needs of their clients may actually increase rather than decrease reoffending.

The Correctional Program Assessment Inventory (CPAI) was designed to assess, in a fairly structured and objective manner, the degree to which a program has been adequately designed and implemented. It is sensitive to the three principles of risk, need and responsivity, as derived from empirical research. The instrument is still being developed and studied, but it has demonstrated its usefulness in a wide variety of correctional settings so far.[8]

Basically, the CPAI assesses a specific program by tabulating the presence, number and variety of the best-validated elements of effective correctional programs. The instrument is composed of nine sections with a total of 56 scorable items:

1. *Program Description/Demographics:* e.g., number of years in operation, physical setting (institutional/community), number of clients, number of staff, program budget, authority (government/private).

2. *Program Implementation* (11 items): e.g., qualifications and experience of Program Director, whether a thorough literature review has been conducted to identify relevant program design features, whether a need for this program has been documented, whether program values are consistent with existing values in the larger institution or community, whether funding is adequate for the task and goals of the program.

3. *Client Pre-service Assessment* (7 items): e.g., whether a reasonable assessment of risk factors and criminogenic needs is undertaken, whether risk factors and needs are assessed with recognized psychometric scales or tests, whether assessed offender risks and needs are appropriate to the style and method of treatment offered.

4. *Program Characteristics* (4 items): e.g., the degree to which the program targets 19 specific criminogenic behaviors and attitudes, the type of treatment approach used (e.g., social skills therapy, family therapy, cognitive restructuring), whether printed treatment manuals are available.

5. *Therapeutic Integrity* (9 items): e.g., whether program participants are separated from the rest of the institutional population, whether clients participate in treatment services regularly and frequently, whether intensive service is provided for high-risk cases, whether staff are assigned to clients with which they work most effectively, whether clients have any input into program structure, whether a variety of rewards are available.

Case Study 6.1, *continued*

6. *Relapse Prevention* (6 items): e.g., whether the client is trained to observe and anticipate problem situations, whether the client practices and rehearses alternative prosocial responses, whether the client is referred to other services to aid in readjustment, whether "booster sessions" are provided to relearn/reinforce skills taught in the formal treatment phase.

7. *Staff Characteristics* (9 items): e.g., education, experience and training of staff, whether staff turnover is low or high, whether staff are assessed yearly on clinical skills related to service delivery, whether staff have any input into program structure or specifics.

8. *Evaluation* (6 items): e.g., whether clients are periodically assessed on target behaviors, whether a management audit system is in place, whether client satisfaction is assessed, whether client reoffending data are gathered at six months or more after leaving the program, whether an acceptable research design has been used to evaluate outcome.

9. *Other* (4 items): e.g., whether ethical guidelines for treatment are recorded and practiced, whether positive changes in the program are planned or underway, whether community support is positive and stable.

Each item is scored as not applicable ("NA"), not known ("NK"), element absent ("0") or element present ("1"). For each of the nine subsections, a subtotal is obtained by counting the percentage of elements present relative to the total number of elements assessed (e.g., if four out of six evaluation items are present, the program receives a score of 66 percent on the evaluation section). Each subsection is scored as either "very satisfactory" (70% or higher), "satisfactory" (60 - 90%), "satisfactory, but needs improvement" (50 - 59%), or "unsatisfactory" (less than 50%). An overall "total score" is also obtained by summarizing across all nine subsections. A variety of data sources are used to gather information for a CPAI assessment: program site visits, file reviews, interviews and responses to structured questionnaires.

An actual summary chart for a CPAI assessment of a halfway house program is provided below. We will refer to the program as the "Community Corrections Program."[9] This is a residential pre-release program that serves offenders released by the state Department of Corrections. It is operated by a stable nonprofit agency with an excellent record of community service. The program has been in operation for 11 years. Eighty-five male felony offenders were in the program at the time of the assessment. There are 18 full-time and six part-time employees. Funding is provided through a state contract.

While a detailed report explained the CPAI consultant's findings and recommendations in detail, the chart below summarizes several interesting highlights. On the overall score, the program did not quite reach the "satisfactory" level of 50 percent. The program scored poorly on pre-service assessment, program characteristics, and evaluation. However, this program scored relatively well on program implementation, staff characteristics, and "other."

Specific strengths and weaknesses were noted by the consultant who conducted the CPAI assessment. For example, areas of weakness included the following:

Pre-Service Assessment: The program does not conduct an assessment of risk or responsivity factors associated with recidivism. Staff assessment of client needs are not standardized. Most clients receive the same treatment; appropriate distinctions between clients are not made.

Program Characteristics: Target behaviors and attitudes are not well-defined. Appropriate criminogenic behaviors and attitudes are not adequately addressed. A glaring deficiency is the lack of a clearly defined theoretical model of treatment. On the positive side, the whereabouts of clients are closely monitored, and clients spend more than 40 percent of their time in therapeutic activities.

Evaluation: Formal program completion criteria need to be developed: distinctions need to be made between those who successfully complete and those who do not. Individual client progress is reviewed, but the review is subjective and limited. No recidivism data are gathered on program clients.

Areas of strength included the following:

Program Implementation: The program director has a master's degree and is directly involved in selecting, training and supervising staff. An assessment of the need for the program and its compatibility with the values of the community, judges and others, showed that the program is held in high regard.

Staff Characteristics: Staff are well-educated and the program has a very low staff turnover rate. The program's administrative office supports increased educational attainment for staff. Direct service staff showed empathy, broad life experiences, fairness, firmness and clear communication skills. Staff are assessed yearly on their clinical skills.

Other: Client records contain extensive information on social history, problem areas, and case plans and notes. Records are kept in confidential files.

Case Study 6.1, *continued*

A CPAI assessment provides valuable data for programs to articulate what they are about: for example, who is served, with what intent, in what ways, and what intermediate and long-term changes are expected. Similar to the process of "evaluability assessment,"[10] examination and clarification of program goals and structure can provide valuable learning opportunities for program staff and directors and can inform useful and necessary program adjustments prior to undertaking formal outcome evaluation. What Andrews, Gendreau and their colleagues describe for correctional programs may also be applicable to a wider variety of interventions: drug treatment programs, delinquency prevention programs, counseling programs for domestic violence offenders, and so on. Their approach is based on sound principles of program development, and it utilizes a scientific approach that reduces the subjectivity of judgments about adequate program functioning.

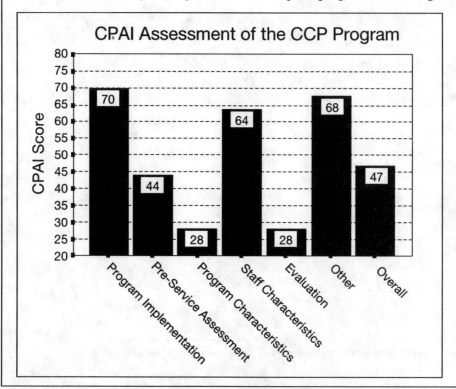

Questions

1. Describe how the CPAI assesses basic dimensions of program design and monitoring. Using Figure 6.4 ("Monitoring Analysis") as a guide, briefly describe one example for each of the cells in Column 1 ("what was intended": clients, staff and program services) and Column 4 ("gaps": clients, staff and program services).

Case Study 6.2

Monitoring Presale Firearm Checks Specified by the Brady Act

Instructions: Read the case study below, then answer the questions at the end of the selection. You will find it helpful to review concepts in Chapter 4 (especially "Designing the Policy") and Chapter 5 (Case Study 5.2).

Recall in Case Study 5.2 that the Brady Handgun Violence Prevention Act (P.L. 103-159) went into effect on February 28, 1994. The interim provisions of the act require that licensed firearm dealers request a presale check from the Chief Law Enforcement Officer (CLEO) on all potential handgun purchasers in the jurisdiction where the prospective purchaser resides. Recall also that the Firearm Inquiry Statistics (FIST) program was established to develop data on the impact of presale firearm checks on the identification of prohibited firearm purchasers. FIST provides crucial monitoring data on presale firearm checks, as specified by the Brady Act.

This type of data collection is absolutely essential to planned change. We want to determine the degree to which a policy is actually used and enacted as planned (i.e., the policy as specified on paper by the provisions of the Brady Act). Of course, we are also interested in the degree to which there are any gaps between what was planned and what was actually done (i.e., the policy "in action").

Presale Firearm Checks[11]

Findings are based on data collected by the Bureau of Alcohol, Tobacco and Firearms (ATF) and the Bureau of Justice Statistics (BJS). Data for 1994 and 1995, provided by ATF, were calculated using the number of firearm-coded inquiries to the FBI's criminal history database. The percentage of denials used for ATF estimates was based on the experiences of jurisdictions that had implemented presale firearms check procedures prior to the Brady Act. Data for the first half of 1996 were collected under the BJS Firearm Inquiry Statistics (FIST) program. The results were from a survey of 600 law enforcement agencies, of which 176 in 44 states responded. Major findings are reported in Table 6.1 below.

On average each month, an estimated 6,600 firearm purchases were prevented by background checks of potential gun buyers during the 28 months after the effective date of the Brady Handgun Violence Prevention Act. The checks revealed purchasers' ineligibility under federal or state laws to buy a handgun or other firearm. More than 70 percent of the rejected purchasers were convicted or indicted felons.

Between March 1994 and June 1996, for all states together, there were almost 9 million applications to purchase firearms and an estimated 186,000 rejections. The data do not indicate whether rejected purchasers later obtained a firearm through other means.

Case Study 6.2, *continued*

On average each month, an estimated 3,100 applications were rejected in the 32 states that followed the review procedures set forth in the Brady Act when it became effective in February 1994 ("original Brady States"). During the period from March 1994 through June 1996, there were 86,000 rejections from a total of about 4.2 million applications or inquiries.

These are the first BJS statistics from an ongoing survey to assess the impact of presale checks on preventing sales of handguns and long guns to persons in prohibited categories. The categories are defined in the Federal Gun Control Act of 1968 or in related state legislation. The provisions of the Federal Gun Control Act (18 U.S.C. sec. 922 (g) and (n) as amended) prohibit the sale of firearms to an individual who:

- is under indictment for, or has been convicted of, a crime punishable by imprisonment for more than one year;

- is a fugitive from justice;

- is an unlawful user of a controlled substance;

- has been adjudicated as a mental defective or committed to a mental institution;

- is an alien unlawfully in the United States;

- was discharged from the armed forces under dishonorable conditions;

- has renounced United States citizenship;

- is subject to a court order restraining him or her from harassing, stalking or threatening an intimate partner or child; or

- is a person convicted of domestic violence.

In the most recent six months for which national data were collected (January to June 1996), gun dealers made more than 1.3 million inquiries about the eligibility of potential buyers of handguns. About 34,000 ineligible customers were identified, a rejection rate of 2.6 percent. For the original Brady States during the most recent period, 570,000 inquiries or applications resulted in 16,000 rejections. This represented a 2.8 percent rejection rate.

During the first half of 1996, almost three-fourths of rejections of a handgun purchase were based on a finding of a felony conviction or indictment. Although not all states have the ability to check nonfelony categories, fugitives from justice (6%), persons who violated state laws (4%) and persons under court restraining or protective orders (2%) accounted for the next largest reasons for rejections.

Case Study 6.2, *continued*

Rejected applications, (all states) 1/1/96-6/30/96	100
Felon (convicted/indicted)	72
Fugitive	6
State law prohibition	4
Restraining order	2
Mental illness or disability	1
Other*	15

*Includes persons addicted to illegal drugs, juveniles, aliens, violators of local ordinances, those who have renounced citizenship, persons dishonorably discharged, and unspecified.

As of midyear 1996, 14 states reported that presale checks included a check of outstanding restraining orders; 11 states reported that checks of mental health records were made in connection with presale firearm checks. When only those states that reported searching databases for reasons other than felony status are considered, rejections for such reasons accounted for the following:

Nonfelony reason	Percent of rejections in states that search records for specific nonfelony reasons
Fugitive	6%
Restraining orders	4%
Mental illness	2%

Case Study 6.2, *continued*

Table 6.1: Presale Firearms Checks: Estimates of Inquiries and Rejections

	Bureau of Alcohol, Tobacco and Firearms[a]				Bureau of Justice Statistics[b]	
	3/1/94 - 12/31/94		1/1/95 - 12/31/95		1/1/96 - 6/30/96	
	All States	Original Brady States[c]	All States	Original Brady States[c]	All States	Original Brady States[c]
Inquiries and Rejections						
Inquiries/applications	3,679,000	1,696,000	4,009,000	1,884,000	1,308,000	570,000
rejected	92,000	42,000	60,000	28,000	34,000	16,000
Rejection Rate	2.5%	2.5%	1.5%	1.5%	2.6%	2.8%
Reasons for rejection						
Felony indictment/conviction	65,000	30,000	43,000	20,000	24,000	13,000
Other	26,000	12,000	17,000	8,000	9,000	3,000

Note: All estimated counts are rounded. Percentages were calculated from unrounded data. Detail may not add to total because of rounding.

[a] Information was provided by the Bureau of Alcohol, Tobacco and Firearms. The estimates include all types of guns.

[b] Based on 176 sources in 44 states. The estimates reflect only applications for purchase of handguns.

[c] Original Brady States are the 32 states required to follow presale review procedures set out in the Brady Act. When the Brady Act became effective on February 28, 1994, 32 states and Puerto Rico were required to follow presale review procedures set out in the act. The remaining States were Brady-alternative states. Since then, 10 more states have enacted legislation to become Brady-alternative states (Colorado, March 1994; Georgia, January 1996; Idaho, June 1994; Louisiana, May 1996; Minnesota, August 1994; New Hampshire, January 1995; North Carolina, December 1995; Tennessee, May 1994; Utah, March 1994; and Washington, June 1996).

Questions

When we are monitoring, we want to find out the degree to which the policy design was actually carried out as planned. Review the section in Chapter 4 titled "Designing a Policy." Recall that at this stage the change agent typically identifies: (1) the *target population*, or who will be affected by the policy; (2) the *provisions* of the policy, or what the members of the target population will receive; (3) the *decision authority*, or who has the authority to carry out the policy; and (4) the *procedures* that must be followed by the decision authority.

1. Review Case Study 5.2, and briefly describe the four policy components of the Brady Act (i.e., "policy design").

2. Now, using the Monitoring Analysis in Figure 6.4 as a guide, describe the degree to which these four design components have been carried out, and describe any gaps that you find. For example: Is the Brady Act doing what it is designed to do, and are state officials doing what they are supposed to be doing? What specific data reported in Case Study 6.2 helps to answer these questions?

Endnotes

1   Cannon, Angie (1996). "Survey: 'Three-Strikes' Laws Aren't Affecting Crime. The Federal Government and States Aren't Hastening to Use Them. California is the Notable Exception." *The Philadelphia Inquirer*, 10 September 1996. Reprinted with permission from *The Philadelphia Inquirer*, Sept. 10, 1996.

2   Rossi, Peter H., and Howard E. Freeman (eds.) (1993). *Evaluation: A Systematic Approach*, 5th ed. Thousand Oaks, CA: Sage.

3   Sherman, Lawrence W., and Richard A. Berk (1984). "The Specific Deterrent Effects of Arrest for Domestic Assault." *American Sociological Review*, 49:261-272.

4   Ibid, note 2.

5   Ringwalt, Christopher L., Jody M. Greene, Susan T. Ennett, Ronaldo Iachan, Richard R. Clayton, and Carl G. Leukefeld (1994). *Past and Future Directions of the D.A.R.E. Program: An Evaluation Review*. Draft Final Report, September 1994. Washington, DC: U.S. Department of Justice, Office of Justice Programs, National Institute of Justice.

6   Maxfield, Michael G., and Terry L. Baumer (1990). "Home Detention with Electronic Monitoring: Comparing Pretrial and Postconviction Programs." *Crime & Delinquency*, 36:521-536.

7   Andrews, Donald, Ivan Zinger, Robert D. Hoge, James Bonta, Paul Gendreau, and Francis T. Cullen (1990). "Does Correctional Treatment Work? A Clinically Relevant and Psychologically Informed Meta-Analysis." *Criminology*, 28:369-404.

8   Andrews, Donald A. (1995). "Assessing Program Elements for Risk Reduction: The Correctional Program Assessment Inventory (CPAI)." Paper presented at the "Research to Results" conference, sponsored by IARCA, Ottawa, Canada, October 11-14, 1995.

9   This name is a pseudonym. This CPAI assessment was based on an earlier version of the CPAI. Although only six scales were used, the items assessed were quite similar to those described in the nine-scale version.

10 See: Rutman, Leonard (1984). *Planning Useful Evaluations: Evaluability Assessment*. Beverly Hills: Sage; Wholey, J. S. (1994). "Assessing the Feasibility and Likely Usefulness of Evaluation." In J.S. Wholey, H.P. Hatry, and K.E. Newcomer (eds.) (1994). *Handbook of Practical Evaluation*, pp. 15-39. San Francisco: Jossey-Bass.

11 Adapted from: Manson, Don, and Gene Lauver (1997). *Presale Firearm Checks* (NCJ-162787). Washington, DC: U.S. Department of Justice, Office of Justice Programs, Bureau of Justice Statistics.

CHAPTER 7

DEVELOPING A PLAN FOR EVALUATING OUTCOMES

CHAPTER OUTLINE

▶ *Evaluations can measure impact, continuous outcomes, or efficiency:* More specifically, is the program or policy achieving its objectives, how do outcomes change over time, and is it worth the investment of resources devoted to its implementation?

▶ *Impact evaluation:* This most common type of evaluation attempts to establish causality between intervention (program or policy) and outcome (a specific change in the problem).

▶ *Two prerequisites for evaluation must be met:* (1) Objectives must be clearly defined and measurable, and (2) the intervention must be sufficiently well designed and well implemented.

▶ *Develop outcome measures based on objectives:* Good outcome measures should be *valid* and *reliable*.

▶ *Specify the research design to be used:* Examples include: the simple pretest-posttest design, the pretest-posttest design with a control group, the pretest-posttest design with multiple pretests, the longitudinal design with treatment and control groups and the cohort design.

▶ *Identify potential confounding factors* (factors other than the intervention that may have biased the observed outcomes): Common confounding factors include biased selection, biased attrition and history.

▶ *The two major techniques for minimizing confounding effects are random assignment and nonequivalent comparison groups:* Each involves creating some kind of comparison or control group.

▶ *Identify users and uses of evaluation results:* Who is the intended audience, and how can results be effectively and efficiently communicated? How will the results be used?

▶ *Reassess the entire program or policy plan:* Review the entire planning process from start to finish, looking for any inconsistencies, contradictions or inadequacies.

Now the time has come to measure the impact of the intervention: has the program or policy achieved its intended effect(s)? How can we tell? The goal at this stage is to develop a research design for measuring program or policy outcome (a specific, intended change in the problem, defined by objectives). Did the program or policy achieve its intended objectives? Why or why not?

In spite of the obvious need for evaluation, many programs and policies have never been evaluated. Cost is often given as a reason for not conducting evaluations, but we must also recognize that evaluation can be threatening to stakeholders, because their public image, political power and/or agency budget is linked to the success or failure of a specific program or policy. Sometimes *not* evaluating is an effective means of avoiding accountability.

Increasingly, however, funding agencies are demanding accountability for outcomes. Grants made to public and private agencies by federal agencies such as the National Institute of Justice typically require an evaluation component, and often an independent researcher must do the evaluation. In the fields of health and mental health, managed-care agencies carefully measure outcomes and costs in order to ensure that the money they manage is being used effectively. This kind of thinking is making its way into the criminal justice system.

Remember that all stages of planning, including the formulation of an evaluation plan, should precede the actual start-up of the program or policy. Evaluation should never be an afterthought. In most cases, the research design depends critically on the design stage, in which crucial decisions are made about target recruitment or selection. Evaluation is a critical component of the planning stage, not an activity that should be done "after the facts are in."

Types of Evaluation

Before you define what kind of evaluation data to collect, it is important to know about different approaches to evaluation. We need to be clear about the kinds of evaluative questions we are going to ask before designing the evaluation. Evaluations of programs and policies typically take one of three major approaches: (1) impact assessment, (2) continuous evaluation, or (3) efficiency analyses.

Note that we do not intend (or pretend) in this chapter to cover evaluation methods in all their complexity.[1] We do intend for readers to become familiar with the basic concepts necessary for understanding evaluation. We will not attempt to teach students or practitioners how to design their own measures in this book. That is a task for a good course in research methods.

Impact Evaluation

The most common type of evaluation, and the type we focus on mainly in this chapter, is an *impact evaluation*. To assess impact, we want to compare actual outcomes to desired outcomes (objectives). In order to do this, we will need valid measures of the desired outcomes, as well as information about the status of clients on these measures prior to their exposure to the intervention. For example, the fact that a high proportion of clients of a delinquency prevention program end the program with high self-esteem is meaningless if those clients started the program with high self-esteem. It is not sufficient to know simply that a change occurred: we need to determine whether the program or policy in question caused the observed change. We need to know that this change would not have happened without the intervention. To know this, we will also need information on similar types of persons who were not exposed to the intervention. If the same change occurred in this second group, then we are unable to attribute the change to the intervention.

Continuous Evaluation: Outcome-Based Information Systems

One weakness of many impact evaluations is that their results are limited to a specific point in time. Programs, in particular, are constantly changing in terms of their staff, clients, services and goals. Staff turnover, intervention fads, changes in the political environment and changes in the characteristics of incoming clients can all produce changes in program outcomes. The results of even the best-designed impact evaluation gradually become obsolete. Continuous evaluation offers an alternative: why not collect and analyze outcome information on all clients on a permanent basis? This way, stakeholders could learn from the outcome data, make adjustments and see the consequences of their responses over time. The growth of computerized information systems within criminal justice is making this approach increasingly viable and useful.

This incremental learning process incorporates much of what we talked about in the last chapter with regard to monitoring, but the focus is on improving outcomes rather than assessing the adequacy of implementation. Moreover, this interactive approach to evaluation incorporates the concept of action research that was introduced by Kurt Lewin (see Chapter 2). In terms of design, an outcome-based information system is a multiple cohort design (see the section called "Specify the Research Design" in this chapter) in which the outcomes for each cohort (a specific group of clients) can be compared as a trend over time.

Let's add one more step to this idea: such a system of learning is even stronger when outcome information is monitored in an entire system of programs. For example, a city or state could monitor specific outcome data on all programs that serve a specific population of clients, such as drug offenders or juvenile delinquents. With this information, comparisons of programs over time generate more information about why certain outcomes are being produced. The control group is then not made up of clients who receive no services, but clients who are similar in many ways (a matched control group) and who receive different services.

Computerized information systems are increasingly common within criminal justice. Although the focus of such systems is typically on management needs—for example, personnel, finance and case control—client-specific outcome information can easily be added to enhance the ability of the organization to assess a program or policy's success. One example of such a system is ProDES, Philadelphia's Program Development and Evaluation System (see Case Study 7.1).

Efficiency Analysis

Lastly, we may want to know how efficient a given program or policy is. Two types of analyses are useful for this purpose: *cost-benefit analyses* and *cost-effectiveness analyses*. In cost-benefit analysis, we ask if the amount of change that is being produced (the benefit) is worth the cost (usually in monetary terms). Cost-effectiveness analyses, in contrast, express outcomes in substantive terms, so as to compare programs and policies that produce similar outcomes.

For example, let's look at a three-month school-based curriculum for teaching problem-solving skills to eighth graders determined to be at high risk for delinquency. If desired changes are taking place, then various measures of benefit can be established (e.g., a unit increase in problem-solving skills as measured by a standardized test; the number of children who avoid any subsequent arrest up to age 18). The costs, some of which may be less obvious than others, must now be accurately measured. For example, how much money did it cost to buy course materials (notebooks, videos, etc.) and train classroom teachers to administer the curriculum? Was there a cost in terms of what students did not get (e.g., a reduction in mathematics or science training to make way for the problem-solving skills curriculum)? We may then compare the difference between total dollars saved by preventing each arrest (e.g., costs of arresting, processing, charging and supervising each adjudicated delinquent) and dollars expended on operating the problem-solving skills curriculum. In other words, we calculate ratios of costs to benefits. If there is no benefit, the cost is irrelevant. However, a moderate gain at a low cost may often signal a more worthwhile program than a slightly higher gain at a much more substantial cost. A cost-effectiveness analysis of the same program might estimate the total dollars spent to convert each delinquent into a nondelinquent, and then compare this approach with others that attempt to produce similar outcomes (e.g., secure detention).

We can also compare actual costs against projected costs: an "efficient" program might be one that remained within budget or under budget but produced a tangible benefit. In many cases, the costs of achieving the same level of benefit can be compared across different programs, policies or settings. Efficiency analyses, therefore, can provide valuable information to assist stakeholders and policymakers in making choices from among competing programs, policies and projects.

As you may suspect, exactly *how* specific costs and benefits should be defined, and exactly *what* is defined as a cost or a benefit is a matter of some controversy. These definitions are not straightforward, and actual procedures for conducting efficiency analyses tend to be quite complex. For all three types of evaluation, we expect our readers to be aware of why, how and where such analyses are used, but their actual conduct requires sophisticated training and expertise. This is particularly true of efficiency analyses.[2]

Two Prerequisites for Evaluation

Before actually evaluating a program or policy, two main criteria (prerequisites) must be satisfied. If either prerequisite is not met, any attempt at evaluation is likely to be unsuccessful, and the results will be unconvincing. Indeed, an entire methodology called "evaluability assessment"[3] has been developed to address these critical concerns.

Figure 7.1

Two Prerequisites for Evaluation

1. Program or policy objectives must have been clearly specified, and those objectives must be measurable (see Chapter 3).

2. The intervention should have been sufficiently well designed (see Chapter 4) and sufficiently implemented for there to be no question that its critical elements (activities) were delivered to clients as planned. Remember, this is why you do monitoring: to find out whether the program or policy in action matches the program or policy on paper (see Chapter 6).

Develop Outcome Measures

To develop outcome measures, refer back to objectives. How will these objectives be measured adequately? Remember that an objective contains four components (see Chapter 3): (1) time frame, (2) target population, (3) a key result, and (4) a criterion for measurement. We are trying to determine whether a specific intervention (program or policy) produces an intended change in the problem. Recall from Chapter 3 that an impact model specifies such a prediction or hypothesis.

Establishing the impact of a program amounts to establishing causality. In other words, we want to determine whether the intervention actually produces a specific effect, an intended change in the problem. To do so, we need adequate measures and an adequate research design.

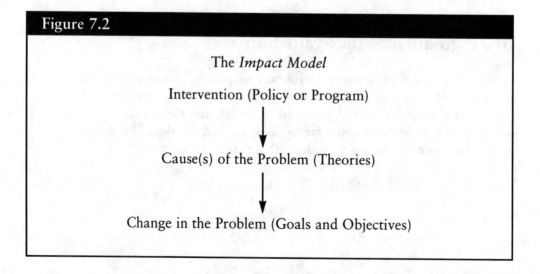

Figure 7.2

The *Impact Model*

Intervention (Policy or Program)

↓

Cause(s) of the Problem (Theories)

↓

Change in the Problem (Goals and Objectives)

The validity of a measure refers to the degree to which the measure or procedure succeeds in doing (measuring) what it purports to do. Most experts refer to this type of validity as *construct validity*. In other words, how can you tell whether your measure actually assesses the construct or concept that it is supposed to assess?

For example, we might be using a measure of self-esteem, such as the Rosenberg Self-Esteem Scale,[4] or we might be using a measure of self-reported drug use, such as the National Household Survey on Drug Abuse.[5] The question is: How accurate is each measure? Is it a good indicator of the construct you are trying to measure? These questions are often investigated through research that attempts to demonstrate that the measure relates to another known indicator of the same concept. We might measure a student's self-esteem, then correlate self-ratings with ratings from that student's friends and family members. We want to see if there is a relationship between our measure and another indicator of the same concept. Or, we might validate self-reported drug use with actual drug testing technology to determine if self-reports are under- or over-inflated. Wherever possible, we usually try to use existing measures for which previous research has indicated reasonable evidence of validity.

The *reliability* of a measure refers to its consistency. For example, what is the probability of obtaining the same results upon repeated use of the same measuring instrument (i.e., test-retest reliability)? We want to be sure that the measure is somewhat consistent over time and that results do not vary dramatically from one time to the next. For example, self-esteem is seen as a relatively stable personality trait. Any reliable measure should not yield wildly disparate results about a person's self-esteem from one week to the next. Attempts to establish reliability of a self-report measure such as self-esteem usually examine, through research, the internal consistency of the items in a measure (i.e., do items correlate with one another?) or relationships between scores obtained from two or more separate administrations of the same test.

Identify Potential Confounding Factors

Establishing the impact of a program, as we noted above, amounts to an attempt to establish causality. Did the intervention produce an observed change in the problem? Before we look at a few basic research designs, we need to discuss confounding factors (sometimes called *confounds*). These refer to any factors, other than your program, that may account for observed changes on the outcome measure (e.g., an increase or decrease in the problem). Confounding factors bias the measurement of program outcomes. In research design textbooks, these confounding factors are often labeled threats to the internal validity of the experiment.

Biased selection is a common confound of which to be careful. In many criminal justice interventions, especially offender treatment and post-release programs, researchers view reducing recidivism as a primary objective. However, upon close inspection of many interventions, we often find out that many of the clients who were selected to receive the treatment were not at high risk at the start. If youths in a delinquency prevention program had no observable risk factors at the start (such as previous arrests, truancy, academic failure or family problems), it is not surprising if such youths, upon graduation from the program, show a low rate of recidivism. Does this mean that the intervention worked? Or does it mean that client selection was so biased we have no way of knowing whether the program actually works?

When we refer to confounding factors, we are saying that something else (other than the intervention itself) may have caused the observed change in the problem, or something may have disrupted ("confounded") the way we measured a change in the problem. Confounding factors introduce bias into our measurement of outcomes. You must try to anticipate potential confounds and design your evaluation to minimize them. The evaluation of each intervention should address potential confounds. The following are three of the most typical confounds:

1. *Biased selection:* Systematic bias in client selection procedures results in the treatment group not including adequate numbers of clients with demonstrated needs or problems. Sometimes called "creaming," this problem occurs when a program deliberately or unknowingly selects those clients most likely to show a favorable outcome, rather than those clients most in need of the intervention. For example, many private drug treatment programs claim phenomenal rates of success, but we often find that they have limited their client selection to those with the least severe problems. In other words, clients most in need were not selected, and our suspicions are further aroused if no control group was used to compare program outcomes. We have no faith whatsoever in such results.

2. *Biased attrition:* Bias is introduced into the outcome measure because subjects dropped out of one comparison group at higher rates than subjects in other comparison groups. For example, it is a common difficulty in drug treatment programs that those with the most severe problems drop out before the end of program. The observed result is that those who remained in the treatment program had lower rates of relapse than similar subjects in a control group. The result is biased, however, because the treatment program lost those subjects who were most likely to show the highest rates of relapse.

3. *History:* Some unanticipated event, occurring between the beginning and the end of the intervention, introduces bias into the measurement of program objectives. For example, if a major change in a state's criminal laws occurred during the course of a mandatory arrest experiment, the new law, rather than the intervention, might explain the observed result of increased arrests for domestic abuse.

Example 7.1

Potential Confounds in the Minneapolis Domestic Violence Experiment

The Minneapolis Domestic Violence Experiment[6] has been criticized for not sufficiently addressing confounding factors. Some suggest that we cannot adequately determine from this experiment whether a mandatory arrest policy works better than mediation or separation. One measure used was a follow-up interview with victims to ask about victimization following the police intervention. Victims were interviewed immediately after the intervention, then every two weeks for 24 weeks. Researchers reported a decrease in the problem, as measured by fewer victim reports of repeat abuse. Of couples who received the mandatory arrest intervention, only 19 percent of victims reported further abuse in the follow-up study, compared to recidivism rates of 33 percent and 37 percent, respectively, in the separation and mediation interventions.

Here is the difficulty: what if women were scared to report further incidents of abuse because they had been threatened or beaten by their spouse following the previous police intervention (arrest, mediation or separation)? Sherman and Berk reported that a substantial number of victims in their sample dropped out of the study. Initial interviews with victims were completed in only 62 percent of all cases. Others could not be found, or refused to be interviewed. Biweekly interviews were completed for only 49 percent of subjects in the original sample. The study may have lost many of those who were victims of repeat abuse following the experiment.

Maybe some of these victims who refused to be interviewed were reluctant to talk to the interviewers for fear of retaliation by their spouse. Perhaps some of these women had already experienced retaliation from spouses who had been temporarily detained under mandatory arrest provisions but were subsequently released a day or two later.

Sherman and Berk reported that of those victims they actually contacted, there was no "differential" attrition (i.e., the victim dropout rate for the experiment was about the same for each of the three interventions).[7] However, we have no way of knowing how many of those not contacted actually experienced further abuse. Critics expressed doubts about the experimental results because of this potential confound.[8] In addition, attempts to replicate the results of the Minneapolis experiment in other jurisdictions have not been very successful.[9]

In summary, it is not entirely clear that the intervention (mandatory arrest) was responsible for the observed results (a decrease in reported incidents of abuse). We cannot entirely rule out the possibility that the results were biased due to the attrition (dropping out) of more than one-half of the original subjects. We are suspicious that those victims who refused to be interviewed in the follow-up study might have been more likely to experience further victimization than those who agreed to be interviewed. The observed reduction in repeated incidents of abuse may be due to the fact that victims who dropped out of the experiment were afraid to report further incidents of abuse to police or interviewers.

Two Techniques for Minimizing Confounding Effects

There are two major techniques for minimizing confounding effects: (1) *random assignment*, and (2) *nonequivalent comparison groups*. Each involves creating a comparison group, a different group of clients that is equivalent to the treatment group, on any factors that might influence the outcome measure (e.g., recidivism) but does not receive the intervention.

Random Assignment

Random assignment means that researchers randomly assign eligible clients to separate treatment and control groups. This is not the same as *random selection*. Students often have a difficult time keeping these two concepts separate. As a sampling strategy, one might randomly select subjects to participate in a survey or opinion poll. The purpose would be to obtain a representative random sample of the population. In contrast, nobody would ever randomly select clients for an intervention; they would instead determine who is eligible for the program and who needs the program. Once the eligible pool of clients is determined, one might then randomly assign subjects to the treatment and control groups. Clients in any intervention are deliberately selected on the basis of need and eligibility. It is only once they are selected that they might be randomly assigned to treatment or control groups.

What random assignment does, in theory, is equalize two different groups on unknown differences (e.g., intelligence, previous criminal history, etc.) that might bias the outcome results. With a large enough sample, the chances of equally distributing characteristics of subjects across the treatment and control groups is very good. This is the best method for dealing with confounds, when possible. For ethical and practical reasons, however, random assignment is not always possible. In many social interventions, those most in need of the intervention must be selected, and randomization would be unfair or even unethical (see Case Study 7.2 at the end of this chapter).

Nonequivalent Comparison Groups

Often we cannot randomly assign subjects to treatment and control groups, but we can attempt to construct treatment and comparison groups made up of clients with similar characteristics. It is especially important that the two groups are similar in terms of their level of need, and in terms of characteristics that might influence the outcome of interest (e.g., recidivism). We must decide with care exactly which factors might be important to control for. We usually look to previous research to determine important variables. We might then attempt to create *matched control groups*, so that average client characteristics are distributed relatively equally across the two groups (aggregate matching), or so that every client in the treatment group is matched one-to-one with a similar nonclient in the control group (individual matching). Aggregate matching is much easier than individual matching, unless one is dealing with an extremely large pool of eligible clients. Individual matching is more precise, but we lose a very large number of potential cases as we try to match individuals, rather than groups, on a large number of variables. For example, we may be measuring recidivism as a program outcome. It would be important to match our treatment and control groups on variables known to influence recidivism, such as previous criminal behavior, age of offender, employment and job skills, and so on.

Specify the Research Design

In this section, we attempt to acquaint readers with a few of the most basic research designs used to evaluate program impacts. In general, such designs specify when and how measures will be collected to assess program impact. Each involves comparisons of certain groups of subjects and the measurement of specific variables over particular time periods to evaluate outcome. We will diagram and describe several of the most commonly used research designs.

You might want to think of an example as you go through the diagrams and descriptions of different research designs. Imagine, for example, a six-week prevention program designed for adolescents at high risk of abusing drugs. The program attempts to raise youths' self-esteem. The program's rationale is that increasing self-esteem is a means of increasing one's ability to make independent decisions without being unduly influenced by one's peers. A self-report self-esteem measure such as the Rosenberg Self-Esteem Scale is used.[10]

Figure 7.3

Legend For Diagrams of Research Designs

In each of the diagrams in this chapter:
"X" represents the intervention or treatment,
"O" represents the observation or measure,
"PRE" refers to a pre-intervention observation, and
"POST" refers to a post-treatment observation.

The Simple Pretest-Posttest Design

Figure 7.4

$$O_1 \qquad\qquad X \qquad\qquad O_2$$

PRE	TREATMENT	POST

PASSAGE OF TIME →

This is a simple, easy-to-use design, but it is not a good one. Because there is no comparison or control group, we cannot adequately determine whether the program or some other unmeasured influence (confounding factor) produced the observed change from O_1 to O_2. How do we know, for example, that self-esteem wouldn't have increased (or decreased) even without the intervention? How do we know whether clients were high or low on this measure at the start? How do these clients compare to a similar group who did not receive the intervention?

The Pretest-Posttest Design with a Control Group

Figure 7.5

$$O_1 \qquad\qquad X \qquad\qquad O_{2 \text{ (treatment group)}}$$
$$O_1 \qquad\qquad\qquad\qquad O_{2 \text{ (control group)}}$$

PRE	TREATMENT	POST

PASSAGE OF TIME →

This is a much better design than the simple pretest-posttest design. A control group gives us some means of comparing initial measures with later measures. If the two groups are relatively equivalent with regard to variables likely to influence the outcome measure, we can compare the outcomes observed for the two groups to evaluate program impact.

The Pretest-Posttest Design with Multiple Pretests

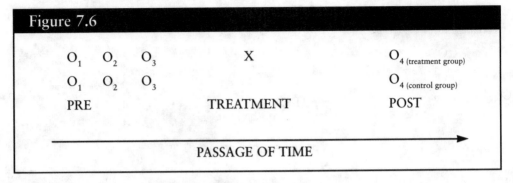

Figure 7.6

O_1 O_2 O_3 X $O_{4 \text{ (treatment group)}}$

O_1 O_2 O_3 $O_{4 \text{ (control group)}}$

PRE   TREATMENT   POST

PASSAGE OF TIME

This design is a slight improvement over the second one. It gives us a better assessment of clients' and nonclients' condition before treatment. This design allows us to obtain a baseline of behavior or attitudes for each group before the intervention begins. A baseline is always preferable to a one-shot (cross-sectional) assessment of pre-intervention characteristics. It is valuable because it gives us a much better indication of how stable or unstable any specific behavior is and whether treatment or comparison groups differ in their baselines prior to treatment.

The Longitudinal Design with Treatment and Control Groups

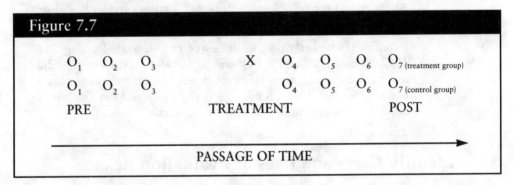

Figure 7.7

O_1 O_2 O_3 X O_4 O_5 O_6 $O_{7 \text{ (treatment group)}}$

O_1 O_2 O_3 O_4 O_5 O_6 $O_{7 \text{ (control group)}}$

PRE   TREATMENT   POST

PASSAGE OF TIME

This is the most favorable design, but it tends to be expensive. It takes a long time and it is difficult to conduct. It is best because it gives us a baseline for both the treatment and the control groups, both before and after the intervention begins.

The Cohort Design

Figure 7.8

O_1 X $O_{2\ (1997\text{-}98\ Cohort)}$

O_1 $O_{2\ (1996\text{-}97\ Cohort)}$

PRE   TREATMENT   POST

PASSAGE OF TIME →

When it is difficult to assign clients to treatment and control groups, the evaluator may decide to follow different *cohorts*: similar groups of people who go through the same system or experience, but at different times. One cohort receives the intervention program, the other cohort (the control group) does not. This design is often used for school studies. For example, you have identified the ninth grade in one school as a group particularly vulnerable to experimentation with drugs, but still "reachable." The following steps might be taken to set up a cohort design.

1. Measure self-reported drug use of the ninth-grade class in 1996-97.

2. At the beginning of the next school year (1997-98), start a drug awareness education program.

3. At the end of the school year (1997-98), measure the level of drug use in this second cohort.

4. Determine whether drug use is lower in the second group (the 1997-98 cohort) than the first cohort (1996-97), the one that did not receive the program. This design assumes that all other conditions in the school (e.g., funding, security measures) have remained relatively constant from one year to the next.

Identify Users and Uses of Evaluation Results

Who will be interested in the results of this evaluation, and how will they use the information? If any evaluation is to be useful, it should serve the information needs of the program or policy and its stakeholders (see Chapter 2). The funding agency is a major stakeholder, but any intervention will have multiple stakeholders such as citizens, politicians, criminal justice officials, volunteers, targets, and so on. The time spent previously (at Stage 1) identifying stakeholders should not be wasted. Evaluation is a critical means of demonstrating accountability and (hopefully) effectiveness to stakeholders.

The change agent should develop plans and assign responsibility for packaging and communicating evaluation results to different users. It is particularly important to find means of communication that can be understood by different audiences. Even at academic conferences, for instance, many eyes in the audience glaze over when a presenter puts up overheads cluttered with complicated statistical results. If the results are to be useful—and used—one must create means of communication that audiences can understand and to which they can react. Stakeholders must be able to participate in a dialogue with the report writer or presenter.

Reassess the Entire Program Plan

At this point, we review the entire planning process, from Stage 1 (problem analysis) through Stage 7 (evaluation). Remember that (ideally) we are doing all this planning before the program is actually implemented. Too many program developers, researchers and funding agencies still fail to see that critical decisions that have been made at earlier stages affect later stages. For example, if an evaluator has had no input into decisions regarding client selection processes, he or she often finds it impossible to construct an adequate comparison group. This is particularly true when selection processes are biased in favor of low-risk clients, there are multiple referral sources, or selection criteria are simply too vague to define any specific target population.

This is just one example of the type of problem that can occur if one fails to examine how all the different planning pieces fit together. Now that the plan is complete, it is time to review the entire planning process from start to finish. No doubt there will be inconsistencies, contradictions or inadequacies. The whole puzzle rarely fits together perfectly on the first try. Taking this step of review and reassessment, however, is much less burdensome now (before the program starts) than later (when program operations demand constant attention and stakeholders expect results, not excuses). Review and reassessment of the entire program planning process is a step that must be taken with deliberation and care. Answering the questions that follow Case Study 7.2 will provide a good test of how well you understand some of the major concepts presented in this chapter.

DISCUSSION QUESTIONS

1. What is meant by the term *evaluation*?

2. What are the main differences between *continuous evaluation* and *impact evaluation*?

3. How can an automated information system increase the availability of evaluation data?

4. Define and describe an example of *efficiency analysis*.

5. What are the two prerequisites for evaluation? Explain.

6. Define: (a) *reliability*, and (b) *validity*.

7. (a) Define *confounding factors*. (b) Describe the three most common types of confounding factors.

8. Refer back to Example 7.1 (the Minneapolis Domestic Violence Experiment). How were confounding factors illustrated by this example?

9. How does one minimize possible confounding effects in an evaluation? Make sure you discuss the two major techniques.

10. Describe each of the following research designs: (a) *simple pretest-posttest*, (b) *pretest-posttest with a control group*, (c) *pretest-posttest with multiple pretests*, (d) *longitudinal design with treatment and control groups*, and (e) *cohort design*.

EXERCISE 7.1

Your instructor may ask you to analyze a published evaluation study. One good example is provided by Frank Pearson's article on intensive supervision probation in New Jersey.[11] Read the article and answer the following questions: (a) What were the program's intended outcome objectives? (hint: remember the distinction between process versus outcome objectives; see Chapter 3). (b) To what degree, if any, did the program achieve its intended outcome objectives? Give specific examples and evidence from the article to support your answer.

Case Study 7.1

ProDES: An Information System for Developing and Evaluating Services to Delinquent Youths

Philip W. Harris and Peter R. Jones[12]

Instructions: Read the case study below, then answer the questions that follow.

ProDES (the Program Development and Evaluation System) is an outcome-based information system that tracks every Philadelphia delinquent for the duration of his or her involvement with the juvenile justice system. Its primary focus is development of the entire system of *programs* that serve delinquent youth. That is, it provides programs and the system as a whole with a continuous flow of intermediate (changes during the program) and ultimate (recidivism and community adjustment) outcome information. The information is then used for program development, matching youths to programs, and assessments of the program resources available to system-level decision makers, such as judges and probation officers.

ProDES was also designed to study key *policy* questions. Questions such as whether more resources are needed for female delinquents or sex offenders already have been investigated with these data. Trend information produced by ProDES, such as the growing number of delinquent youths with drug and alcohol abuse problems and the dramatic increase in the number of Hispanic youths entering the system, lead to the need for new policies. Moreover, because information is collected continuously, ProDES can measure the impact of policy and program changes on specific outcomes. ProDES is the product of a unique effort in Philadelphia to enhance existing juvenile correctional programs and simultaneously develop new programs and approaches that are more effective in meeting the goals of the system. ProDES has three goals:

1. To facilitate the development of intervention programs for delinquent youths by providing those programs with continuous outcome information that is relevant to the ways in which program personnel think about change,

2. To facilitate planning of the entire array of delinquency services provided by the Department of Juvenile Justice Services through the provision of program-level outcome information that identifies program strengths and weaknesses as well as strengths and weaknesses in the entire array of services available, and

3. To facilitate the rational matching by probation officers and judges of adjudicated youths to programs that can meet their needs and the needs of the community.

Most students of corrections are familiar with the term "recidivism." Among the definitions of recidivism are re-offending, new arrests, new charges, new adjudications and new commitments. The usefulness of these measures for program development, however, is extremely limited. Thus, while recidivism data are important for some purposes, we recognized from the beginning the need for outcome measures that would speak directly to the purposes of those persons directly serving delinquent youths. Harris and Jones found, too, that these service providers needed more than descriptions of their clients. They needed multiple measures that demonstrated change over time.

The first phase of the developing ProDES involved visits to 15 agencies selected to represent the broad range of programs. Within each program, *evaluability assessments* were conducted that sought to articulate the goals and objectives of the various programs, their measures of success or failure and the range of information they routinely collected and utilized. These assessments demonstrated that no common base of information existed across all community programs. However, commonalities did exist in terms of information that agencies thought to be important to the evaluation of their own programs and to the system as a whole. Agreement was also found in terms of the ideal structure of an information system—one that went beyond simply describing program clients at one point in time (usually at intake) and included multiple measures to demonstrate change over time.

The second phase of the research involved the testing of *outcome measures* and the development and implementation of an information system that monitors case-level outcomes and provides data previously identified as central to the mission of individual programs, to Department of Human Services and to Family Court. With this in mind, a system of data collection, analysis and feedback was designed that would use case-level data collected at four points in time: (1) record data are collected immediately by ProDES staff following disposition in Juvenile Court, (2) program intake data are collected by program staff shortly after a youth was admitted into the program, (3) discharge data are collected by program staff shortly before release from a program, and (4) follow-up data, including recidivism measures and interviews with the youths and caregivers whose cases are being analyzed, are collected by ProDES staff six months following departure from the program.

The content of the ProDES database includes the entire court record of the youth:

- current offense and related decisions,
- prior offenses and related decisions,
- sociodemographic variables,
- family and educational information, and
- psychological assessments.

Case Study 7.1, *continued*

Shortly after the youth arrives at the program, staff of the program collect the intake information:

- a risk assessment
- a needs assessment
- family structure and attitudes toward family
- self-esteem
- values
- school bonding (7 dimensions)
- family bonding (5 dimensions)
- drug and alcohol use
- employment experience

At discharge, all of the intake information is repeated in order to determine if changes on these key outcome dimensions have taken place during the course of the program. In addition, information is collected on the interventions that were used, in-program behavior, program completion and reason for discharge.

Six months after a youth leaves the program, a follow-up is conducted. The follow-up includes a record check to see if there have been new juvenile or adult charges filed, and telephone interviews are conducted with the youth and a parent concerning community adjustment and satisfaction with the program.

As of January 1994, ProDES became fully operational. Currently 64 programs feed data into the system and receive case-level and aggregate reports. Data are fed back to programs, Family Court, Probation staff and the Department of Human Services on a continual basis. Additionally, multivariate analyses of data are conducted to focus attention on *policy issues* of importance to the field, and system-wide trends are reported regularly. Most importantly, each ProDES program receives an annual report of its outcome information.

In designing ProDES, Harris and Jones gave recognition to potential *confounding factors*. One such factor is the risk of future recidivism that already existed before the program started. That is, one youth might begin the program with a high risk of future offending (usually based on past behavior such as previous arrests), while another presents a low risk. If the high-risk youth recidivates and the low-risk youth does not, how would we know that the program was making a difference? ProDES, using an empirically developed scale, predicts risk of recidivism for each youth and controls for risk statistically when examining program outcomes.

A second *confounding factor* is that the attitudes, values, perceptions and complexity of a youth's view of the world can affect a youth's reaction to the program. It is well recognized that not all youths respond to a partic-

Case Study 7.1, *continued*

ular program in the same way. Maturity, personality characteristics and cultural background can affect whether a youth relates to program staff, feels comfortable in the program's environment, finds the program content stimulating, enjoys the experiences and learns from the program's interventions. ProDES contains a typology of delinquent youths, based on self-reported standardized scales. By analyzing the responses of more than 2,500 youths on 14 scales, ranging from a measure of values to several scales that measure family bonding and school bonding, Harris and Jones identified five types of youths. Program outcomes are then assessed for each type, with the expectation that patterns of outcomes will vary by type.

ProDES was designed from the beginning as an information system that would support performance evaluation research. As such, it can serve as an adjunct to a management information system, but is not a substitute for a good management information system. It collects more than 800 items of information on every case, and is, therefore, a tremendous resource for developing systems of programs and for examining complex policy questions.

Questions

1. Discuss the usefulness of ProDES, using concepts from Chapter 7. How is ProDES useful for evaluating programs? How about policies?

2. How did Harris and Jones account for confounding factors that might bias observed outcomes?

3. Do you see any problem with a six-month follow-up? Explain.

Case Study 7.2

Evaluating Outcomes of Community-Based Delinquency Prevention[13]

Instructions: Read the case study below, then answer the question that follows.

The Problem, Program Design and Goals

To assess concerns of minority overrepresentation in the Pennsylvania juvenile justice system, and to respond to changes in federal guidelines for states participating in the Juvenile Justice and Delinquency Prevention (JJDP) Formula Grant Program, the Minority Confinement Subcommittee of the Pennsylvania Commission on Crime and Delinquency (PCCD) Juvenile Advisory Committee concluded that some action could be taken to slow the entry or re-entry of minorities into the juvenile justice system. They recommended the development and support of community-based intervention activities. Five programs were funded in Dauphin County (Harrisburg) beginning in 1991-92; those programs concluded their third and final year of PCCD funding early in 1994. It was expected that programs would obtain their own funding after two and one-half years of initial funding from PCCD.

All programs stressed the value of supervised activities to keep youths out of trouble. All provided "life skills training," which often included training in problem-solving skills, conflict resolution and cultural diversity and awareness. Most provided homework or tutoring assistance, structured recreation and/or field trips, some form of career development or vocational training, and community service. All programs, as requirements of their PCCD funding, had two mandated goals: (1) to reduce future involvement with the juvenile justice system, and (2) to improve school behavior and performance.

Research Design

We were contracted as evaluators quite some time after the programs began operations, and agencies were already utilizing diverse referral sources. Because neither randomization nor matched constructed control groups were possible, our choices for forming comparison groups were limited. We had no control over client selection and referrals, and referrals came from different sources (e.g., self and family, probation, school and police). Requirements of informed consent also limited research design options. To gain access to agency records (e.g., police, probation, school) for individual program clients, we were required to obtain a release form signed by the client and a parent. As a result, a strict "control" group was not possible (i.e., one that was identical to the intervention group in all respects except that no treatment was delivered). It was not possible to obtain police and school records for nonclients unless they had already granted consent but never subsequently participated in any of the programs.

Comparison groups were constructed on the basis of frequency of client participation in the programs. Numerous studies have suggested that the

Case Study 7.2, *continued*

intensity of treatment (e.g., frequency of contacts; number of contact hours) is one of the most crucial variables influencing the success of intervention, including drug and alcohol treatment and delinquency prevention.[14] We would expect that if a program works at all, a critical variable affecting client outcome is treatment intensity or degree of exposure to the program. We were aided by the fact that many of the clients who were referred to the programs signed a release-of-information form, but they never attended the programs.

To determine the adequacy of these constructed comparison groups for each cohort, we examined the possibility of biased selection (i.e., did the groups differ on critical preselection variables that might affect the outcomes of interest?). While our data allow us to examine group differences on numerous risk factors, the most crucial factors to examine are those most likely to affect the dependent variables. Recidivism, for example, is known to be related to previous delinquent activity and age (older juveniles are at greater risk of arrest and rearrest). Sources of referral could potentially bias comparison groups (e.g., probation referrals may be more likely to have been arrested than other referrals). For analyses of school outcomes, it is advisable to examine possible preselection differences that could influence educational outcomes (suspensions, truancy and core GPA). We also examined demographic factors that could have influenced selection (e.g., ethnicity, family structure, parental employment).

We report results for two separate client groups in Harrisburg: (1) those who attended programs during the 1992-93 school year, and (2) those who attended programs during the 1993-94 school year.

The 1992-93 sample consisted of 187 clients. Our first comparison group (the "control" group) was made up of 80 clients (43%) who never participated in any program. The second comparison group was made up of 45 clients (24%) who participated occasionally but accumulated less than 30 total program hours over the 1992-93 school year. Our third comparison group was made up of 62 clients (33%) who accumulated greater than 30 program hours during the 1992-93 school year. The three groups did not differ significantly in terms of prior arrests, gender, family structure, parental employment, previous truancy or prior suspensions. However, the comparison groups did differ in terms of age (high attenders were slightly younger), referral source (probation referrals had poorer attendance, while self or family referrals had higher rates of attendance), ethnicity (75% of the total sample were African-American, but Latino children were slightly overrepresented in the low and high attendance groups), whether the student was promoted the previous school year and academic performance the previous year (nonattenders had slightly lower grades and were less likely to have been promoted). Because randomized assignment of subjects to comparison groups was not possible, we cannot rule out the possibility that comparison groups differed on other, unmeasured pre-intervention variables related to the dependent variables of interest. For analyses of recidivism and educational outcomes, we can be assured that factors of most concern (prior arrests,

Case Study 7.2, *continued*

suspensions and truancy) do not contaminate the results. All pre-selection factors that statistically differentiated the comparison groups (e.g., age, referral source, ethnicity, previous school promotions and grades) were examined in statistical analyses as control variables.

In the 1993-94 sample, 97 clients were examined. Our first comparison group (the "control" group) was made up of 32 students (33%) who never participated in the programs. The second comparison group was made up of 31 clients (32%) who participated occasionally, but accumulated less than 50 total program hours over the 1993-94 school year. Our third comparison group was made up of 34 clients (34%) who accumulated greater than 50 program hours during the 1993-94 school year. To determine the adequacy of these constructed comparison groups, we examined the possibility of biased selection (i.e., did the groups differ on critical pre-selection variables that might affect the outcomes of interest?). Upon intake, the three comparison groups did not differ significantly in terms of prior arrests, age, gender, ethnicity, family structure, parental employment, academic retention (92-93 SY), prior suspensions (92-93 SY) or core GPA (92-93 SY). The comparison groups did differ in terms of referral source (probation and police referrals had poorer attendance, while self or family referrals had higher rates of attendance and referrals from human services had the highest rates of attendance) and truancy the previous school year (non-attenders and low-attenders had higher rates of truancy than high attenders). Once again, because randomized assignment of subjects to comparison groups was not possible, we cannot rule out the possibility that comparison groups differed on other, unmeasured pre-selection variables related to the dependent variables of interest. For analyses of recidivism and educational outcomes, then, critical factors (prior arrests, age, previous suspensions, previous grades) do not contaminate the results. All pre-selection factors that differentiated the comparison groups (i.e., referral source, truancy) were examined in statistical analyses as control variables.

Results

Recidivism. Results for the 1992-93 Harrisburg sample suggest that programs had success in reducing recidivism for high-risk clients. The rate of recidivism over a three-year period for the high-attendance group (25.8%) was impressive, especially considering that nearly one-half of these clients had previous arrests prior to their referral. In contrast, the control group had a recidivism rate of 53 percent for the same period.

Recidivism results for the 1993-94 Harrisburg sample were less positive. The rate of recidivism over a two-year period for the high-attendance group (23.5%) was satisfactory, but nearly the same proportion (about one-fourth) of these clients had previous arrests prior to their referral. Prior arrests, then, rather than programmatic intervention, was the strongest influence of recidivism. Compared to the previous year (1992-93), programs in 1993-94 targeted clients who were much younger and much less likely to have previous arrests.

Case Study 7.2, *continued*

Academic Performance. Impacts on academic performance were somewhat disappointing, although missing data resulted in smaller samples than desirable for multivariate tests. For both the 1992-93 and 1993-94 samples, Harrisburg programs had no significant effects on academic performance. For the 1993-94 sample, academic performance either remained stable or declined slightly for all comparison groups over a two-year period, and statistical analyses suggested that programs had no significant effect on grades. The absence of any directional improvement in grades over time suggests that programs have made little progress in impacting their clients' educational performance.

Dropout Rates. For the 1992-93 sample, Harrisburg programs had no significant effects on dropout rates. Only previously poor academic performance significantly explained dropout rates. Although the 1993-94 sample was young and the follow-up period brief, results did not reveal any statistically significant program effect on dropout rates. However, results for the 1993-94 sample were positive (the regular program attendees had a dropout rate of 4.3 percent, compared to 26.9 percent for the control group).

Truancy. For the 1992-93 sample, Harrisburg programs had no significant effects on truancy. All comparison groups showed a large increase in truancy from 1991-92 to 1993-94. Although the sample was young and the follow-up period brief, results for the 1993-94 sample were similarly disappointing. However, while no statistically significant programmatic effect on truancy was found, results were positive (i.e., there was a slight but statistically nonsignificant decrease in truancy from 1993-94 to 1994-95). The only significant predictor of post-intervention truancy for the 1993-94 sample was previous (pre-intervention) truancy.

Implications

Although the results were somewhat disappointing, it is important to recognize that results do not reflect the total success or failure of the programs. For example, findings about recidivism are compromised by the fact that there were so few youths with prior arrests in the 1993-94 sample. Academic performance, dropout rates and truancy did not improve significantly, but it may be unrealistic to expect dramatic changes in youths who participated in the programs only sporadically. Further, programs may influence educational outcomes only to a small degree, as compared to the more pervasive effects exerted by schools and families.

Results may be influenced by various factors, some of which we can account for in our data (e.g., gaps in the delivery of program services, inconsistent patterns of youth participation in programs, insufficient program resources, inadequate measures of client skills and attitudes) and some that lie outside the parameters of our evaluation (e.g., inadequate funding for public schools, poverty and family trauma). It may also be the case that some programs evaluated individually, rather than as a combined sample, would produce more positive results. Unfortunately, because the number of clients

Case Study 7.2, *continued*

in each program was so small, and there was so much missing data, we could not effectively evaluate outcomes for individual programs.

Another problem is presented by the need for adequate measurement of additional objectives that programs attempt to achieve (e.g., improved self-esteem, problem-solving skills and interpersonal behavior). We vigorously attempted to measure such outcomes using self-report measures and staff ratings of client behavior in the 1994-95 cohort, but program staff did not have the time or resources to complete the assessment process at required three-month intervals. Thus, there may be areas of program impact that we were unable to measure adequately.

Concern was raised by the diverse nature of referral sources during the 1993-94 school year. Rather than selecting clients on the basis of their suitability for each program, intakes during the 1993-94 school year were marked by a high diversity of client characteristics and needs, perhaps indicating a desperate attempt by the coalition to get referrals from anywhere possible. Program funding, therefore, may not yet have stabilized to the degree necessary for programs to concentrate intensively on defining their intended target population and strengthening their service delivery to meet specified client needs.

Question

1. Explain how Case Study 7.2 illustrates concepts discussed in Chapter 7, providing evidence to support your answer: (a) reliability and validity, (b) non-equivalent comparison groups, (c) confounding factors, and (d) reassessing the entire program or policy plan.

Endnotes

[1] For more thorough discussions of evaluation concepts and methods, we recommend the following works: Berk, Richard A., and Peter H. Rossi (1990). *Thinking About Program Evaluation.* Newbury Park, CA: Sage; Patton, Michael Quinn (1997). *Utilization-Focused Evaluation: The New Century Text.* Thousand Oaks, CA: Sage; Rossi, Peter H., and Howard E. Freeman (eds.) (1993). *Evaluation: A Systematic Approach.* (5th ed.) Thousand Oaks, CA: Sage; Wholey, Joseph S., Harry P. Hatry, and Kathryn E. Newcomer (eds.) (1994). *Handbook of Practical Evaluation.* San Francisco: Jossey-Bass.

[2] See for example: Thompson, M. (1980). *Benefit-Cost Analysis for Program Evaluation.* Beverly Hills: Sage; Stokey, E., and R. Zeckhauser (1978). *A Primer For Policy Analyses.* New York: Norton.

3   Rossi, Peter H., and Howard E. Freeman (1993). *Evaluation: A Systematic Approach.* (5th ed.) Thousand Oaks, CA: Sage; Rutman, Leonard (1984). *Planning Useful Evaluations: Evaluability Assessment.* Beverly Hills: Sage; Wholey, Joseph S., Harry P. Hatry, and Kathryn E. Newcomer (eds.) (1994). *Handbook of Practical Evaluation.* San Francisco: Jossey-Bass.

4   Rosenberg, Morris (1965). *Society and the Adolescent Self-Image.* Princeton, NJ: Princeton University Press.

5   Johnston, Lloyd D., Patrick M. O'Malley, and Jerald G. Bachman (1997). *National Survey Results on Drug Use From the "Monitoring the Future" Study, 1975-1996.* Vol. 1, Secondary School Students. Washington, DC: U.S. Department of Health and Human Services, National Institute on Drug Abuse.

6   Sherman, Lawrence W,. and Richard A. Berk (1984). "The Specific Deterrent Effects of Arrest for Domestic Assault." *American Sociological Review,* 49:261-272.

7   Ibid, note 6.

8   Lempert, Richard (1989). "Humility is a Virtue: On the Publicization of Policy-Relevant Research." *Law and Society Review,* 23:145-161.

9   Sherman, Lawrence W. (1992). *Policing Domestic Violence: Experiments and Dilemmas.* New York: Free Press.

10   Ibid, note 4.

11   Pearson, Frank S. (1988). "Evaluation of New Jersey's Intensive Supervision Program." *Crime & Delinquency,* 34:437-448.

12   Philip W. Harris and Peter R. Jones are professors of criminal justice at Temple University in Philadelphia. ProDES is operated by the Crime and Justice Research Institute. Reprinted with permission of authors.

13   Adapted from: Welsh, Wayne N., Patricia H. Jenkins, and Philip W. Harris (1997). *Reducing Minority Overrepresentation in Juvenile Justice: Results of Community-Based Intervention in Pennsylvania, 1992-95.* Philadelphia: Temple University, Department of Criminal Justice. See also: Welsh, Wayne N., Patricia H. Jenkins, and Philip W. Harris (in press). "Reducing Minority Overrepresentation in Juvenile Justice: Results of Community-Based Delinquency Prevention in Harrisburg." *Journal of Research in Crime and Delinquency,* 36(1).

14   Palmer, Ted (1992). *The Re-Emergence of Correctional Intervention.* Newbury Park, CA: Sage.

CHAPTER 8

INITIATING THE PROGRAM OR POLICY PLAN

At this point, the program or policy is ready to be launched. Ideally, all six stages of planning should be completed prior to the initial start date for the intervention. We recognize, however, that time constraints imposed on the planning process may result in less-than-optimal program designs and action plans. Nonetheless, at this stage, for the first time, our program or policy comes alive. While planning and reviewing is a process that will continue throughout the life of the program, it is now that we begin doing what we have planned.

Of course, we rarely have any control over the environments within which policies and programs are implemented: they have lives of their own, driven by visions and goals that may be independent of our new innovation. Alternatively, they may be wholly driven by political and financial arrangements that often appear irrational and chaotic. Because our program or policy operates in a dynamic organizational or system environment, we need to pay attention to changes that occur in areas such as political climate, fiscal health of funding sources, key policy-makers and policies related to our intervention. Sometimes these changes will occur independently of our intervention, but in other cases our interventions will cause reactions that require adaptation. As we discussed in Chapter 2 in relation to force field analysis, some of the forces that sustain a problem or issue over time are more potent than others. As these potent forces shift in strength, it becomes critical for programs and policies to change. As an example, consider the potential impact of the Welfare Reform Act that President Clinton signed into law in 1996.

Example 8.1

The Welfare Reform Act

The Welfare Reform Act substantially reduces the ability of individual states to provide welfare benefits to its neediest citizens. In Pennsylvania, the state has created what has been termed "the toughest test of welfare reform in the nation."[1] March 3, 1999, is the date on which 38,000 adults will lose their welfare benefits unless they are working at least 20 hours a week. This reality has meant that states have had to scramble to develop programs to induce welfare recipients to work. Even with new welfare-to-work programs, though, more than one-half of current heads of households on welfare will not be working. Will this new economic reality affect criminal justice programs? What impact will it have on families of prison inmates, on ex-inmates returning to the community, on young people whose parents can no longer provide for them? This scenario suggests that there is information about the program or policy environment that is crucial to anticipating implementation problems, as well as understanding why program administrators add activities to a program design or modify existing ones. On the other hand, innovators can cause innovations to fail at this stage.

We repeat our warning from Chapter 1: planned change improves the likelihood of successful intervention, but it cannot guarantee it. Good planning increases the odds of success by explicitly considering important factors that might lead to failure or success.

Example 8.2

Criminal Justice Planning and the Lesson of Jurassic Park

Our preference for rational planning is a value that guides our writing and research. We are not so naïve, however, to believe that careful planning always produces successful outcomes. Even the most carefully crafted plans can have no effect, make problems worse or create unintended effects. There are other times when energy and resources are wasted because planning processes are terminated prematurely. In general, subtle facets of the criminal justice system (see Chapter 2) can frustrate good planning. In real life, systems do not always behave the way we want them to.

In the 1993 film *Jurassic Park*,[2] Ian Malcolm, a mathematician (played by Jeff Goldblum[3]), warns of the larger, more powerful natural rhythms of nature that can undermine what appear to be great scientific advancements. "My point is that life on earth can take care of itself," he rants. "In the thinking of a human being, a hundred years is a long time. . . . But to the earth, a hundred years is nothing. A million years is nothing. This planet lives and breathes on a much vaster scale. We can't imagine its slow and powerful rhythms, and we haven't got the humility to try. We have been residents here for the blink of an eye. If we are gone tomorrow, the earth will not miss us."

Eugene Doleschal[4] sounded a similar warning, this one directed at criminal justice reform efforts. He argues that forces that continually shape the justice system should be allowed to interact naturally. When reforms are implemented, the results are often the opposite of those intended. For example, many efforts intended to reduce prison populations through the creation of community-based programs have failed to do so. Instead, community programs have often extended supervision and control of less serious offenders. Other examples include policy changes intended to reduce discretion that only moved discretion to other, less visible decision points in the system. Doleschal likens these reforms to a program conducted in Alaska and Canada to protect herds of caribou from their natural predator, the wolf. By shooting the wolves, environmentalists hoped to increase the caribou population. Instead, old and sick caribou that previously were killed and eaten by the wolves faced death by starvation and disease.

Rather than give up on planning, we can learn from these experiences. In many cases, failures become the means for discovering the nature and strengths of forces we are trying to change. Sometimes we may decide that our knowledge and resources are inadequate for the task, but in other cases we become better equipped to try again.

Planning for Failure

Failure of any program or policy is related to two broad types of difficulties: (1) insurmountable obstacles within the implementing agency or its environment; and (2) breakdowns or omissions in the planning process.

First of all, it is possible for a program or policy to fail even when its designers have planned thoroughly and carefully. It may be the case that certain obstacles are too big or too powerful to overcome or that inadequate resources are available to do so. As we discussed in Chapter 2, such obstacles may be *physical* (e.g., the physical design of a courthouse precludes more efficient case processing), *social* (e.g., exisiting barriers related to class, gender or race are unchanged by the program or policy), *economic* (lack of sufficient funding), *educational* (e.g., special training or education is required to implement an intervention), *legal* (e.g., criminal justice agencies are legally obligated to do certain things and prohibited from doing other things), *political* (e.g., motivations of partisan stakeholders can block a specific change) or *technological* (e.g., problems with managing the information system required to implement a new policy). A criminal justice systems analysis and a force field analysis should help planners anticipate such obstacles and develop strategies to overcome them. Such activities increase the probability of success.

The second set of difficulties concerns planning breakdowns, omissions or deficits: one or more critical planning tasks have not been properly executed. The examples and case studies presented in Chapters 2 through 7 illustrate some of the most likely deficits in the planning process. We reiterate here common difficulties at each stage.

Figure 8.2

Common Planning Deficits at Each Stage

Stage 1: Analyzing the Problem

- Insufficient information about the problem has been examined. We do not really know how big the problem is, where it is or who is affected. We may not even have a clear definition of the problem.
- No theory guided the intervention. We do not know how or why the expected change should have occurred.
- Inadequate examination of previous interventions: we may have recreated the wheel or recycled an old, broken wheel by failing to learn about previous attempts to change the problem.
- Important stakeholders were not identified or included in the planning process.
- Inadequate examination of the larger system or environment was conducted.

Stage 2: Setting Goals and Objectives

- Goals and objectives were not clearly stated.
- Substantial disagreement about goals or objectives persists among stakeholders.

Figure 8.2, *continued*

- Incompatible goals or values in the larger system were not identified.
- Needs for interagency collaboration were not sufficiently addressed.

Stage 3: Designing the Program or Policy

- No specific intervention approach was identified.
- Target populations and selection were not adequately identified.
- Program components or policy provisions and procedures were unclear.
- Responsibilities of program staff or policy authorities were unclear.

Stage 4: Developing an Action Plan

- Required resources have not been properly identified.
- Required resources have not been acquired.
- Responsibilities for implementation have not been clearly assigned.
- Insufficient attention was devoted to maintaining support and anticipating resistance.

Stage 5: Developing a Plan for Monitoring Program/Policy Implementation

- No monitoring of program or policy implementation was attempted.
- Information systems for monitoring were inadequate.
- Monitoring instruments were unreliable.
- Responsibilities for data collection, storage or analysis were unclear.
- Monitoring data was not used to make necessary adjustments to the program or policy.

Stage 6: Develop a Plan for Evaluating Outcomes

- Prerequisites for evaluation were not adequately met.
- Outcome measures were not reliable or valid.
- The research design was inadequate for determining outcomes.
- Confounding factors were not adequately addressed.
- Users of evaluation results were not adequately identified or consulted.

Stage 7: Initiating the Program or Policy Plan

- Inadequate review of the planning process was undertaken before implementation began.
- Substantial obstacles within the implementing agency or its environment subverted the aims of the program or policy.
- Planning breakdowns, errors or omissions occurred.
- The change agent failed to learn and adapt during implementation.
- The change agent failed to properly execute plans.

Consider the following example. Implementation failure easily occurs when leaders overstate the goals of a program or policy (Stage 2) in order to garner support from stakeholders in the larger political environment (Stage 1). When innovations are oversold, stakeholders feel deceived and cheated. Todd Clear and his colleagues[5] observe with humor the range of promises attached to Intensive Probation Services (IPS): "Advocates of IPS programs are not humble in the claims they made for these programs. Commonly, IPS is expected to reduce prison crowding, increase public protection, rehabilitate the offender, demonstrate the value of probation, and save money. Even a skeptic is bound to be impressed" (p. 32). These exaggerated objectives eventually spelled trouble for the evaluation (Stage 6). Petersilia and Turner[6] found in their evaluation of 14 IPS programs that the primary purposes of intensive supervision were rarely achieved:

- The programs did not alleviate prison crowding and may have increased it in some sites.

- They cost considerably more than is generally realized (Stage 5).

- They were no more effective than routine probation and parole in reducing recidivism.

The best that can be hoped for in the wake of such disappointing outcomes is a careful reassessment of the entire planning process, followed by necessary adjustments (Stage 7)—especially a more realistic accounting of goals and objectives (Stage 2).

Planning for Success

The important point to keep in mind at the implementation stage is that the planning process has not yet ended. In fact, it never will. New information pertinent to the program or policy will emerge, some of it though evaluation research, that may suggest modification to the original design. This is what learning is about. The organization's capacity to learn will largely determine the extent to which the goals of the innovation are achieved. There are four tasks that need emphasis at this point in order to increase the chances of success.

1. *Communicate:* Continually communicate to constituents and potential opponents the need for the program or policy. Develop advocates for the program or policy from among a wide range of public officials, so that the vision of what you are up to is passed on to others who may be asked about the need for it. Publicize widely and frequently information on the program and its performance.

2. *Build internal capacities for leading and learning:* Those persons who are carrying out the activities articulated in the design are your most valuable assets. Their command of the vision, goals and activities described in the design are critical to the innovation's success. Their ability to lead, support each other, think strategically, adapt and carry out their assigned tasks are essential to a program's success. Your organization needs to invest in their development.

3. *Study:* The need for information is essential for learning to occur. Data regarding implementation of the program or policy's design, data on performance and data on changes in the environment need to be tracked and brought into discussions among key stakeholders.

4. *Increase the fit:* Purposefully permit the innovation to take shape as new information about the needs and characteristics of the environment emerge and as the capacities of the program or policy develop. The better it fits the needs and priorities of the political environment, the greater will be the level of acceptance.

Learning and Adapting

In Chapter 1, we mentioned the concept of mutual adaptation; the program (or policy) and the organizational environment in which it operates will both change during the implementation process. Programs change over time. Not only is there continual reshaping of a program design before it is put into action, but programs continue to change after the point at which "the tire meets the road." It is this kind of change that makes the components of program design poor predictors of program success. Then, too, program staff, program clients and decisionmakers, rather than being passive participants in the implementation process, directly affect how the innovations are used by adapting the innovation to existing organizational structures and norms and using it to serve their own purposes.

In addition, the same program design can produce drastically different results in different settings, thus supporting the conclusion that context is critical to outcome. You may recall from our discussion in Chapter 2 regarding systems analysis that the private sector has played a critical role in criminal justice for many years. Some local criminal justice systems, however, have had disastrous experiences with private-sector programs. In corrections, for example, the promised fiscal advantages of private corrections have not always materialized.[7]

It is not only innovations that undergo change during the implementation process; the organization within which the innovation is used also undergoes change. A new program for sex offenders is not installed in a vacuum; rather, this innovation must be accepted by a living system in which the balance is necessarily disrupted. Specifically, with regard to a probation program in Texas, Markley[8] observed that when program management personnel changed, line staff became "demoralized." Their commitment to the program was dependent on the leadership provided by a few individuals. Other common disruptions include the transfer of personnel to a new program, the hiring of outsiders (new personnel) to staff the new program, and the requirement that staff acquire new skills in order to continue doing their jobs.

Implementation of a program or policy in any organizational setting requires both adaptation by individuals and adaptation of the innovation in order for the implementation process to succeed.[9] This process of mutual adaptation implies that the same innovation can look very different across different settings.[10] The crucial point to be made is that unless a program or policy is carefully tailored to the setting in which it is to be used, successful implementation is unlikely.

An excellent example of this kind of tailoring of the innovation can be seen in the approach that the Center for Alternative Sentencing and Employment Services (CASES) in New York City has taken to ensure that its clients fit their target population: jail-bound, rather than probation-bound, offenders. Data on sentencing in New York revealed that sentencing practices differed across the five boroughs. Judges in Queens, for example, require fewer misdemeanor offenses than do those in Manhattan before sentencing an offender to serve significant jail time. In order to prevent use of the CASES Community Service Sentencing Project (CSSP) from becoming a replacement for probation, criteria for accepting offenders into CSSP are adjusted to borough-level sentencing patterns.[11]

Not only does tailoring itself promote effective adaptation, but so do the structural characteristics of organizations. Decentralization of program control, for example, permits different sites to develop a program design at their own pace and allows the program to adapt to the idiosyncrasies of each site in ways that improve chances for successful implementation. It may be that a program is more effective under some conditions than others, but it may also be the case that different modes of adaptation make it possible for an innovation to adapt to a variety of organizational environments.

It is critical during implementation to uncover any changes in the intended program or policy design and describe them. These changes are deviations from the original plan and must be understood before a sound evaluation can be conducted.

The Tasks of Implementation

Implementing the program or policy plan (Stage 7) involves putting into motion the program design (Stage 3) and the action plan (Stage 4), monitoring implementation (Stage 5) and, if appropriate, evaluating outcomes (Stage 6). Once evaluation data are analyzed, feedback is provided to all stakeholders, and the program should be thoroughly reassessed to determine where revisions are necessary. At the end of the process, the change agent asks whether further adjustments are necessary to meet program objectives. What are the strengths and weaknesses of the program? Decisions may have to be made about whether the program should be continued and whether it should receive further funding. Reassessment and review of the program or policy should occur periodically from this point forward.

Initiating the Program/Policy Design

In Chapter 4, we examined how a program or policy is constructed. Every program or policy must have a clearly defined design that includes: targets (e.g., eligibility, numbers to be served, access, screening, intake); program staff or individuals responsible for implementing the program or policy (e.g., selection, training, duties); and program components or policy provisions (e.g., specific goods, services, opportunities or interventions to be delivered). Initiating the design, then, requires doing everything that was previously specified. Together with the action plan, the design maps out the major tasks for implementation.

Initiating the Action Plan

In Chapter 5, you learned how to develop an action plan that specified the entire sequence of tasks that need to be completed in order to launch or implement the program or policy successfully. These included technical and interpersonal tasks (e.g., identifying and acquiring the necessary resources, locating office space and/or meeting space, hiring and training staff, designing client intake and reporting forms, purchasing equipment and supplies, setting dates and assigning responsibility for the completion of specific tasks). The action plan is, in essence, a "blueprint" explaining how to translate a vision of the program or policy into reality.

Like the director of an orchestra, the change agent must coordinate the program or policy activities of all the different individuals and groups associated with the program or policy. Managers must hire and train their staff, they must build good relationships with potential referral sources (e.g., police, schools, probation), they must train staff to use required intake forms and keep client records, they must build good relationships with citizens and businesses in the neighborhood, and they must provide regular reports of progress to their funding providers. Three guidelines will ensure smooth coordination: (1) maintain consistency between staff job descriptions and actual tasks, (2) maintain clear and frequent communication among staff members, and between staff and supervisors, and (3) keep an eye on the timeline (that is, make sure that activities required for successful progression from one step to the next are carried out on time—e.g., make sure that staff are hired and trained by the dates specified in the action plan, that all record-keeping forms are printed and that procedures are clearly understood by staff).

Remember that some resistance is inevitable with the start-up of a new program or policy. Resistance may come from any of the participants involved: clients, targets, even the intervention's own staff (i.e., the action system). Any resistance that appears should be dealt with fairly and seriously. Conflict is *not* something to be avoided at all costs. It may provide the opportunity to identify and resolve misunderstandings, and it may also point out difficulties in implementation that truly deserve attention.

Monitoring Program/Policy Implementation

At Stage 6 (see Chapter 5), you laid out a plan for monitoring program or policy implementation. As program or policy operations begin, it is time to start monitoring. *Implementation* refers to the initiation, management and administration of the action plan. Once the intervention actually begins, we want to minimize discrepancies between what was planned (i.e., the program or policy on paper) and what is actually done (i.e., the program or policy in action). *Monitoring* attempts to determine whether program/policy implementation is proceeding as planned. Monitoring is a process that attempts to identify any gaps between the program or policy on paper (design) and the program or policy in action (implementation).

For the target population, monitoring data should assess the following questions: What were the characteristics of the actual individuals targeted by the intervention? Were targets that were truly in need or at risk selected? Is the intervention meeting its specified criteria in terms of target eligibility (e.g., age, sex, income, region) and numbers to be served? Were proper recruiting, screening and intake procedures followed? How were referrals made? For program components, monitoring data should answer the following questions: Who did what to whom in what order, how much, and how often? Were there variations in service delivery or activities? Did different staff deliver programming in a different manner? Was there more than one program site or location, and if so, were program activities administered consistently across different sites? Make sure that monitoring data also provide information about service tasks and responsible authorities: Were proper staff or authorities identified? Did they fit the specified roles and job descriptions? Did they understand their duties and perform them as expected?

Evaluating and Providing Feedback to Users and Stakeholders

If any evaluation is to be useful, it should serve the information needs of the intervention and its stakeholders (see Chapter 2). The program or policy's major stakeholders include its funding agency, as well as the community, businesses, politicians, criminal justice agencies, volunteers, clients, and so on. The time spent previously (at Stage 1) identifying stakeholders should not be wasted. Evaluation (Stage 6) is a critical means of demonstrating accountability—and, hopefully, effectiveness—to stakeholders. The change agent should now assign individual responsibility for packaging and communicating evaluation results to different users. If the results are to be useful, and used, one must create means of communication that intended audiences can understand and to which they can react.

Conclusion

Implementation is an ongoing process of adaptation, negotiation and communication. In order to maximize the mutual fit between a program or policy and the environment within which it is initiated and allowed to develop, both the innovation and the environment must change.

At this point, we hope that students and practitioners have a good idea of the kind of analyses and kind of questions we need to ask to figure out "what works" in reducing or preventing any specific problem. We have argued throughout this book that many criminal justice interventions fall short of their goals because of poor planning, poor implementation and poor evaluation. What we truly need is not more programs and policies, or new programs and policies; we need better programs and policies. We need a better understanding of planned change to improve the effectiveness of criminal justice interventions. Such change is ubiquitous in governmental, community, private and nonprofit agencies. This book has attempted to provide a systematic, seven-stage framework for analyzing and improving existing interventions, but also for planning new ones so as to maximize chances of success. Major steps of analysis were summarized in Figure 1.1.

Which of the following interventions are effective? How would you know, or how would you find out?

- Intermediate sanctions to reduce jail overcrowding (e.g., intensive supervision probation, boot camps, electronic monitoring)

- After-school delinquency prevention programs

- Drug treatment programs for convicted offenders

- Drug Awareness Resistance Education (DARE)

- Operation Weed and Seed (dual policy of first stamping out drug sales and distribution in specific communities, then "seeding" community with protective, economic and social resources)

- Shelters, counseling and victim assistance for abused women

- "Three strikes and you're out" legislation, which aims to put away repeat offenders for long periods of time

- Mandatory arrest policies for suspected spouse abusers

- "Megan's Laws" (laws specifying the public's right to know where released child molesters are going to live)

- Juvenile waiver laws (serious juvenile offenses may be raised to adult courts)

We reiterate a few major propositions to conclude this endeavor. First, we need a systematic plan for any change effort. Interventions both new and old need to be subjected to thorough scrutiny and analysis. Successful interventions are a product of hard work, careful planning and a willingness to revise where necessary. Second, good intentions are rarely enough to bring about successful change. Beware of the "activist bias,"[12] by which well-intentioned advocates of change assume that they already know what the problem is and what is needed. Such advocates may insist that we desist all this prolonged planning and simply "get on with it." The perils of unplanned or poorly planned change should by now be obvious: expensive, poorly articulated, poorly implemented, ineffective programs and policies that are unable to compete successfully for scarce funds. Third, program or policy planning is an interactive and ongoing process. It is crucial to review and modify planning (where needed) at each stage of the analysis. This takes time, but it is time well spent. Fourth, a rational planning approach provides a framework for developing logical and effective programs and policies. The default (very often) is to use unarticulated and untested assumptions to guide planning. Finally, participation of and communication with all key actors or stakeholders (e.g., program staff, clients, individuals or agencies whose cooperation is needed, funding sources, citizens affected by the intervention, elected representatives) throughout the change process are keys to success. While careful planning and analysis cannot guarantee success, it will increase the probability of success.

DISCUSSION QUESTIONS

1. Why should program planning and management occur on a regular basis? Why is it necessary to continually revise and reassess?

2. What can be done to increase the chances that an innovation will succeed? What factors increase the chances of failure?

3. What steps (activities) are involved in initiating the program or policy plan?

4. What is meant by the phrase "coordinating program activities"? Give two or three examples to illustrate your answer.

5. How do different organizational structures affect the ability of a program or policy to adapt to environmental demands?

6. What is mutual adaptation and why is it important? Give an example.

7. How can you tell when a program or policy is ready to be evaluated?

Case Study 8.1

The Best Laid Plans:
The Success and Failure of Sentencing Guidelines

Instructions: First read the background below, then read the article that follows. Answer the questions at the end of the case study.

"The best laid plans 'o mice and men gang aft aglay . . ." Scottish poet Robbie Burns said it well. No matter how carefully "wee timorous beasties" or humans plan for the future, things never work out exactly as planned. Even when planned change is successful, it may not be permanent. Why not, you may ask. People who play critical roles ("stakeholders")—including leadership roles—come and go over time; initial enthusiasm abates; the political environment changes; the priority assigned to a specific public problem shifts; and the actual change that resulted may not have been dramatic enough to maintain or recruit new support. Planned change is dynamic, like the problems it seeks to address. The following case study illustrates how successful planning for the Oregon sentencing guidelines gave way over time to political tampering and eventual abolishment. It is a story of both success and failure, not one or the other.

Background[13]

In 1989, Oregon developed felony sentencing guidelines to address four main policy goals:

1. to provide proportional punishments based on sanctions that became more severe as the seriousness of crimes increased and as defendants' criminal histories became more extensive;

2. to provide truth-in-sentencing, so that offenders served the imposed prison terms rather than a fraction of the sentence imposed;

3. to provide sentence uniformity and reduced disparity in sentencing by using narrow sentencing ranges, so that similar offenders received similar sentences; and

4. to maintain a sentencing policy consistent with correctional capacity.

The guidelines appeared to be achieve their goals well. In a 1990 survey of judges, prosecutors and defense attorneys, 90 percent agreed with the goals of fairness, proportionality and truth-in-sentencing. Seventy percent rated the guidelines as successful at achieving their goals. Over a six-year period from 1989 to 1995, offenders sentenced under the guidelines served an average of 83 percent of their sentences, up from a previous average of 24 percent. Judges departed from presumptive guidelines in only 6 percent of cases in 1990, although this departure rate had crept up to 12.5 percent by 1995. The Criminal Justice Council estimated that sentencing disparity based on race and gender (controlling for crime seriousness and criminal history scores) was reduced by 45 percent in 1990, the first full year

Case Study 8.1, *continued*

of guidelines operation. Other benefits included reductions in the number of trials and in time spent by offenders awaiting sentencing, as well as reduced pressure on local jails due to a decline in the number of felons serving time in local jails.

In Oregon, an important aim of sentencing guidelines was to operate an expanded prison system in which the population remained within 97 percent of capacity. Prison population forecasts relied on the use of a Criminal Justice Council database, which contained felony sentencing data received from state courts. Over a 40-month period ending in April 1995, forecasts had been accurate within 1 percent.

The goal to control growing prison populations had a successful precedent. Minnesota's sentencing guidelines, implemented several years earlier, had required impact analyses of new crime legislation: any new bills introduced in the state legislature that proposed to increase sentences had to analyze the projected impact on prison beds and available capacity. No longer could legislators freely jack up criminal penalties without taking responsibility for the fiscal consequences of their decisions. Provisions in Minnesota had worked well to control overcrowding,[14] but shifts toward "getting tough" with offenders in recent years have compromised the stability of the guidelines and strained prison capacity.[15]

The political environment in Oregon also changed over time. Due to a 1990 property tax limitation measure adopted by Oregon voters, the prison construction plan was never completed. Initially, legislators chose to modify probation revocation procedures and authorize use of boot camp programs rather than disturb the sentencing guidelines. Passage in 1994 of a mandatory minimum sentencing measure by voter initiative further destabilized the system and upset population projections and planned capacity. Other setbacks followed.

In spite of remarkable success over a six-year period from 1989 to 1995, sentencing guidelines in Oregon were severely weakened by changes in the political environment. In the article below, Judy Greene describes these events with insight, wit and precision.

Wisconsin Guidelines Killed, Oregon's Weakened[16]

Recent political developments have profoundly affected well-established guidelines systems in two states. In Wisconsin, the governor and the Republican-controlled legislature abolished the state's guidelines, and axed the sentencing commission and its staff, principally to save money.

Oregon's guidelines remain in place, but the politicization of sentencing policy has weakened the guidelines as a mechanism for controlling prison population levels and achieving fair and proportionate sentencing.

On the heels of a ballot initiative which "trumped" many of the Oregon guidelines' presumptive sentences with stiff mandatory prison terms, the legislature abolished the ten-year-old Oregon Criminal Justice Council ("OCJC"), the agency which created and managed the guidelines system, replacing it with a new citizen policy board.

Case Study 8.1, *continued*

Development of Guidelines in Oregon

Oregon in the mid-1970s experienced a sharp rise in prison populations. Prison crowding was challenged in the federal court, resulting in 1980 in a court-imposed population cap (later rescinded). To reduce overcrowding, bond measures were proposed in 1980, 1983, and 1986 to finance new prison beds. Each was defeated. By 1987, prisons were operating at almost 200 percent of capacity, and corrections officials began to use an early release program to ease the crunch.

Governor Neil Goldschmidt in 1987 initiated a building program designed to double capacity at a cost of $85 million. The legislature also called for a strict set of sentencing guidelines that would increase incarceration levels for violent offenders, sharply decrease use of prison sentences for non-violent offenders, and hold the overall population within the planned expansion. OCJC was directed to develop the guidelines.

The council was established by the legislature in 1985 to serve as a non-partisan policy-planning body that included state-level officials from all branches of government and key local criminal justice professionals. Sentencing guidelines were formulated by the Sentencing Guidelines Board, an OCJC subcommittee, with assistance from council staff.

Guidelines legislation was approved in 1989, establishing "truth in sentencing" and setting presumptive sentences for felonies, based on crime seriousness and offenders' criminal histories. Judges may depart from the guidelines for "substantial and compelling" reasons—imposing up to twice the recommended prison sentence if aggravating factors are found, and reducing the term, or imposing probation, when mitigating circumstances apply. Appeals may be filed by both defendants and prosecutors.

Implementation of the guidelines from 1989 to 1994 was very successful. Judicial compliance was high. There were dramatic increases in prison admissions and average time served for violent offenses. Guidelines offenders now serve an average of 83 percent of the sentence imposed, compared with 24 percent before the guidelines (see April 1995 *Overcrowded Times*). Because, however, prison use declined for property and driving offenses, the prison population was projected to remain within planned capacity.

Introduction of sentencing guidelines was not a hot political issue. Media coverage was positive. An evaluation by the National Council on Crime and Delinquency of intermediate sanctions programs operated under Oregon's community corrections act found that the system was achieving its goals. Findings highlighted the effectiveness of efforts to target the more expensive, surveillance-, or treatment-oriented sanctions for offenders with higher risk scores. With both incarceration and violent crime rates declining, state officials believed that considerable progress had been made.

Budget Woes: Ballot Measure 5

The prison expansion initiated by Neil Goldschmidt stopped under governor Barbara Roberts when a 1990 ballot threw Oregon state government into a fiscal crisis. Ballot measure 5 stripped significant portions of the property-tax base for education, but mandated that the state cover the revenue losses—drawing state income-tax resources away from other sectors of state government. Governor Roberts sheltered the corrections operating budget, but failed to convince voters that a sales tax was needed to provide additional resources to the state. Prison building stopped about 1,000 beds shy of the original 1999 goal of 7,894 beds. To address population pressures and free up prison beds, legislators authorized a boot camp for selected prison-bound offenders and modified probation revocation procedures.

But population pressures mounted and electoral politics became increasingly polarized. Governor Roberts declined to run for a second term. And despite the guidelines" overall effectiveness, proposals to revamp the sentencing system were introduced by representative Kevin Mannix (a Democrat from Salem) during the 1993 legislative session. He proposed a web of mandatory minimums which would require imprisonment of most offenders; his ideas were brushed off and the bill died.

Sentencing Policy by Ballot Initiative

In 1994, Mannix won his revenge. He recast his ideas into ballot measures, and—bankrolled by a small group of conservative businessmen—launched a campaign to place them on the November ballot. Fueled by "get tough" rhetoric and public concern over parole release of *preguidelines* prisoners, Ballot Measure 11 passed by a two-thirds margin. It set a stiff schedule of mandatory minimums which override the sentencing guidelines for 16 serious felonies. The measure will double the prison population by the year 2000, requiring an estimated $1 billion in prison construction.

The 1994 election also brought sweeping changes in the legislature. Many incumbents, frustrated by the tax-revolt-driven dismantling of much of the state's service-delivery system, declined to run for re-election. Others lost in hotly contested races. The result was a turnover of 40 percent, with a shift to Republican leadership in the state senate. The leadership group which had approved and defended the guidelines was dispersed, along with the council and its staff.

Building Up Community Corrections

The newly-elected Democratic governor, John Kitzhaber, in response to Ballot Measure 11, outlined a major policy shift. State prison space would be reserved for violent and "career" offenders committed for terms of more than one year, including all those sentenced under Measure 11. Offenders sentenced to 12 months or less (90 percent of whom are parole or probation violators) would remain in county community corrections systems.

Case Study 8.1, *continued*

The new plans provides community corrections funding directly to the counties on a block grant basis. It was sold as "deregulation," providing counties with more flexibility and control. This entailed eliminating the community corrections administrative staff in the state department of corrections, and transferring field positions to community corrections agencies in the counties.

Kitzhaber has promised to build thousands of new prison and jail beds. Senate Bill 1145. proposed by Kitzhaber and passed by the Oregon legislature in 1995, authorized his plan to transfer responsibility for felony offenders sentenced to twelve months or less to the counties. This is expected to free up about 1,400 state prison beds. The measure provides funding to support both jail expansion and operation of county-level treatment programs and work release centers. For example, SB 1145 is projected to transfer responsibility to Multnomah County for 700 prisoners who would have been sent to state prisons. The county will receive state support to expand jail capacity by 330 beds and create 150 new beds for drug and alcohol treatment.

Abolishing the Criminal Justice Council

The Criminal Justice Council was abolished during the fractious debates about SB 1145. The council and its staff had been adrift for some time. Criminal justice issues had not been center stage for Governor Roberts, who relied primarily on her corrections director, Frank Hall, for leadership in this area. When the term of the council's chairman expired, she left the slot open for over a year. The new chairman was soon appointed to the circuit court bench, again leaving the council without a leader. The council came to be seen by many as a waste of time and resources.

Early in the 1995 session, Bob Tiernan, a conservative legislative member of the council, who had never attended any of its meetings—and viewed it as too liberal, introduced a bill to abolish it, transferring its functions to the department of corrections. The proposal might have been defeated, but for a mishap between council staff and the governor's office. Just after the 1994 election, prison admissions shot up. The governor's office requested a quick estimate of projected population growth. Council staff prepared a simple trend analysis—and promised a more thorough, reliable forecast later on. But the trend data, once released, were used in budgeting and dollar figures were attached to the estimate and passed along to the legislative leadership. At a subsequent budget meeting, consternation ensued when a council staff indicated that the still-expected forecast might deflate the previous estimate by as a many as 2,000 beds.

Some of the governor's advisors had urged him to move the criminal justice policy-planning function into the executive branch, arguing that the governor has to take heat for the problems, and should take control of formulating the solutions. Broad support for the council was expressed at legislative hearings from virtually all sectors of the justice system, including many victims' rights advocates, but with Republican leaders in both houses

Case Study 8.1, *continued*

set against the council, the issue did not die. The governor intervened and proposed a new seven-member Oregon Criminal Justice Commission to preserve the idea of long-term criminal justice planning while letting the council die.

"In my view the Council needed to be abolished because it was just too large to be effective," says Dale Penn, district attorney in Salem and chair of the new commission. "Members were constantly complaining that they went to meetings only to find that there was no quorum and no work could be accomplished. We have envisioned that some of the same inclusiveness of the old council can be retained through establishment of various subcommittees to draw in a broader representation. So the only change we've made is to cut the numbers of actual commissioners back to a workable size."

Responsibility for the guidelines was transferred to the new commission, while prison population forecasting was moved to the executive office that prepares state revenue projections. David Factor, staff director of the council at the time of its demise, says that the move had little to do with sentencing guidelines *per se*. "The guidelines were never an issue that generated public outcry. These changes, coupled with cuts in funding and staff, were motivated by desire to concentrate power in the executive branch."

The new commission got off to a rocky start. Senate confirmation was blocked for two of the governor's seven nominees by opposition from the victims' advocate community. The five members who originally won appointment constituted a quorum, but only one—the chair—had professional experience within the criminal justice system. In January, 1996, two new nominees—Portland's police chief, Charles Moose, and Bill Gary, a former deputy attorney general—were confirmed.

Factor expresses continued concern about the future of Oregon's guidelines. He fears that they have lost much of their policy-shaping potency, given the intense politicization of sentencing policy associated with Ballot Measure 11. "I worry that guidelines will no longer be viewed as a critical medium for structuring sentencing policy. Without the council, the governor will have a lot more control over this arena, but a lot less political cover."

Kathleen Bogan, Factor's predecessor, agrees. "When they demolished this independent powerhouse made up of the state's most respected criminal justice policy makers, they wiped out a *lot* of institutional memory. As Voltaire said, 'If God did not exist, it would be necessary to invent him.' I think they will eventually find it necessary to recreate the council in some form."

Phillip Lemman, director of the new commission, offers reassurance. "We plan to establish a guidelines subcommittee which will involve the same range of public safety professionals as served on the old council. It's just that now a *citizen* board will have the final say-so on recommendations that go to the legislature. Given an entirely new membership, the learning curve will be steep. But Oregon has a strong tradition of effective lay boards. We can point, for example, to those established for higher education and forestry, where citizen involvement provides a useful and needed reality check."

Case Study 8.1, *continued*

Factor believes that the guideline concept was never adequately institutionalized as *the* mechanism for controlling prison population levels. "In the face of Ballot Measure 11, there's no alternative but to build bed capacity. Measure 11 is now forcing the state to expand the Snake River facility to its 3,000 bed capacity, with another new 1,500 bed facility in the planning stage—and it won't stop there."

Dale Penn says that it is hard to predict the future impact of the initiative process on the sentencing guidelines, but thinks there is still solid support for them in the legislature. "Given the current legislative configuration, we are not at a point where I would foresee any serious changes from that body—no major tinkering with the system we have in place. People here recognize that guidelines give us the ability to plan strategically and the mechanism to decide what the impact of our reforms will be."

A budget bill to authorize expenditure of $94,000,000 for expanded local corrections under SB 1145 was passed in a special session of the legislature in early February1996. The transfer of supervision of the targeted offenders to the counties takes effect on January 1, 1997.

Heading into the special session, Kevin Mannix opposed the plan—offering instead a proposal to contract with a private firm to build four 500-bed-barracks-style prisons. His proposal was soundly rejected, but Mannix is mounting yet another initiative. His "Son of 11" proposal would create a new schedule of minimum sentences for "major crimes"—including many nonviolent property offenses—starting at an 18-month presumptive minimum for targeted offenders, requiring an 18-month mandatory term for those with a prior conviction in the same crime class, and stacking additional terms in prison for each additional prior. The measure would swell the state's prison population by an additional 5,000 offenders.

A second measure enacted during the special session may help head off the proposed initiative. A chronic property offender crime bill was devised by the new commission because some legislators were not prepared to vote for SB 1145 unless it was coupled with an attempt to identify "career thieves" and provide prison terms long enough to keep them incarcerated at the state level. The new law targets property crimes (felony theft, criminal mischief, car theft, burglary). For most targeted offenders, after *four* prior convictions the judge would impose a 13-month sentence, or after a *second* conviction if the prior conviction is for a serious property offense. For residential burglary, similar patterns would require 19 months.

According to Penn, the bill was crafted as a "addendum" to the guidelines. It does not change the sentences in the grid, nor does it actually establish mandatory minimum sentences. Instead, it provides that regardless of the normal guidelines presumptive sentences, the minimum sentence will be 13 (or 19) months in prison—but it also provides that a *departure* sentence may be imposed, as "authorized by the rules of the Oregon Criminal Justice Commission."

Case Study 8.1, *continued*

> "Our bill won the support we needed for 1145, but it also will lay the ground for those who will oppose Kevin's ballot measure," says Penn. "Legislators will be able to say, 'Is this necessary now? Hasn't something already been done to address this problem?'"

Question

1. Using the chart in Chapter 1 (Figure 1.1) as a guide, identify two major steps in the seven-stage model of planned change that could help explain what happened in Oregon. Use specific concepts from the text, and provide evidence from the article to support your answer.

Endnotes

[1]   Goodman, H. (1992). "Rendell Hopes 'Philadelphia Works' Works for Poor, But Even if it Does, He Warns, Much More Needs to be Done." *The Philadelphia Inquirer*, 19 April 1998, p. D1.

[2]   Crichton, Michael (1990). *Jurassic Park*. New York: Ballantine.

[3]   Universal Films (1993). *Jurassic Park*. Directed by Steven Spielberg. Produced by Kathleen Kennedy and Gerald R. Molen. Written by Michael Crichton and David Koepp. Based on the novel by Michael Crichton. Photographed by Dean Cundey. Edited by Michael Kahn. Music by John Williams.

[4]   Doleschal, Eugene (1992). "The Dangers of Criminal Justice Reform." *Criminal Justice Abstracts*, March, 133-152.

[5]   Clear, T., S. Flynn, and C. Shapiro (1987). "Intensive Supervision in Probation: A Comparison of Three Projects." In B. McCarthy (ed.) *Intermediate Punishments: Intensive Supervision, Home Confinement, and Electronic Surveillance*, pp. 31-51. Monsey, NY: Criminal Justice Press.

[6]   Petersilia, Joan, and Susan Turner (1990). "Comparing Intensive and Regular Supervision for High-Risk Probationers: Early Results From an Experiment in California." *Crime & Delinquency*, 36:87-111.

[7]   Shichor, David (1995). *Punishment for Profit: Private Prisons/Public Concerns*. Thousand Oaks, CA: Sage.

[8]   Markley, Greg (1989). "The Marriage of Mission, Management, Marketing and Measurement." *Research in Corrections*, 2.

9   Berman, P. (1981). "Thinking About Programmed and Adaptive Implementation: Matching Strategies to Situations." In H. Ingram, and D. Mann (eds.) *Why Policies Succeed or Fail*. Beverly Hills. CA: Sage; McLaughlin, M. (1976). "Implementation as Mutual Adaptation: Change in Classroom Organization." In W. Williams, and R.F. Elmore (eds.) *Social Program Evaluation*. Academic Press.

10   Ellickson, P., and J. Petersilia (1983). *Implementing New Ideas in Criminal Justice*. Santa Monica, CA: RAND.

11   Neises, E. (1993). *Report: The Center for Alternative Sentencing and Employment Services*. New York: The Center for Alternative Sentencing and Employment Services.

12   Sieber, Sam D. (1981). *Fatal Remedies*. New York: Plenum.

13   Adapted from: Bogan, Kathleen, and David Factor (1995). "Oregon Guidelines 1989-1994." *Overcrowded Times*, 6(2):1, 13-15.

14   Miethe, Terance D., and Charles A. Moore (1989). *Sentencing Guidelines: Their Effect in Minnesota*. NIJ Research in Brief (NCJ-111381). Washington, DC: U.S. Department of Justice, Office of Justice Programs, National Institute of Justice.

15   Dailey, Debra (1995). "Minnesota's Guidelines: Past and Proposed Changes." *Overcrowded Times*, 6 (6):1, 7-9.

16   Greene, Judy (1996). "Wisconsin Guidelines Killed, Oregon's Weakened." *Overcrowded Times*, 7(1): 1, 14-18, 20. Reprinted with permission from Castine Research Corporation, Castine, ME.

Appendix 1:
A Seven-Stage Checklist for
Program and Policy Planning

Stage 1: Analyzing the Problem

❑ **A.** *Document the need for change:* Collect and analyze data to define what the problem is, where it is, how big it is and who is affected by it. What evidence of the problem exists?

❑ **B.** *Describe the history of the problem:* How long has the problem existed? How has it changed over time?

❑ **C.** *Examine potential causes of the problem:* What causes the problem? What theories do we have? The intervention to be chosen must target one or more specific causes supported by research.

❑ **D.** *Examine previous interventions* that have been implemented to change this problem: Identify the most promising interventions and choose a preferred intervention approach.

❑ **E.** *Identify relevant stakeholders:* Do different groups of people have different definitions of the problem? Who is affected by the problem?

❑ **F.** *Conduct a systems analysis:* Conduct research on the justice system in which the problem exists, and determine how the system may create, contribute to or maintain the problem.

❑ **G.** *Identify barriers to change and supports for change:* Who is likely to support a certain course of action? Who is likely to resist it?

Stage 2: Setting Goals and Objectives

❑ **A.** *Write goal statements* specifying the general outcome to be obtained: Consider the goals of criminal sanctions and normative values driving desired outcomes.

❑ **B.** *Write specific outcome objectives for each goal:* These should include a time frame for measuring impact, a target population, a key result intended and a specific criterion or measure of impact.

❑   C. *Seek participation* from different individuals and agencies in goal setting: Consider top-down versus bottom-up approaches.

❑   D. *Specify an impact model:* An impact model is a description of how the intervention will act upon a specific cause, so as to bring about a change in the problem.

❑   E. *Identify compatible and incompatible goals in the larger system:* Where do values of different stakeholders overlap or conflict?

❑   F. *Identify needs and opportunities for interagency collaboration:* Whose cooperation and participation is needed to achieve the goals of this program or policy?

Stage 3: Designing the Program or Policy

❑   A. *Choose an intervention approach:* Integrate the information collected at previous stages to decide what the substance of an intervention will be. Decide whether a program or policy approach is appropriate.

❑   B. **Program design** requires four major activities:

   ❑   (1) *Define the target population:* Who is to be served, or changed?

   ❑   (2) *Define client selection and intake procedures:* How are clients selected and recruited for the intervention?

   ❑   (3) *Define program components:* The precise nature, amount and sequence of services provided must be specified. Who does what to whom, in what order, and how much?

   ❑   (4) *Write job descriptions of staff, and define the skills and training required.*

❑   C. **Policy design** requires four major activities:

   ❑   (1) *Define the target population of the policy:* Which persons or groups are included and which are not?

   ❑   (2) *Identify the responsible authority:* Who is required to carry out the policy, and what will their responsibilities be?

   ❑   (3) *Define the provisions of the policy:* A policy should identify the goods, services, opportunities or interventions that will be delivered, and the conditions that must be met in order for the provisions to be carried out.

   ❑   (4) *Delineate the procedures that must be followed:* Individuals responsible for implementing a specific set of rules must clearly understand the specific steps and actions to be taken to ensure that the policy is carried out consistently.

Stage 4: Developing an Action Plan

❑   A. *Identify resources needed and make cost projections:* How much funding is needed to implement a specific intervention? Identify the kinds of resources needed, estimate costs and make projections, and develop a resource plan.

❑   B. *Plan to acquire or reallocate resources:* How will funding be acquired? Identify resource providers, and be prepared for making adjustments to the resource plan.

❑   C. *Specify dates by which implementation tasks will be accomplished, and assign responsibilities to staff members for carrying out tasks:* A Gantt chart is particularly useful for this purpose.

❑   D. *Develop mechanisms of self-regulation:* Create mechanisms to monitor staff performance and enhance communication, including procedures for orienting participants, coordinating activities and managing resistance and conflict.

❑   E. *Specify a plan to build and maintain support:* Anticipate sources of resistance and develop responses.

Stage 5: Developing a Plan for Monitoring Program/Policy Implementation

❑   A. *Design a monitoring system* to assess to what degree the program or policy design (see Chapter 4) is being carried out as planned: Is the intended target population being reached? Are program/policy activities or provisions actually being carried out as planned? Are appropriate staff or responsible authorities selected and trained, and are they carrying out their assigned duties?

❑   B. *Design monitoring instruments to collect data* (e.g., observations, surveys, interviews): Collect data to find out what is actually being delivered to clients or targets. The purpose is to identify gaps between the program/policy on paper (design) and the program/policy in action.

❑   C. *Designate responsibility for data collection, storage and analysis:* Ensure that there is no ambiguity about what information is to be collected, who is responsible for collecting it or how it is to be collected, stored and analyzed.

❑   D. *Develop information system capacities:* Information systems may consist of written forms and records that are filed, or fully computerized data entry and storage systems.

❑   **E.** *Develop mechanisms to provide feedback to staff, clients and stakeholders:* Depending on the results of monitoring analyses, it may be necessary to make adjustments either to what is being done (the program or policy in action) or to the intended design (the program or policy on paper).

Stage 6: Develop a Plan for Evaluating Outcomes

❑   **A.** *Decide which type of evaluation is appropriate and why:* Do major stakeholders (including those funding the evaluation) want to know whether the program or policy is achieving its objectives (impact), how outcomes change over time (continuous outcomes) or whether it is worth the investment of resources devoted to its implementation (efficiency)?

❑   **B.** *Determine whether two prerequisites for evaluation have been met:* (1) Are objectives clearly defined and measurable? (2) Has the intervention been sufficiently well designed and well implemented?

❑   **C.** *Develop outcome measures based on objectives:* Good outcome measures should be valid and reliable.

❑   **D.** *Identify potential confounding factors* (factors other than the intervention that may have biased observed outcomes): Common confounding factors include biased selection, biased attrition and history.

❑   **E.** *Determine which technique for minimizing confounding effects can be used—random assignment or nonequivalent comparison groups:* Each involves creating some kind of comparison or control group.

❑   **F.** *Specify the appropriate research design to be used:* Examples include: the simple pretest-posttest design; the pretest-posttest design with a control group; the pretest-posttest design with multiple pretests; the longitudinal design with treatment and control groups; and the cohort design.

❑   **G.** *Identify users and uses of evaluation results:* Who is the intended audience, and how can results be effectively and efficiently communicated? How will the results be used?

❑   **H.** *Reassess the entire program or policy plan:* Review the entire planning process from start to finish, looking for any inconsistencies, contradictions or inadequacies.

Stage 7: Initiating the Program or Policy Plan

❑   **A.** *Initiate the program or policy design and the action plan* developed at Stages 3 and 4: Make sure that specific individuals are responsible for coordinating all program or policy activities.

❑   **B.** *Begin monitoring program/policy implementation* according to plans developed at Stage 5.

❏   C. *Make adjustments* to program or policy design as monitoring detects gaps.

❏   D. *Determine whether the program or policy is ready to be evaluated.*

❏   E. *Implement the research design* developed at Stage 6: Collect and analyze evaluation data.

❏   F. *Provide feedback to stakeholders.*

❏   G. *Reassess the entire program/policy plan and make necessary modifications* to increase fit with the program or policy's environment.

Index

About the Authors

Wayne N. Welsh is an Associate Professor of Criminal Justice at Temple University. He received his Ph.D. in Social Ecology from the University of California, Irvine, in 1990 and his M.A. in Applied Social Psychology from the University of Saskatchewan (Canada) in 1986. Undergraduate courses he has taught include Introduction to Criminal Justice; Violence, Crime and Justice; Environmental Criminology; and Planned Change in Criminal Justice. Graduate courses include Violence, Crime and Aggression; and Criminal Justice Organizations: Structure, Process and Change. Welsh has conducted research in two broad areas: (1) applications of organizational theory to criminal justice and examinations of organizational change, and (2) theories of violent behavior and intervention/prevention programs.

Welsh is the author of *Counties in Court: Jail Overcrowding and Court-Ordered Reform* (Temple University Press, 1995). In this book and in various journal articles, he has examined the impacts of court-ordered correctional reform, especially responses and adaptations by criminal justice agencies. His recent research has focused on delinquency prevention and school violence. He was Principal Investigator on a three-year study (1992-95) evaluating an initiative to reduce disproportionate minority confinement'in Pennsylvania's juvenile justice system. Funded by the Pennsylvania Commission on Crime and Delinquency, this study evaluated nine community-based delinquency prevention programs in Philadelphia and Harrisburg. A 1996 study funded by the National Institute of Justice examined multi-level predictors of school violence in Philadelphia, and examined recommendations for violence prevention. Currently, he is Principal Investigator on an NIJ-funded project titled: "Building an Effective Research Collaboration Between the Pennsylvania Department of Corrections and The Center for Public Policy at Temple University." The purpose of this project is to develop a collaborative research partnership between researchers and practitioners, with a demonstration research project that includes three main elements: (1) a descriptive assessment of Drug and Alcohol programming, (2) an intensive on-site process evaluation of representative drug and alcohol programs at two institutions, and (3) design of an outcome evaluation based on analyses of data collected. Recent articles have appeared in *Criminology*, the *Journal of Research in Crime and Delinquency* and *Crime and Delinquency*. Welsh is currently working on a book with Marc Riedel that will present an interdisciplinary approach to the study of violence that cuts across research and theories at the individual, group, organizational, community and social structural levels.

Philip W. Harris is an Associate Professor of Criminal Justice at Temple University and a Principal at the Crime and Justice Research Institute. He received his Ph.D. from the School of Criminal Justice at the University of Albany in 1979 and has been a member of the Temple faculty since 1980. He has directed research on police and correctional decisionmaking regarding juveniles, evaluations of juvenile delinquency programs, and development of management information systems. From 1989 to 1995, Harris also directed the Juvenile Corrections Leadership Forum (JCLF), a program of leadership development for state-level juvenile corrections directors, funded by the Edna McConnell Clark Foundation. JCLF was the platform for launching the Council of Juvenile Correctional Administrators. Beginning in 1992, he and Peter Jones designed and have now implemented a permanent information system, ProDES, that provides a continuous flow of outcome information on all programs that receive youths from Philadelphia's Family Court. Output from this system has included evaluations of more than 60 programs, reports on system trends, and policy papers dealing with female offenders, substance abuse and race, and dispositions of first-time offenders, Harris and Jones recently implemented a similar outcome-based information system, PrOMIS, for a system of 18 delinquency prevention programs and are assisting the American Humane Association in the development of an outcome-based information system for a child welfare system.

Prior to coming to Temple, Harris spent four years as a juvenile corrections administrator in Canada. There he directed the assessment department of a large private agency, developed training for staff and designed the agency's management information system. He has contributed several book chapters, journal articles and research reports on juvenile justice, program implementation and information systems, and has provided consultation and technical assistance to juvenile delinquency agencies, police departments, courts and criminal justice advocacy groups.